Footfalls Echo

Footfalls Echo

Sally Breach

authorHOUSE®

AuthorHouse™
1663 Liberty Drive
Bloomington, IN 47403
www.authorhouse.com
Phone: 1-800-839-8640

Published by AuthorHouse   06/15/2012

ISBN: 978-1-4772-1366-7 (sc)
ISBN: 978-1-4772-1367-4 (e)

. . . Footfalls echo through the memory
Down the road we did not take
Towards the door we never opened
T.S Eliot Four Quartets

For all the Lizzie's
Embrace the truth

Acknowledgements

This is the point where I find myself wishing I'd remembered to write down every time someone helps me during book research, which would make this bit considerably easier!

So . . . I'll do my best, and apologies in advance if I miss somebody; but be assured, each and every one of you, that I am forever in your debt, because in this instance revisiting the village of Frincham in order to bring Lizzie Fidler to life has been a long and often challenging, but at the same time deeply satisfying journey for me, and I couldn't have done it without you.

First of all I would like to thank everyone at the West Berkshire Council Domestic Abuse Reduction programme, and the Women's refuge, for all of the help and encouragement you gave me during this project. You only made me make one promise to you and I hope you like how I kept it. No names for obvious reasons. You all know who you are and I am hugely grateful.

Thanks to everyone at DEFRA for helping me wade through difficult planning issues and thanks to Suzanne and her fellow protestors for explaining their side of a planning argument too.

To the very helpful people at the Commonwealth War graves commission I offer my grateful thanks and will always admire the way you continue to care so deeply for those who give their lives in wars, and for their families.

On a more personal note I would like to thank my far flung siblings Cheryl and Simon and certain of their offspring for nagging at me constantly to get on with this book because at times it became so hard to write I feared more than once that I might fail.

My best friends Gill, Lesley and Heather and all of you who keep me giggling in my slimming class continue to spur me on and encourage me in all I do, for which I will be eternally grateful because a girl will always need her friends 'through thick and thin' . . . and especially when at times she's both . . .

Writing, for all its richly satisfying enjoyment, is a very solitary activity that at times can be pretty lonely and the need for support and encouragement from other writers when I *invariably* get stuck I could never underestimate or take for granted. So to Betty my writing e-buddy in America I say, here you are as promised and get well soon because I need you in my life just as much as ever. To Tony Henderson-Newport, Khellan Payne and Catherine Ellison; the gifted writers hiding their lights under laptops at the Vodafone World Headquarters in Newbury, I say thanks for all your support too (and for all the coffee . . .). I appreciate your help way beyond the confines of these words because you're the only ones who really know just what I mean when I say I'm stuck, and if I have learned one thing on this particularly difficult journey it's that the answer to writer's block is 'Grab an Americano and run it past Tony, Khellan and Catherine'!

STB 2012

Chapter one

Life appeared much as usual in the village of Frincham, a place of little significance except to those who choose to live there. Barely a spot on the local map, it sits there, struggling to retain its integrity in the 21st century, situated in leafy West Berkshire and nestling quietly between its neighbouring village of Yattley, and the larger market town of Newbury.

Since the dawn of time English villages are traditionally agricultural in origin and were at some point constructed on private land, normally owned by the local squire, to provide housing and a community for workers on his country estate, and normally tied to their employment. So if they moved on or lost their job, they became instantly homeless too.

These small pockets of former agricultural industry usually include a village square, or main street, where the traders and the pub, or pubs, might be found, but in this particular village, the village square is actually more of a slightly wonky triangle. Dominating one side of it is an imposing and extremely old Michelin starred and thatched bar stroke hotel and restaurant called the Royal Oak: named after a legend that King Charles II, during an escape from Cromwell's Roundheads via a tunnel from nearby Shaw House to Donnington Castle during the second Battle of Newbury in 1644, (by what must have been quite a circuitous route), apparently hid in the tree at an unspecified moment. The bar stroke hotel now leans slightly drunkenly to one side from hundreds of years of subsidence, and its leaded window panes all twinkle like fairy lights in the sun from slightly different angles. The remaining tree stump from which the Royal Oak takes its name forms the centre of a modern mini roundabout in the centre of the triangle, and cars now park in regimented herring bone pattern parking spaces up the centre of a main through road that once saw only horse drawn carriages, and the occasional bicycle.

The butcher's shop stands on the corner of the second angle. Double fronted, it still boasts its two huge Dickensian and rather saggy bow windows, through which one can daily see the array of meats and homemade sausages and pies that are temptingly on offer. Very much a family run business with traditional values, on entry to the premises one can be assured a hearty greeting from the current custodian, Ken

Griffin, and probably a free pie, or a bone for your dog in addition to your purchases when you leave too.

Directly opposite the Royal Oak, and along the third angle, stands a row of three terraced 'chocolate box' style Elizabethan black and white cottages. These are numbers one to three Stanton Cottages: thatched as one building, and all with their downstairs bathrooms built onto to the back as flat roof extensions rather as a second thought after indoor plumbing became the norm. Their emerald green external paintwork identifies them as still belonging to the local squire, which in this case means the owner of the rather imposing Stanton Court Estate, an impressive stone mansion that stands alone in its many acres of manicured park outside the village, on the rather aptly named Stanton Court Road.

At the far end of the triangle, by the grocer's shop, Mattesons, (also the post office), stands a fairly large property, set farther back with a sweeping semi circular and deeply gravelled driveway. The original Manor House for the village, it is Jacobean in style with characteristic windows and lintels, and it has a front door right in its centre that on first sight makes one wonder if the owners still use its original key; that must be the size of a spanner.

The village has a second pub called the White Hart, which is most popular with lesser mortals than those that frequent the Royal Oak, though its regulars do include the Oak's esteemed chef, Gareth Carey, who has a slight addiction to the Landlord's Irish stew. The Hart, as it is known locally, stands to the side of the road just down the lane from the square, sitting comfortably between the slightly dilapidated village hall, and the school.

Opposite the school and set back with a slightly raised aspect of very old churchyard and a war memorial, stands the square towered and quintessentially English looking St Mary's church, whose pews still have little doors on them to keep out the riff raff (and the draught), and whose clock chimes every quarter of an hour with comforting regularity, but only until 10pm. The Rectory, a rather old and shabby house of somewhat confused and wildly unsympathetic vintages stands adjacent, but with what remains of a convenient garden gate between the two to ease the Rector's commute time to and from work from roughly three minutes to roughly one.

Directly behind St Mary's Church flows the gently meandering River Kennet, still dotted along its entirety with concrete gun emplacements, or 'pill boxes,' dating back to the unrealised threat of German invasion during World War II, and including one at the very bottom of the Rectory garden that makes a convenient play den for the Rector's children.

As a gift from the river that adds to St Mary's many charms, the churchyard also boasts a regular congregation of all creatures great and small to bask in the sunshine, or eat the leftovers from the church kitchen. The particular favourites are the numerous wildfowl, especially when accompanied by a row of chicks that take advantage of all the peaceable nooks and crannies and provide an excellent topic for sermons around Easter time.

On this particular day, the school day had finished and all the children had gone home, when the recently restored afternoon peace was broken as a rather battered old Ford Escort pulling a trailer of mysterious bulges secreted beneath some shabby bed sheets made its way noisily into what passed as the square, and eventually pulled into the little lay-by at side of the road outside the post office. There were just three occupants inside the car: the driver, a man smoking a roll up cigarette, who had greasy black hair and a face that made you reach into your pocket for your wallet to make sure it was still there. In the passenger seat next to him sat a teenage boy of about seventeen. Gypsy, with strikingly hypnotic black eyes, he had a mop of jet black hair that fell in tight curls to the neck of his black T shirt, but without quite concealing a small gold hoop earring through one ear. Completing the family trio and seated in the back was a woman whose cheap and dowdy appearance showed her age to be quite a bit older than she actually was: her grubby blonde head cast downwards, she was visibly mouse like in her timidity and she worried constantly at the nail on her left thumb.

It was the boy who stepped out of the car, looking around himself moodily. His jeans were way beyond distressed, being considerably more hole than whole and, heading for the doorway of the shop; he hawked and spat disgustingly on the pavement just in front of him.

'Just find the notice board and see what cards they've got Dan . . . window cleaning, gardening, that sort of thing . . .' said his father from inside the car.

'I know what I'm doing . . . !' the boy replied shortly, turning impatiently back towards the car. Then, pushing the shop door open he mumbled, 'I'm getting to be a friggin' expert . . .'

A woman and her three young children were leaving the shop as he tried to enter, but he pushed himself rudely on past them without holding the door, as if he had not even seen them there. Shaking her head in disbelief at his lack of manners, the woman was dressed in what looked at first glance like an ordinary dark pink skirt suit; but she was, on closer inspection, wearing the badge of office of a vicar; the dog collar, poked through the buttoned up neck of her pale pink clergy shirt. With her, and clamouring together so as not to become separated in the traffic jam at the door were three little girls, all dressed in the local school uniform of a grey skirt with a red cardigan and socks, and by their features and equality of their height, presumably triplets. All were equally anxious for her to open the ice pops that she had just bought for them, and from the back seat of the car the woman watched her has she stood there, effortlessly ripping open the ice pops with her teeth and handing them around to stop the arguing over which child apparently got the only cola flavoured one.

It was otherwise a quiet and sunny afternoon, and once the vicar and her children moved away towards the Rectory happily sucking, the only other sound to break the silence outside the shop apart from birdsong was the clip-clop sound of approaching horses on the road behind her. The woman in the car looked in the cracked door mirror with guarded interest as two of them came into view from a side lane, just as the boy came back out of the post office carrying a few advertisement cards in one hand. On board the highly polished and expensive looking horses were two young teenage girls: one being the fourteen year old Amy Palmer, who lived in the aforementioned Jacobean spanner house, and the other, older girl by two years, was Hannah Derby, daughter of the local squire, the successfully knighted businessman, Sir Christopher Derby.

Danny Fidler looked from one to the other with a slight smile, but his black eyed gaze involuntarily returned to the much prettier Hannah as she passed him by, with her long blonde hair tied neatly back underneath her riding helmet; and he also noted a very nice pair of legs sensuously encased in tight cream jodhpurs and shiny brown leather boots.

Very nice . . .

And then he wolf whistled.

She looked back at him instinctively before effortlessly correcting her horse as he jumped at the unexpected sound but, hotly embarrassed by the wink and the wolfish look he gave her to go with the whistle, she turned away with a tut of her tongue and a hopefully visibly disinterested toss of her head.

'Stuck up cow . . .' said Danny, loudly breaking the peace of the afternoon, but she succeeded in ignoring him this time. Her face burning with embarrassment though, she kicked her horse easily into a trot and headed out of the square, with the other horse and rider following suit just behind her.

Once back on the road, the car passed the two girls again about half a mile further out towards the next village.

Danny's black eyes glinted as he watched them in the car's filthy door mirror, as they turned onto a bridleway, took off at a gentle canter into the woods, and out of sight.

*   *   *

On the very outskirts of Frincham and geographically nearer the next village sits a Social Housing development called, somewhat euphemistically, the Flowergarden Estate; but to the locals, quite simply, as 'Bandit Country'. Here lives the other end of the residential chain: the families that have mostly been moved out of nearby Newbury's estates for various reasons such as antisocial behaviour; apart from the few stalwarts that have bought their homes from the local council and consequently have lived there since they were built in the mid 1960's. These privately owned homes are instantly recognisable by their assortment of white plastic front doors, a few additions here and there, and by their block paved or gravelled front lawns, enabling them the luxury of off road parking once the evening joy riders come out. It has a pretty grim reputation and so consequently it is where the local police head every time something goes wrong and, on the whole, where nobody really wants to live unless there is no alternative.

It was into here that the car turned off the main road, and moved slowly and purposefully down and around until it reached its final destination, Hyacinth Close.

First sight of number 27, their new home, was a faded blue wooden front door with two square frosted glass panels; the bottom pane having been replaced by a sheet of plywood, presumably after it had suffered fatal injury on some previous occasion. The front garden was bordered, as were most of the others, by a low wooden fence with just two wide planks, mostly broken at one end or missing altogether, and sundry overgrown shrubs and weeds mostly growing over and around a skip that was still full of the previous occupant's belongings, still holding resolutely on to the hope of collection. A wooden and rather ramshackle garage with a flaky asbestos roof stood to the side of the house; its doors held together by the placement of the dustbin, and closer inspection proved that this was because the door hinges were all missing bar one.

Lizzie Fidler sat in the back of the car and tried to think positive as she looked out at her new home. This was to be their new start; a clean sheet. Everything was going to be better from now on. He'd promised. But even as its frontage misted into soft focus from her breath on the inside of the car window, she could not hide her feelings of trepidation and despondency.

'You got the keys Lizzie, or what?' her husband asked, leaning one arm over the back of the driver's seat and fixing his eyes on hers briefly, before turning away with an impatient huff when she had instantly withdrawn her gaze, and opened his door with a shove against its stubborn resistance.

First inside, the front door opened before her into a decent sized hallway with a view either up the naked wooden stairs or straight through to the kitchen. The sitting room led off to the right of the door, and had a set of frosted glass sliding doors leading through to the kitchen. It showed some signs of effort on behalf of the housing association, having been freshly painted an anonymous magnolia, but otherwise the curtains hung in a garish and uneven orange droop, and the brown carpet was threadbare and worn, apart from where heavy furniture had stood in the past, giving a tiny echo as to it's original depth and pattern.

The kitchen paid homage to the 1960's with a chipped Formica table in the centre of the floor, and under the window stood a cracked Belfast sink; its overflow channel a sinister murky mass of thick black mould, and it had a positively furry old wooden drainer to one side. The windowsill and walls had been painted with white gloss over the original ceramic tiles at some point but the paint was now flaking, and mouldy underneath, revealing garish brown and orange patterned tiles.

She reached over the sink on her tip toes and tugged back some very dirty thin cotton curtains, forcing them along their stubborn and sticky wire, to take a look at her new back garden, and pulled a face. Nature had been given a free rein over a long period here, and a tangle of weeds had choked what had at one time been a fairly decent sized garden, albeit far from private and surrounded by other houses. There was a seriously listing greenhouse at the bottom but she couldn't see a single pane of glass unbroken, and the detritus of the previous occupants of this house lay in a graveyard of decades of undisturbed peace buried in elder, dandelions and nettles. The only other things she could see out there were a few abandoned house bricks that had most likely been used as missiles on the greenhouse, a metal pail laying on its side with a rusted out and delicately lacey base, an old tin bath, similarly rusty, and a beheaded garden gnome, with his still smiling face lying grotesquely alongside while the rest of him was still fishing into thin air.

She stood lost in thought as to what on earth she could do out there to make the garden half decent, when a shout from upstairs broke her chain of thought.

'I'm having this room!' It was Danny, breaking the silence and bringing her focus starkly back inside the house again. Turning with a sigh she followed his voice and went up a flight of stairs,that practically all creaked, to find him in one of the three bedrooms; which had a built in wardrobe on one wall and a large window overlooking the road at the front.

'Where's Dad?' she asked him, nodding slightly at his choice and looking around his chosen room.

'In your room,' he said, pointing down the landing to another bedroom, at the back of the house and partially above the kitchen. Pausing briefly to look in the bathroom with a push at the door and her first view of a sickly pink bathroom suite and orange walls, she found Len in the second of the double rooms, trying to fix the door on a fitted wardrobe, unsuccessfully, and giving up with a shove of impatience as she entered.

'This do?' he asked. She pursed her lips and nodded with raised eyebrows at the totally characterless square box of a room with one wide window quite high up the wall, that she knew she'd have to stand on her tip toes to look out of and certainly wouldn't be able to open without standing on the bed. The windowsill was tiled in thick earthenware and very chipped, and her eyes took in a whole cemetery of dead flies that had not managed to escape through the window to a greater freedom outside.

The third and final room was the small one incorporating the headroom at the top of the stairs. It had a cupboard almost at her waist height just inside the door that she also recognised she'd never be able to reach anything in without the aid of a chair, and the room was otherwise hardly big enough to house even a single bed, should one ever be needed again. She glanced at the uncarpeted floor space, pictured Len's beer making equipment there, and nodded to herself.

'Dan! Lizzie! There're a load of kids out the front! Get down here! We need to get all our stuff in before it gets nicked!' Len was shouting angrily at them from halfway up the stairs. Not a good start . . .

Lizzie quickly headed back down the creaky stairs and out of the front door, instantly conscious of the openly hostile eyes fixed on her from a group of children no more than eleven or twelve years old, with either bicycles or skateboards, and all hanging around the car trailer. They continued to watch belligerently as Len began to unload their belongings and pass them to her one by one until she couldn't carry any more, and despite his threats to them all, until Danny appeared from inside the house with his eyes set firmly straight at them, and they moved silently away.

Chapter two

Dizzy Hardy-Mitchell pushed open the front gate at the Rectory and let the children through noisily ahead of her to find their daddy, and render his concentration impossible for the rest of the day. Frincham Rectory had been her home for almost nine years now, though it was her husband Hector who was the actual incumbent at St. Mary's, the parish church. Dizzy worked for the glory of God and expenses, because the diocese didn't know what to do with double acts that had families, in a church that didn't warrant the stipends of two clergy. Their IVF produced triplets were six years old now, and attended the village school just opposite home, allowing their father to time the Telegraph crossword perfectly from the beginning of the morning playtime bell, to the one at the end, very neatly. A proud descendant of world renowned novelist and poet Thomas Hardy, author of such great works as Tess of the D'Urbervilles, and Far from the Madding Crowd, and one of his most devoted fans, he had named his daughters after three of Hardy's best known characters, namely, Tess, Liza-Lu and . . . Bathsheba. They had quickly become known, thanks to their mother's sometimes rather unwelcome habit of re-jigging names to something more personally satisfying, as Tesco, Looby-Loo and Batty, and all had very differing personalities, insofar as to seem entirely unrelated at times.

Batty was the robust, tomboy leader of the pack, utterly fearless and always up to something not quite sensible. Her second in command, some of the time, and her identical twin being Tesco; and Looby-Loo, the non-twin of the trio and a little smaller in stature, being the one for ever playing catch up in whatever scheme Batty had planned.

Looby-Loo was the quiet and studious one; the one that actually enjoyed learning her spellings, and loved practically any kind of craftwork she could do in her room on her own, while Tesco was the animal lover and spent most of her after school day walking someone else's Jack Russell, or was to be found in the Rectory garden with a tufty guinea pig or two clutched passionately, though not always willingly, to her chest.

Rector Hector was in his study, situated adjacent to the kitchen, so he always knew when a meal was ready because his wife would simply bang on his wall with one end of a large black pepper grinder to attract his attention. He was wrestling with a difficult sermon for the coming Sunday morning and had been staring at his computer screen for almost an hour. Cardiganed elbows resting on his desk, his hands were clasped together in a prayerful position with his index fingers gently bouncing against his upper incisors; and all without typing a single word.

Distracted once and for all, he pushed back his chair, stood slowly, and looked out of his study window, watching for a moment as cartoon clouds scudded in the wind across the pale blue sky.

He was a worried man.

It was no secret locally now that Sir Christopher Derby, chair of the Parish Council as well as one of his Churchwardens, (the other being Sarah Palmer, Amy's rather 'well padded' mother), had been negotiating with Watson's, the national supermarket chain, to purchase some of his less profitable land; and as a result it had recently been announced in the press that they were planning to build one of their ugly great mega stores on the site, right on Frincham's metaphorical front doormat.

Sir Christopher, a widower who very proudly resided in his four hundred year old family seat, lived there with his teenage daughter Hannah, whom we have already met, and a small staff that included a formidable housekeeper called Mrs Higgins; long ago a young woman, but now rather eccentric, who spent a prodigious amount of her time indulging in her passion for road traffic reports on the radio in the kitchen, and constantly bemoaned the hold up's on the M25, or spaghetti junction in Birmingham, as if all of their lives depended upon it.

Sir Christopher's estate was no longer quite its original size after what had been a few lean years for him, but it still boasted almost 15,000 acres of land, included a sizable farm, and some of the cottages and shops in the village.

Hector was aware that Christopher had been hit hard by both the global recession, and more than a few cases of 'bad day at the stock exchange' after many a heart to heart with him after the monthly Rector and Warden's meetings at the Rectory, and it was obvious again now that he was trying to raise funds to keep his estate running by selling off yet more of his land to the highest bidder.

This came as no surprise to the local community because, for one, it's notoriously hard to keep any kind of secret in a village, and also, when a previous attempt to gain planning permission to build three hundred houses on the same piece of land two years ago: considered locally as well away from his house but mightily close to everyone else's had been foiled following local protests, his aristocratic feathers had been well and truly ruffled. And his pride was extremely well known thereabouts.

Hector had been put in a tricky position with his senior Churchwarden on that occasion because Dizzy had been one of the main objectors at the resultant public meeting, voicing her concern on local amenities such as the school being severely over stretched, and pointing out the fact that the single track road approaching the site bordered the churchyard on one side and a similarly grade two listed building on the other; so it couldn't be widened. He afforded himself a little smile though, at the memory of Christopher's unwise attempt to imply to Dizzy that she shouldn't compromise her husband's neutral standing in the community by protesting, was met with her rather succinct reply of:

'I married the man Christopher, not his job . . . And I'm not his outboard motor, I'm another boat . . .'

The impact that a mega store would undoubtedly have on village community life and businesses quite honestly went without saying. Sarah Palmer, as well as being his other Churchwarden, was a robustly fearless woman who'd been the local activist who had headed up the housing protest campaign last time around, and now she was beginning to make identical noises again. Since her boxes of the previous documents had been brought up from the cellar at the Manor House and dusted off, Rector and Wardens meetings were becoming very frosty affairs, and already a local residents meeting had been called by her and held in the village hall.

The hall, usually perfectly adequate for village meetings, had been full to capacity that night, and an overflow of around eighty people had to listen to proceedings via a hastily rigged up sound system, normally used for Tuesday afternoon pensioner's Bingo, being piped out to the car park.

The local villages' residents and, in particular, local business owners were, on the whole, as one up in arms and ready to fight the application that now apparently included the construction of a brand new road to ease the traffic problems of the previous one; eating up even more valuable green fields.

Sir Christopher had, grudgingly, attended that first protest meeting, and brought along two representatives from Watsons, to answer questions chiefly, and they had brought drawings and computer generated images of their proposals for the villagers to see.

From the very start the atmosphere was charged and as soon as challenged, Sir Christopher had not made things any easier for himself by adopting a defensive attitude as to his own right to sell off his own land in any way he chose. Argument that the parcel of land was considered an area of outstanding natural beauty and included significant areas of ancient broadleaf woodland; and that the new road would destroy a centuries old flood and wildflower meadow, fell foul after he reminded them that the removal of similar woodland on the estate in his great-grandfather's time to make way for their cricket pitch and pavilion had met with little or no resistance by villagers at the time, who obviously believed cricket more important than a few trees when it suited them.

Ashley Phillips, and overweight and balding forty something in an expensively cut suit representing Watsons, had then positively ignited the meeting after stating; 'It is true that the transport hub forms a key aspect of the Watsons proposal; but despite the flood meadow being locally considered to be an area of outstanding natural beauty, you all need to understand that it is not legally recognised as such . . . and our surveyors have found nothing whatsoever of note or rarity living there . . . it's just a plain old flood meadow on land that can be put to much better use as a car park . . . And as for the trees . . . I can announce tonight that Watsons has committed to the planting of *50* new trees elsewhere on the site to replace those few, mostly decayed or diseased trees that must be felled . . . So we are entirely confident: as we are also confident, that the

21

proposed development's close proximity to the M4 motorway will satisfactorily boost our chances of a successful application . . .'

Hector had tried to chair the meeting in order to give everyone a fair hearing but once that had been said, and despite his best efforts, proceedings had ended up a complete free for all. Sarah suggested creating a protest sit-in in the disputed trees, reminiscent of the protests over the building of the Newbury Bypass some years previously that soon began to really look like happening, and muttering was coming thick and fast as to whether Swampy and his old Newbury Bypass friends and descendents might be interested in hearing about their protest too.

Before things got totally out of hand, local celebrity Artist resident Paul Taylor, sitting alongside his wife Jules, calmly reminded them that no formal application had even been lodged yet. He suggested that people were getting ahead of themselves, but this was met with little confidence either.

The protestors had even thought up a name for themselves now, and 'FLAWS' (Frincham locals against Watsons Supermarket), had had several meetings since that night. They had set up a website and an online petition that already had hundreds of signatures. They had started a fighting fund to pay for things like photocopying flyers and printing posters for distribution. They had sought legal advice, hired larger venues for their meetings as more and more people heard of the plans, and they were now holding fundraising events in the pub (quiz and curry night every Tuesday), and the village hall (bring and buy sales, jumble sales, and old favourites like bingo, beetle and whist drives). They had set up online giving to the fund and had given themselves a massive fundraising target of £80,000, in case they needed to fund professional representation should the formal application go to public enquiry.

In short, Sarah Palmer was a force to be reckoned with, and a woman now on a mission. Rumour had it, she had even managed to retain a copy of the Watsons Scoping document while wearing her other 'hat' as vice chair of the Parish Council, that she'd slipped into the agenda at a recent meeting she had fortuitously chaired in Sir Christopher's absence: (a scoping document being a request to the council to provide details of what information would be needed for an environmental analysis prior to any formal application being made). That meeting had triggered significant local interest too; and the press, the local MP Peter Cooper, and the local TV and radio stations had all become involved now.

FLAWS had posted their Mission Statement on their professionally created website last week as: '*We will do whatever it takes within our control and funds available to ensure that we achieve our objective to stop the Watsons supermarkets Frincham development and thereby retain the integrity of our village for future generations.'*

Hector sighed at the storm that was undoubtedly heading their way and was concerned about his wardens. Sir Christopher, although very committed to the church, if not his colleague since all this, was a very proud man, and respected, but not well liked in the village; and he could see that Sarah obviously found it slightly awkward that her daughter Amy, and his daughter Hannah, were good friends who often rode out together. But Sir Christopher's title and general manner were alienating and frankly unchristian to the majority, and conversation always stopped dead now the second he entered any shop or room.

And rather disconcertingly, Hector had noticed, it had also begun to include the church on Sundays.

The door to his study burst open behind him and a whirlwind of little girls scattering book bags and colourful rucksacks descended on him, all chattering at once, and he smiled at his daughters gratefully for breaking his chain of thought.

Pulling at him purposefully, Batty took his hand and led him out into the garden for a quick game of hide-and-seek, while Dizzy began mashing bananas and brown sugar together with a fork to make a pile of sandwiches for their tea.

Chapter three

Hannah and Amy meanwhile, had reached the end of the two mile ride and made their way down the adjoining bridle path back towards the village now, eventually taking the fork in the wooded path that leads down to the expanse of water known as Clearwater Lake. Chatting and giggling in the way that only teenage girls do about the dark eyed gypsy boy, they made their way along the shoreline, allowing their horses to cool their hot feet after their exertions and stop for a drink along the way. Then they turned into the gravel driveway of an imposing house near the water's edge that belonged to Paul and Jules Taylor; Clearwater House, and dismounted respectfully to walk their horses the rest of their way. Amy's horse, a spirited piebald gelding called Jethro with one blue eye and one brown one, lived on land to the side of the house here, despite Hannah's attempts to encourage her to move him to Stanton Court, and in the domain that once was the favourite place of the Taylor's grown up daughter Jemmie, with her own succession of past equine friends. Jethro's predecessor, an affectionate little pony called Whisper, had also lived at the Taylor's until Amy had outgrown him last year and he had been sold on.

Paul Taylor was home at the moment rather than off on one of his numerous trips abroad, and they waved up to him standing at the large picture window in his studio that overlooked the lake, above their enormous garage. Wiping his hands on a paint rag with a paintbrush lodged conveniently behind one of his ears, he waved back at them and smiled before turning back to his latest canvas.

The back door opened and Jules Taylor appeared to shake a post late lunch tablecloth free of breadcrumbs as they approached her. As she did so a large and overweight black Labrador hauled himself up from his favourite sunspot by the back door and lumbered down the path to greet them with his head down and his tail wagging furiously.

'Hello Barney!' said Amy, bending down to rub his ears, as Jethro's ears went back sharply and he stamped a foot at the approaching dog. Amy checked him easily with a slight tug on his reins and called over her shoulder to Jules.

'Hi Mrs Taylor, is my Dad still here do you know?'

'As far as I know he's still over there,' she called back, indicating with a sideways tilt of her head to an area to the rear of the house. 'But be careful because he said he was going to be opening up the hives to see how they're doing today . . .'

The previously overgrown and neglected old kitchen garden had been converted into five, brick wall protected, and therefore mostly frost free allotments for local residents three years ago. Amy's father, Chris Palmer, was head of the local allotments committee and spending quite a lot of his time in there too; tending his own vegetables and soft fruits, being assisted this year by the recent addition of three bee hives from the local beekeepers 'Honeycomb Club', of which he was also a proud member.

Jules watched as Hannah took Jethro so Amy could pop in to say hello to her father, who waved to her from under his hood as he tended his bees, before she jogged off to rejoin Hannah as she trailed Jethro and made her way over to the two adjoining stables. Hannah loosely tethered her horse in the shade adjacent to a tasty hay net and a bucket of water for a while, and then settled herself on a straw bale, while Amy unsaddled and prepared to groom Jethro; taking a welcome gulp from a can of coke from the fridge in the tack room first. She passed the can over to Hannah before taking a hoof pick from a hook on the wall, as the sound of pop music began to drift across the air from the stables and Jules turned away.

Going back into the kitchen, she folded the tablecloth and looked across at the dresser to a photograph of Jemmie, baptised Jemima, radiant and shining on her wedding day just last year. It still made her smile to think that their little tomboy who had once practically lived in those stables had grown into such a beautiful and confident woman. Now a hospital doctor in nearby Reading with designs on becoming a consultant pediatrician, she had married the boy next door, after a bit of a shaky start—and if half a mile still constituted being next door anyway. She and her husband Martin were now both living in his newly extended cottage on the hill with a delinquent Springer Spaniel called Dipstick, and were excitedly anticipating the arrival of their first child in a few months time.

Paul and Jules Taylor had lived in Clearwater House for many years and had actually been married twice; the first for twenty eight years, and the second for almost two, (but with a two year gap in between after a rather public divorce and an even more public reconciliation period of 'Will they, Won't they?' in the national newspapers). Paul was a much sought after artist with a reputation for wanting things 'done his own way' at the time of their break up. After a very 'tabloid fodder' affair with a predatory blonde half his age, Paul had actually quite quickly realised that the grass was green enough for him at home with Jules. Then he had spent the best part of a year, using all his powers of determination, a little romance, and his impressive address book, to win her back. He eventually did, but after much heartache and an almighty struggle, mostly because he thought she seemed to be an awful lot happier without him for a while.

Their second marriage was proving much more of team effort than the first and he spent a lot more time at home these days. He took her with him to receptions and parties, and in school holidays when she was not at her part time school job over at Yattley, she accompanied him abroad. He took much more of a part in the life of the village now as well, and since this inevitably meant he became more approachable generally, he was often being asked to open fetes and pet shows, and recently he'd acted as master of ceremonies at a church fundraising auction of promises up at the church, using the pulpit as the auctioneer's elevated platform, and a tent mallet for a gavel.

They had two grown up children, and Jemmie was the younger. Their son Marcus lived with his wife Sam in London. Marcus was a cosmetic dentist and Sam his practice nurse and manager and, having lost their first child during pregnancy, they'd moved out of their trendy apartment overlooking the River

Thames once Sam became pregnant again. Their twins, Tillie and Jake, were now almost two years old, and the family now lived in Sam's childhood home in the leafy suburb of Barnes. Sam had jumped at the opportunity to move back in once she'd found out her long widowed father wanted to move into a much more manageable retirement bungalow development he'd recently seen on a Bridge tournament weekend in Eastbourne. So they'd quickly bought the house so that he could achieve his wish, and he was now living a contented two minutes dog walk from home to the seafront.

Grandpa Brian had settled into his new home very quickly, taken up Crown Green Bowls, walked the length of the prom every morning with 'Buttons' and 'Poppers' his little west highland terriers, and played his beloved Bridge twice a week at the Burlington Hotel by the pier with a widowed lady called Yvonne that he'd met the first time he'd plucked up the courage to go into the club on his own.

On their frequent visits to see him Marcus surprised even himself by really liking Eastbourne and its quintessentially English charms, and thoroughly enjoyed long walks along the often blustery prom with Brian and his and his new canine companions. The bowling greens, the Martello Towers, the ice cream stalls, cafés, tea rooms; and the pier with its traditional sweet shops and amusement arcades, all had him hooked now. Even the all pervading smell of fish and chips set his taste buds alight these days, despite his being a bit of a fitness freak with an otherwise healthy lifestyle.

Chapter four

The Landlord and sole occupant at the White Hart, apart from a very large and thoroughly soppy German shepherd dog called Belinda, was a Derry born Irishman who, though stereotypically labelled during the first half of his life as 'Paddy', now preferred to be known simply as 'Flynn'. He'd had a Christian name of course, which nobody could ever pronounce, or spell, due to its almost complete absence of related letters compared to what it actually sounded like, so he'd eventually given up and stuck with the easiest option of his surname.

Your typical pale skinned, sandy haired Irishman, he was also labelled as a 'confirmed bachelor', though in truth he was neither confirmed, nor assumed gay, but the victim of doomed love who had so far not found a candidate to come even close to that misty eyed girl of his youth.

Flynn was going through the daily ritual of bottling up the bar ready for the Saturday lunchtime session, steering himself round Belinda at frequent intervals because she knew all the jobs he had to do and felt that he could do them better with her assistance. He'd checked all the barrels in the cellar and stocked up behind the bar, and was now unbolting the doors to let in his first customer of the day; his first customer every day since he'd been there, Jimmy Knapp. Jimmy was a crooked man of almost ninety summers; never seen out of the cottage in the square that he was born in without his customary ancient and very shiny flat cap, and a wooden walking stick. He habitually eased his daily journey from there to the pub on the table nearest the toilets, for his lunchtime treat of a half of Bulmers cider and a cheese and pickle sandwich. Since the death of his old school friend, a lady called Cornelia Bennett, *nee* Bassett, who had lived in the cottage on the hill near the lake now owned by Martin and Jemmie Ryan, he was the oldest resident at this end of the village, and much loved and respected.

'Mornin' Jimmy! How are ya, this fine day?' Flynn said cheerfully, pinning back the double doors to allow the sunshine to freely enlighten the public bar. Belinda's tail wagged enthusiastically in greeting.

'Mustn't grumble Flynn my old mate, mustn't grumble,' said Jimmy wheezily, sucking his false teeth back into place as he shuffled towards his chair, and greeting Belinda as usual with a dog biscuit from his jacket pocket that she knew perfectly well would be there. Flynn went behind the bar and took a half pint pewter tankard down from a hook just above him and shook his head slightly as Belinda crunched her biscuit and dropped crumbs all over the carpet, before beginning to draw Jimmy's cider.

'I wonder how many gallons of Bulmers this little darlin' has held for you over the years eh Jimmy?' he bellowed into Jimmy's good ear, placing his personal tankard in front of him. He loved the fact that Jimmy came in every day, even though their conversations always began with these words, and Jimmy's stories were always the same; the Hart just wouldn't be right without his regular daily visits that had become as much a part of the day as unbolting the double doors.

Flynn's favourite story had actually come out after he'd met Jimmy in the churchyard one morning while he was walking Belinda. Jimmy was sitting on a bench in the churchyard by the war memorial, deep in conversation as he fingered the lettering of one of the names about half way down the list of Second World War dead from the village.

'My half brother . . .' he explained with a little chuckle as Flynn approached him. 'E were a lot older than me, though . . . old enough to be my own father really.' He sucked his teeth back in place as usual before continuing. 'My father's first wife died y'see . . . and he remarried a long while later . . . to my mother, who were all of twenty five years younger than 'im! And when they 'ad me he were almost sixty year old, an' he died when I was ten. Wilf here was a bit of a rogue!' he jerked his head towards the memorial and smiled as Flynn sat down beside him, and Jimmy patted Belinda's head affectionately.

Flynn made himself comfortable. 'A loveable one though, was he? I see you still keep in touch . . .'

'We pass the time of day from time to time . . .' he ran his fingers across his brother's name once more, and then his milky eyes drifted further up the memorial with a twinkle of amusement. 'He were a bugger though . . . he was the only one ever to get his name up twice . . . look . . .' he said, chuckling, 'there he is again!'

Flynn followed his gaze up the list and, sure enough, there he was again, Wilfred Arthur Knapp, in the First World War list of the fallen. Flynn blinked in disbelief, but smiled. 'How was that then Jimmy . . . ?'

'Ah well . . . Wilf joined up as a lad in 1915, and my father got the telegram in 1917 sayin' he was missin' in Holland . . . and presumed dead y'see . . . so when the war was over and nothing more was heard of 'im . . . and the memorial went up, naturally, Wilf went on it, see . . . Father even thought 'ed been put in the tomb of the unknown soldier . . . !' He smiled at the memory

of the story his father had told him as a young child.
'But like I told you . . . old Wilf was a bit of a bugger! 'E
turned up . . .'

'Seriously . . . ?'

Jimmy nodded with a wheezy chuckle. 'It were
years later . . . when I were still a little 'un! Turned out
he'd deserted and run off with some Dutch farmer's
daughter! Then eventually, he'd got caught and court
martialed after the war 'ad been over a bit . . . and he
spent some years at 'is majesty's pleasure . . . because
he had three dependants by then . . . some deserters
didn't fair quite so well . . .'

'Is that right Jimmy . . . ?'

'It is . . . but apparently she found someone else
in his absence . . . and disappeared off the face of the
earth . . . with the two kids an' all . . . so 'e come 'ome!'
Jimmy paused to get his breath before continuing.
'Course, then he got called up again . . . for the second
shout . . . an' all of a year younger than the top end of
the call up. An' he died for real in France . . . on the
Normandy beaches, so natur'ly he went on 'ere again!
He's buried over there somewhere . . . in 'a *corner of
a foreign field that is for ever England*' . . . as they say.
My mother got herself killed in the blitz and I grew up
with her sister in Kent . . . so I've never been to find
it . . .'

Flynn wiped at a spill on the bar, and they continued in easy chatter for a few minutes, with Belinda resting her head loyally on Jimmy's bony knees.

Sir Christopher came in soon afterwards, for a pint of Guinness and a ploughman's lunch, because the Royal Oak, his preferred hostelry, didn't do weekend bar food and the restaurant was reservation only with a very long wait. He was accompanied today by Hannah, in her grubby jodhpurs and leather boots having just spent the morning in the saddle with Amy Palmer as usual. Picking up his order from the bar, her father handed her a diet coke and some crisps and motioned her over to a table so that they could sit and wait for the rest of their lunch. Belinda, in a prime demonstration of cupboard love, left Jimmy and followed her at the sight and sound of a rustly crisp packet, and settled down at Hannah's feet hopefully, as her father nodded to Jimmy on the way by and passed the time of day with his usual booming voice that was devoid of any ability to judge a more suitable volume in the otherwise empty bar.

Just then, two more customers arrived and walked over to the bar: and Len Fidler ordered two pints of beer, one for himself, and the other for his certainly underage son. Hannah raised her eyebrows slightly in disbelief at this as she patted Belinda's head and took a sip of her drink.

Flynn looked from one to the other of the two men, and then directly at Danny.

'You got any ID son?' he asked, his face friendly but firm and his eyes not moving from their target.

'Not on me . . .' Danny replied quietly, dropping his eyes first and mortified that the horse girl who'd blanked him was there and so close that she had to be listening to every word.

'Then how old are ya exactly?'

'Eigh'een . . .' he replied, looking towards his father uncertainly and then back at the Landlord.

'Well now. Let me say to ya, I've been in this business a long time and I reckon you fall a bit short son . . .' He said it with well practiced certainty. 'Tell you what. You have a nice refreshing can of lemonade shandy today . . . bring in your ID for me next time and I'll stand you a beer if I'm wrong . . . how's that?'

Danny shifted from one foot to the other grudgingly, and nodded just once.

Hannah sniggered into her drink behind him, and his face burned indignantly as he stared at his feet.

'That's a good lad. Take a seat where you like gentlemen and I'll bring them over to ya.'

Flynn set about getting their drinks and took them over to the table by the window, with a complimentary bowl of peanuts to show no ill will.

Danny took his can of shandy and sipped at it, pulling a face, before grabbing a handful of nuts, shoving them into his mouth to take the taste away. He'd deliberately sat with his back to Hannah but could still feel her eyes burning into his back.

'You got a tab system running here mate?' said Len hopefully as Flynn turned away.

'Only once the brewery lets me have one too,' he replied, with his stock answer to the same enquiry. Taking the crumpled ten pound note Len then offered him as payment, he went back to the till behind the bar, but keen to put the awkwardness behind them he smiled once more. 'Are you gentlemen new to the neighbourhood or just passing through?' He said it conversationally, passing Len back his change, that Len counted carefully before putting it in his pocket. Flynn continued to stand by their table, a bar towel draped over one shoulder, his arms folded across his chest and his legs astride, awaiting an answer.

'New,' said Len. 'We just moved onto the Flowergarden. We're just checking things out . . . testing then lie of the land . . . you know . . .'

'I do indeed,' said Flynn, looking pointedly at Danny who was studying his distasteful drink carefully.

Changing the subject, Len took a long draught of his beer and asked Flynn if he knew of any jobs going in the village.

'What's your line of work?' Flynn asked.

'We can turn our hands to most things, can't we son?' Danny nodded. 'I'm Len Fidler and this is my son Danny. And the Missis, she's looking for work too, cooking, cleaning . . . she's done bar work before . . .' he looked past Flynn towards the bar and smiled slightly. Flynn turned and followed Len's gaze to a card propped against a beer pump on the bar saying *'Kitchen help needed. Ask Belinda or Flynn for details.'*

'Ask her to come in and see me sometime and I'll see what I think,' he said dubiously. Despite his efforts to the contrary, he was already on his guard: they hadn't made much of an impression on him so far as a family, trying to dodge payment and encouraging underage drinking.

His attention was taken by the sudden arrival of a coach party of American tourists passing through the village who all wanted to taste real English beer and eat ploughman's lunches. Belinda quickly tired of being petted and fled to her basket in the vast but redundant inglenook fireplace, and by the time they'd all gone, so had the Derby's, and so had Len and Danny Fidler.

And after Flynn had been running around like a headless chicken trying to make lunches and serve the drinks that, because it was his barmaid's day off, Jimmy had been pulling for him for the last hour and a half, it struck him that as long as Len's wife could make up a decent ploughman's, she was on.

*   *   *

A couple of days later, just as Flynn unbolted the doors to let Jimmy in, he was surprised to find that it wasn't Jimmy that was waiting outside for a change. Lizzie Fidler smiled timidly and allowed him to let her inside out of the rainy drizzle for her first view of the public bar. She wasn't what he was expecting at all. Whereas Len and his son appeared instantly shifty and cunning, she was the exact opposite. Thin to the point of emaciation, she had her long but unkempt mousy blonde hair tied back with what was quite obviously a postman's red elastic band. Her face was thin and drawn as if she had all the cares in the world, and her hands were thrust deeply into the pockets of a grubby old raincoat. When he put out his right hand to introduce himself properly, her hand, when it appeared briefly from her coat pocket, was ice cold and trembling.

'Would you like a drink while we talk Lizzie? A glass of wine or something?' he asked, instantly recognising the victim in this family and trying to put her at ease.

She shook her head. 'No thank you, I don't drink . . . not at all . . .' she added quietly.

'Just an orange juice, or a nice glass of lemonade then?' he asked.

'I'd like a cup of coffee . . . if it's not too much trouble . . .' she said, eyeing the coffee machine behind the bar. Flynn fetched a cup and placed it in front of her, with a plastic sachet of sugar and a little pot of cream in the saucer.

'I've done lots of bar work . . . and I can cook, and clean,' she said, still nervously avoiding any eye contact.

He watched her as she tried to open the sugar with her teeth, until it tore unexpectedly, spilling sugar in a cascade across the table. Leaping up in horror she jogged the table and managed to spill her coffee too, and it slopped messily down the front of her coat.

'I'm so sorry . . .' she wailed, tears instantly springing to her eyes and now quivering uncontrollably. 'I'm so sorry . . . I . . .'

Flynn smiled slightly and put a hand on her arm, stopping her from frantically wiping at her coat and gently sitting her back down. There was something about her. Her hair scraped back into that harsh ponytail like a cheap facelift, and her eyes, when she dared actually look at him, reached into his heart disconcertingly and reminded him of someone in quite an unsettling way. Reaching back for a bar towel behind him he wiped up the mess and threw the towel over the back of the bar with careless abandon to try and make her smile, but the poor woman was a nervous wreck. He reached across the table once more and put a hand on her wrist very gently.

'I'll be honest with you Lizzie. I need help . . . We've got the quiz and curry fundraiser coming up tomorrow, and after my last week's jar sauce special I reckon there's likely to be a revolt so I reckon you're just perfect. When can you start?'

Finally she smiled, even if just for a fraction of a second, and breathed out very heavily as if she'd been holding her breath the whole time. 'How about now?' she said, standing up. 'If you show me where I can find a wet cloth, I can clean up this sticky mess properly . . . before anyone else comes in . . .'

Once the table was clean again, and now in the kitchen showing Lizzie around, Flynn heard the doors squeak open and grinned as the bristly chinned, day off face of his good friend Gareth Carey, Michelin starred chef from the Royal Oak, walked behind the bar and put his head around the kitchen door. He was carrying a rolled up local newspaper in one hand and tapped it cheerfully against the door frame as he saw Lizzie, grinned, and exclaimed, 'Oh great . . . you've got yourself a new cook Flynn . . . !' putting out his hand to shake hers. She took it with a nervous smile.

'This is Lizzie . . .' said Flynn.

'Hello pet I'm Gareth . . .' His broad Liverpool accent took her by surprise as he took her hand in a firm grip, and shook it so vigorously that her whole

44

body seemed to join in the introduction. 'So, how fast can you unfreeze me an Irish stew and some lovely cheesy mash then, Lizzie? I've been up since seven, I've had no breakfast and I'm so hungry I could eat a scabby horse between two bread lorries . . . !'

Chapter five

Lizzie's hapless husband did nothing unless it was in his favour. A man with an almost inherent drink problem, he was born the result of underage sex whilst his unfortunate mother was drunk at a party in 1973, and quickly realised that he was unwanted by either of his barely teenage parents. He'd grown to the tender age of seven learning how to be a bully in the ideal way; by being bullied, until he'd been spirited away by Social Services and put in a children's home. But even a succession of caring foster homes had failed to break through the defences of the troubled child. By the age of sixteen he'd gained a criminal record for possession and intent to supply drugs, a little habit he'd picked up along the way, but the resultant stay at one of her Majesty's young offender's institutions had taught him not to stay on the straight and narrow; but to box clever. On his release he had got himself a job in the mail room of the Royal Mail Depot in Reading; his legitimate pay packet going most of the way towards funding his recreational drug habit, and allowing him to live in a very dingy bedsit above a Chinese takeaway on the London Road near the Royal Berkshire Hospital. For four years he worked at proving himself trustworthy, and climbed the ladder of promotion steadily until reaching the dizzy heights of Shift Supervisor. He was quite handsome as a young man, but in a disheveled kind of way, and in his spare time he'd never had any trouble finding girlfriends but, a *'love 'em and leave 'em'* kind of man, he had never wanted to be tied down to one person after experiencing first hand, and fist, what it had done to his father.

It was during this period of apparently good behavior at work that he'd met the girl who was to become his wife properly for the first time; though he'd seen her around many times, with a small child in a buggy, because they both lived in the same area. When she'd come into the office that morning to collect a package deemed too large to fit through her letterbox, he'd not needed to hear the sound of the counter bell to draw him out of his back office to attend to her, having seen her walk past his window. Seeing her up close for the first time had almost taken his breath away despite the fact that, pushing her collection card through the glass at him, she was hot and bothered and doing her best to placate the little girl, who was about two years old, in mid tantrum, and creating one hell of a din. She'd apparently wanted some chips from the fish and chip shop next door and the child was red in the face and still grizzling, 'me want chipth . . . .' One hand was clutching a grubby piece of cloth to her mouth, and her fingers were wrapped neatly around her nose, with the accompanying thumb in her mouth being sucked miserably. Her sealed mouth was forcing bubbles of runny snot to burst forth from both nostrils, and the mother had got tears in her own eyes by this time, and looked awfully young. She was stunningly pretty, with long glossy hair falling in cascades around her shoulders, and what he could clearly see to be very impressive breasts defined under her thin t shirt on a cold day that had him almost breathless with lust. Wiping at her eyes with the back of one impatient hand, she'd tugged at the child and muttered 'I haven't got any money for chips.!' under her breath and looked at him briefly as she'd handed him the card.

In those, *what did I do to deserve all this*?' eyes, he saw a kindred spirit for the first time in his life.

Tearing his eyes away from her finally, he'd gone through to the office to locate her package and, passing the vending machines on the way back with it, he'd delved into his back pocket for some loose change. He'd winked at her as he passed the package through the counter glass and she'd almost smiled back, but still looked frazzled. Seizing the moment by opening the counter front, he stooped down to the grizzling child and produced a small packet of Jelly Tots magically from behind his back.

'Ah, ah . . . ! What's your name first?' he said cheekily, as she stopped crying with a ragged sniff and shyly put the hand with the apparently surgically attached cloth towards him to take the packet.

'Amma . . .' she mumbled; the other thumb now defiantly stuck in her mouth.

Len looked at the mother and winked again. 'Well then . . . Anna. If you promise to stop all this noise and be a good girl for your lovely mummy for the rest of today, I just might let you have these . . .' he said.

Out of her buggy now, the child looked a bit dubious at his offer and moved closer to her mother, finally removing her thumb to wrap her arms around one of the girl's denim, and very long, legs.

Having got no agreement he silently opened the packet and popped one of the sweets into his mouth, chewing with exaggerated sounds of enjoyment he offered the packet up to her mother. This was too much for the little girl. 'No . . . Nooo! I be good . . . I be good!' she bleated, furious at the thought of losing any more of the sweets, and especially to her mother, who had denied her what she'd wanted in the first place.

Len finally offered her the packet and she snatched it greedily, stuffing her whole hand inside and shoving practically its entire contents into her little mouth so that she could barely chew.

'That's very kind of you . . . but you shouldn't give in to her you know . . .' the girl said gratefully. 'She's strong willed this one . . . There'll be no controlling her otherwise . . . .'

'Different when someone else does it though . . . and just this once won't hurt love . . .' he laughed. 'So . . . what's the 'E' for in your name then?' he said finally; changing the course of his life for ever.

'Elizabeth' she said with a shy smile.

Of course, he already knew where she was living; he'd seen her go in there often enough: it was a single mother's hostel just off the London Road. He'd gone there that same evening, this time on her invitation, armed with some Brownie point winning chips wrapped in newspaper, and succeeded in becoming the living embodiment of Father Christmas to little Anna and, with one lingering kiss, the means of escape to her mother.

Almost before he knew it they were married and living in a two bedroomed flat, and Len Fidler, on the face of it at least, had finally become respectable.

Len's main problem embarking upon marriage was, of course, insecurity; having never had any. Being married to the sweet natured and lovely Elizabeth; soon shortened to Lizzie, had started out ok, though they were far from being even remotely solvent, and the sad legacy of his lack of any kind of love or security in his life transpired to be that he was a jealously possessive man, who wanted his wife all to himself, and was even jealous of her relationship with her daughter. As time passed it began to drive him increasingly insane when she got the inevitable admiring glances from other men as well, either in the pub with him or when she was out shopping. He knew that happened of course, because that's what he'd done himself in the first place.

Taking control of her body and her soul had started out with small, seemingly innocent things that had just looked like him caring for her, but in truth they were the seeds of his need for complete power over her: restricting her housekeeping to prevent long shopping trips, timing her, asking where she'd been and who she'd spoken to, demanding his meals at very specific times so she'd have to be there, not allowing her a mobile phone once they became the norm, frequently saying he preferred her beautiful hair tied back in an unflattering ponytail, and therefore out of sight, so that she eventually just did it every day until that became the norm too.

In the absence of enough money to buy his drugs he began to drink more; it was cheaper anyway. Then he found that if he drank enough, he calmed down. But the more he became obsessed with his wife's fidelity, or the fear of the lack of it, the more he found he needed to drink to calm down.

By the time Danny was born a couple of years later and he had two children to support, they were so short of money due to his, by now excessive drinking, that he'd fallen back into old habits and started doing what he'd originally planned when he got the job in the mail room; secretly opening mail and stealing cash to try and make ends meet. Specifically he targeted greetings cards in coloured envelopes addressed to children, having identified those years ago as most likely to contain money from loving relatives.

He'd soon been caught of course, and instantly lost his job.

They'd been evicted once they had defaulted on their rental agreement, but at least with the two children they'd been given priority on the housing list, and were moved into Newbury by the council, onto one of the largest estates.

The downward spiral increased in speed as the years passed by, and Lizzie became a victim far too under his control to argue anymore. After an incident involving the still feisty Anna, by then a teenager, when he'd come home roaring drunk from the pub one night, Anna had simply disappeared, and local accusations flew that she'd been murdered. Bricks soon began coming through the windows, and paint cans sprayed badly spelled threats on every reachable wall of their house. For their own safety they'd been moved again, this time to the outskirts of neighbouring Thatcham, and the marriage limped painfully, in poor Lizzie's case, onwards.

After a few more years of troubled existence the family finally got moved to Frincham, in Lizzie's vain hopes that, by then at least it was publicly known that Anna had just run away and never come home, Len would get himself a job on the land somewhere in the fresh air, and stop drinking.

Len and Lizzie's son Danny soon began to find his feet in their new neighbourhood. He had struck up quite a friendship with a boy of about the same age as him, called Baz, who lived at number 41, just down the road from number 27, who had recently bought a battered old pick up truck. They'd soon joined forces and, at Danny's suggestion, had used their combined job seekers allowance to buy a set of ladders and some buckets, and started up a window cleaning business.

Offering a service to clean both outsides and insides, to the instant delight of their customers, word soon got around and the business grew rapidly. The work was easy, if repetitive, but the array of differing personalities among their customers was source of constant amusement to Baz and Danny, and neither boy had ever dreamed of some of the things they saw through windows in their lives before. They saw all kinds of things people didn't think they could. Women tantalisingly sorting out their 'wardrobe malfunctions' when they thought no one was watching, women walking post shower naked from their bathrooms. Couples having rows, couples having sex, couples almost having sex . . . and not always with the people they knew normally lived there either.

To the two hot blooded teenage boys, top of the list was Mrs Doreen (pronounced *Du'reen'*) Jones, the lonely housewife of a certain age from 53 Freesia walk who always stayed in her dressing gown on windows days, until suggestively getting dressed once one of them appeared on the ladder at her bedroom window, to the point of asking Baz, the more confident and flirty one of the pair, inside one day.

He'd developed the habit of whistling 'Me and Mrs Jones' every visit after that . . .

The bored housewives who really knew how to take care of themselves certainly didn't live on the Flowergarden; they lived in the bigger properties along the main through roads with posh cars like Mercedes, Audi's, and big BMW's in their driveways. They were the ones who rarely flirted or made improper suggestions, but would always tempt them inside anyway with trays of real coffee in a tall pot with a plunger, and plates of proper homemade biscuits, often still warm from the Aga. Danny secretly loved these women who spoke so confidently and smelled better than their biscuits, and their huge kitchens, ankle deep carpets and fine antique furniture and ornaments made his mouth water with longing for a similar life.

One of the sources of amusement to the two boys was the imaginative places some of their less streetwise customers kept their spare house keys; should they be out on 'windows' days. They hid them under flowerpots, under strategically placed rocks, garden gnomes, or doormats; in sheds, outside lavatories, and greenhouses, inside little gadgets bought from the *Betterware* man; even on the end of lengths of string that you had to pull through skin-stripping letterboxes in one or two cases.

Before very long they had built up an impressive list of regular customers in the area, and became a familiar sight around the village, which would have been fine with Danny; if he didn't have to keep crossing paths with bloody Hannah Derby about very five minutes, or so it seemed. Frincham was such a tiny village you couldn't go anywhere without her cropping up at every turn; with that snooty look of hers, and it was beginning to drive him nuts. Even when he wasn't cleaning windows and was just minding his own business walking between the estate and the village he saw her too, plodding along on that great brown horse with the paint dipped white legs of hers, whose poncy name, he'd recently discovered, was Beau.

He'd tried not to be intimidated by her, really he had, and usually he succeeded very well, if he encountered her whilst in the company of one or other of his new friends from the estate, and especially if it was Mad Dave. He could really enjoy himself taunting her with Dave's fast wit, and delight in seeing her peaches and cream complexion look more like overcooked beetroot.

But as deeply annoying as she was with the way she looked down on him as she passed him by, there was no doubting the fact that she'd made quite an impression on young Danny Fidler; the boy who generally had no problem at all getting girls to fancy him with his twinkling black eyed gypsy charms . . .

He had to admit, grudgingly, that she was very pretty indeed.

He'd watched her one morning at the beginning of the Easter holidays as he stood perched at the top of his ladders cleaning the windows of the flat above Griffins the butchers. She was standing in the square talking to that Mrs Taylor from Clearwater House, outside the post office. Her long blonde hair was worn loose for a change, and it was shining in the sun like one of those soppy adverts for shampoo. She wasn't dressed for riding that day either, and was wearing the tiniest of denim shorts that showed off her long slim legs, with black leggings and flat suede Ugg boots, and a T shirt with a flowery little unbuttoned flimsy top that had short, puffy sleeves.

Baz whistled softly from his anchor position at the bottom of the ladder as his gaze followed Danny's.

'There she is again Dan! Now she'd be real dream to wake up next to in the mornings wouldn't she?'

Danny looked away with a non committal grunt and slopped the wet cloth against the window; cursing as a stream of water ran down his outstretched arm and inside the sleeve of his T shirt, only to dribble coldly down inside it.

'Nightmare more like: I wouldn't touch her with the other end of this ladder . . . And I bloody swear she's following me!' The last was hissed under his breath bitterly as she passed by the ladder below him, knowing perfectly well he'd be there this morning because she'd heard the butcher say so yesterday.

Her hair bounced off her shoulders glossily, and Danny stole an involuntary look as she disappeared around the corner, and out of sight.

He'd kept his head down and avoided her for most of the rest of that week, but he found himself constantly thinking about her, and her haughty face and her shining blonde hair invaded his dreams. He certainly enjoyed teasing the stuck up cow and making her blush, that was for sure, but that Friday; Baz's van being at the garage having its exhaust replaced after numerous complaints about the mushroom cloud that accompanied their visits to their customers, he and Baz had caught the morning bus into Newbury with the week's takings and, taking advantage of the lovely spring day, were lying on the grass in Victoria Park, killing time by 'watching the girls go by', before catching the one and only bus back to Frincham later that afternoon. The local schools were still off for Easter, and a couple of pretty teenage girls had satisfactorily taken their bait, and were sitting with them while they waited for their friend to arrive, before they headed off to the local cinema for the afternoon.

Danny yawned widely and laid out flat on the grass in an exaggerated stretch, closing his eyes against the bright sun, until the breathless voice of their tardy friend broke into the chatter and the three girls greeted each other.

'Look at you two chatting up the boys! Can't leave you alone for two minutes can I?' she laughed, smiling widely as she hugged them both. 'I'm so sorry I'm late! I had to wait for my dad to get off a conference call before he'd bring me in and . . .' She stopped dead as she realised who they were chatting up.

'Hello gorgeous . . .' said Baz with a wicked grin, patting the grass beside him. 'Dan . . . you're right . . . she is following you!'

Danny opened his eyes and shielded them against the sun.

'Hann-ahhh . . .' he nodded dubiously and attempted bored indifference to her sudden appearance there by re closing his eyes. 'Didn't recognise you without a horse between your thighs . . .'

Katie and Mel giggled. Despite the look on her face it was clear that her friends had no intention of leaving, so she fought hard to look unconcerned, sat down on the grass next to him like an opposing magnet and crossed her legs shyly in her very short shorts, eyeing the prostrate Danny with a heady mixture of bile in the throat horror tinged with quite a bit of rabbit/headlight. She began to fretfully tug at the grass for something to do with her shaking hands.

Danny sighed resolutely as his nostrils caught her sweet flowery scent beside him, crossed one foot lazily over the other, tugged at his earring as if to cure an itch and returned his interlocked hands behind his head as a pillow.

'Hi . . . um . . . Danny . . .' she said quietly, and swallowed hard. 'I . . . haven't seen you in the park before . . .'

'I haven't seen you in the park before either . . .' he said, eyes still closed and mimicking her posh accent. 'Though you seem to crop up everywhere else I am these days . . .'

Katie looked at Mel and raised her eyebrows with a slight smirk.

'I take you two know each other already then?' Mel giggled. 'Ooh Hannah Derby, you're a dark horse!' she laughed, nudging her. 'Not sure your dad would approve though!'

'It's only like red cars Dan . . .' Baz laughed, joining in and winking at Mel. 'You know how it is . . . you decide you really fancy a red car for yourself . . . and then you see them everywhere . . .'

'Are you saying he fancies Hannah too?' Katie sniggered, enjoying Hannah's discomfort as she pulled herself to her feet.

Despite her best efforts to the contrary Hannah flushed crimson and beheaded an innocent daisy. 'Come on you two, let's go or we'll miss the start of the film . . .' she almost whispered, her shirt beginning to stick uncomfortably to her back, and afraid that her pounding heart was visible.

'Danny and Han-nah sitting in a tree . . . K.I.S.S.I.N.G.' Katie sang cheekily, reaching down and jabbing Danny in the ribs.

He was up with the speed of light and took off after her around the boating pond, and she shrieked in delighted horror once he'd caught her, picked her off her feet and held her threateningly over the murky green water while she pleaded with him to put her down and kicked her denim legs frantically. One of her sandals flew off and plopped into the water as an inquisitive swan raised its wings in an arc of high dudgeon and quickly swam away from it.

'I don't . . . I don't fancy him Mel . . . please can we go now . . . I . . .' Hannah's voice cracked as she fought back humiliated tears.

Danny pulled Katie back from the brink of the water, tipped her backwards in a tango dip and stooped to kiss her full on the mouth. Her arms went speedily around his neck as she kissed him back, far too enthusiastically, and they both almost fell in the pond after her sandal as he struggled to balance himself, and her.

The mother of a small boy grabbed him crossly as he stood totally transfixed beside them, holding a football almost as big as he was. She dragged him away muttering about teenagers and antisocial behaviour in the park, while a shaggy dog lifted its leg against an unoccupied bench beside the pair, sniffing at them inquisitively on its pay past.

Baz and Mel were falling about in hysterics, with his arm draped lazily around her shoulders and hers around his naked waist, and poor Hannah couldn't bear to watch anymore. Five was most definitely a crowd. By now she had a lap full of beheaded daisies and was desperate to get away from here. Her eyes fought to look anywhere but at the two of them still vying for entry to the Guinness Book of Records for the longest snog: but as she looked down at the blurring grass once again her eyes caught something metallic glinting in the sunshine, right where Danny had been lying. Wiping at her eyes angrily and checking to make sure nobody was watching her, Hannah picked up the gold hoop earring that must have come undone when he'd tugged at it, twisted it in her fingers for the briefest second, and slipped it unseen into the back pocket of her shorts. She knew it would drive him mad later when he couldn't find it. That'd teach him.

Looking back towards the two of them, she spoke once more before giving up entirely. 'She needs to get her shoe out of the pond before it sinks . . .' she said, pointlessly. Getting no answer she added, 'I've . . . gone off the cinema idea now . . . and anyway we've missed the start . . .'

Standing up and brushing the daisies away, she could see that Mel was too busy messing around with Baz to either notice or hear her and Katie was still otherwise engaged, so she grabbed her bag from the grass, and turned and fled hurriedly back the way she had come before they would notice she'd gone, or call after her.

Danny Fidler opened one eye and watched her go, trying to find out if it was physically possible to smirk whilst snogging.

He saw her take her phone from her bag, press a couple of buttons, and put it to her right ear.

Daddy to the rescue . . . he thought bitterly.

Much to Hannah's continued humiliation she found out that Mrs Higgins had employed Danny and Baz to clean the windows at Stanton Court; all 365 of them: one for every day of the year. There were so many windows that they had to do it in sections and seemed to be there most of the time these days. And while they were there Mrs Higgins would provide them with countless mugs of tea and regale them with tales of contra flows on the M40 in Oxford and multiple pile ups on the clockwise section of the M25.

Baz was delighted to be working at the house and joked that if Danny had any luck he'd catch Hannah walking naked from the ensuite bathroom he'd spotted in her bedroom, once they'd discovered which one was hers, and Danny had taunted her about having a ragged old teddy bear on her pillow at her age. Even it had been, unknown to him, a very valuable antique Steiff bear that had once belonged to her dead mother, and to her mother before that.

Despite himself, Danny took a prodigious amount of effort on Hanna's bedroom windows when they were on that side of the house just in case, but after the teddy bear taunts he thought she was going out of her way to avoid him and had kept her thickly lined curtains pulled together ever since.

But after a day or two he'd found out she wasn't avoiding him at all; she wasn't even there.

Her father had whisked her away abroad for the rest of the school holiday.

Damn.

*   *   *

Sir Christopher had actually had enough of everything that was going on in Frincham when he'd decided to take his moody daughter away. For him, away from the endless meetings and public consultations; and for Hannah of course, to get away from that awful black eyed yob of a boy that kept teasing her and getting her all hot under the collar of her Puffa jacket. So they had dropped everything at a minutes notice and gone to a house he owned and used to rent out as a holiday let, along with several others he still did, in northern France.

As always, they were accompanied by the redoubtable Mrs Higgins.

This house was a barn conversion situated down a narrow lane bordered by an avenue of sweet chestnut trees, and nestling beside its original farmhouse, where a small menagerie of its animals, (namely one sheep two ducks three chickens and a horse), were all either grazing bleating or clucking in its one remaining field. Traditionally built of local granite and slate with one huge window in its centre where the doors used to be, the houses stood on the outskirts of the village of *Colouvray Boisbenatre,* in the beautiful Normandy region.

The village itself was small but adequately kitted out, with a winding road through its centre, a café for long lunches, a *Boulanger,* a little corner shop for essentials, an imposing Roman Catholic church with a very grand churchyard, and a bar for sitting outside of in the evenings eating *Sausisson sech* with hunks of fresh bread, and drinking Cassis or Calvados with the locals. With his flawless French, that never failed to relax him usually, but the spell was not working now, because he was far too preoccupied with his financial problems . . . and his daughter.

Hannah had always loved coming here more than anywhere else in the world. When she was little she would nag at him to cut down the long grass in the back garden as soon as they arrived, so she could roll herself down the steep slope to the swing that was suspended from a tree at the bottom, and moo back at the cows in the field next door. They would buy ice creams from *Madame* in the little shop back then, eat fish and chips from the van that sat outside the bar on Thursday evenings, and they would walk the lanes surrounding the village in the endless sunshine, he lifting her onto his shoulders once her little legs became tired.

She was Daddy's girl in those days; but those days were long gone now, and the swing hanging from the tree at the bottom of the garden had rotted and fallen long ago, and the ropes now swayed forlorn and raggedly in the hazy breeze.

She had been greeted warmly by their elderly neighbours on arrival by the traditional kisses to both cheeks as usual, in reply to which she smiled unconvincingly and nodded her head to their genuine enquiries as to her health and wellbeing, but she'd disappeared up to her room in the eaves, slamming the door ominously the minute he'd opened the front door, stepped over the mountain of junk mail and flicked the light switch.

Apart from wandering aimlessly in the garden with her head down and her hands in the back pockets of her jeans, she had only really appeared for breakfast in the kitchen since they had arrived, because even the moody Hannah found it hard to resist her favourite holiday treat of a *pain au raisin* from the *Boulanger* . . . but a total lack of mobile phone signal, due to the thick walls of locally quarried granite, only added to her moodiness, and he was beginning to wish he hadn't bothered coming.

He stood at her bedroom window now, holding the teddy bear she still would not be without despite her desire to be considered grown up: and only successfully at the window after he had picked his way precariously among her discarded clothes and shoes. So different to the days when he'd picked his way precariously between her Play Mobil gymkhana and her Polly Pocket dolls; he was seemingly appreciating the stunning view down into the valley; but really he was watching her as she nodded her head slightly in rhythm to the unheard music on her iPod as she sat cross legged on the grass, irritably swatting at the flies that accompanied the cows she used to talk to when they grazed near the adjoining fence.

He drew in a deep breath, slowly shaking his head. He'd known in his heart that this time would come all along. The time when his darling little girl would change for ever into the young woman she thought she already was, and undoubtedly finding the fact that nobody else thought so, so deeply annoying.

Damn that black eyed gypsy boy! He was going to ruin her.

He'd seen sulky eyes like the way hers always seemed to be these days before and involuntarily shuddered at the unbidden memory of her mother.

Turning away from the window to break the chain of thought, he picked his way carefully through the debris of her bedroom floor, replaced the teddy bear to her pillow, and left her room to the stillness of the warm afternoon, closing the door behind him.

Chapter six

While they were still away life in the normally peaceful village of Frincham took a nasty turn when a spate of mysterious thefts, practically unheard of previously, succeeded in putting everyone on their guard.

The first incident to be noticed was when Rector Hector found the substantial contents of the church collection plate missing after a funeral service, assumed to have been stolen while everyone was out in the churchyard for the burial. Hector had frequently been warned by the police that there are a growing number of opportunist thieves who attend funeral services; taking advantage of the fact that it is very unlikely anybody would ever ask who they are, and when he reported the theft to the police, they had said as much to him again when they came along to investigate. But then on the same day as the funeral, Jimmy Knapp, who lived in number one Stanton Cottages, by the shop, arrived home from the pub after lunch to discover that his recently collected pension, his father's pocket watch, a very valuable Toby Jug, and Wilf's campaign medals, had all gone.

Old Mrs Cannings from number two, next door to him, lost her late mother's jewellery from her bedroom dressing table, and a pair of fine Staffordshire pottery dogs from her front windowsill. She'd been so upset, and now felt so vulnerable, that she'd immediately given up her cottage, moved out and gone to live with her sister in Guildford.

Bert Collins, Hector's Verger at the church, who lived at number three on the other end of the row, lost his pension too, and his lifelong collection of rare stamps while he was on duty at the funeral.

The biggest burglary, though not surprisingly, was from Stanton Court, when cash and jewellery to the value of several thousand pounds were stolen. So it was that on only the third day of their holiday, and on receipt of a telephone call from his estate manager informing him of the burglary, Sir Christopher booked the first available flight out of Rennes, and they all returned home.

*   *   *

Frincham is a sleepy village, barely changed since the war, with a virtually zero crime rate and a part time police station not too far away; manned by a single officer just two days a week. He spent some of his time processing gun licenses belonging to the local farmers, and the rest of it tending the vegetable patch and hanging baskets but, suddenly faced with such a crime wave, he had immediately called for reinforcements from nearby Newbury.

It soon became apparent though, that the police officers put on the case were all scratching their heads at the moment. No one had reported seeing anything suspicious, none of the properties had had any sign whatsoever of forced entry, and whoever the thief was he, or they, were leaving no fingerprints anywhere.

Flynn had set up a collection at the pub to help Jimmy and Bert replace their stolen pensions, the village jungle drums were well and truly sounding out; and all newcomers to the area were looked at with suspicious eyes.

Hannah Derby had been the first to twig that the connection to all of the thefts was the new window cleaners. They were the only ones who knew where all the victims' house keys were hidden, and even Mrs Higgins when asked, had admitted showing them where to find the spare key to the kitchen door should she be out when they came.

Hannah slipped purposefully into her father's study and called the police while her father was busy with the assessor from his insurance company and, with a healthy portion of smug satisfaction at finally being able to get her own back on Danny Fidler, she told them all about Danny's home life and what she considered to be his obvious motives.

Danny and Baz were immediately taken in to the Newbury Police Station for questioning.

*   *   *

'Tell me again son,' a bored detective sergeant Tidbury said, 'Why you think I should believe you that you two had nothing to do with these thefts?'

They had been sitting at the table in interview room three for almost four hours, without a break.

'Because we didn't, that's why.' Danny said impatiently. He took a deep breath. 'Tell you what, Sergeant Tidbury . . . . You tell me why *you* think we would bite the hands that feed us by thieving from our own customers?'

'Well . . . explain to me why *you* think there was no sign of forced entry at any of the properties . . . they are all your customers and *you* both knew where all their keys were kept . . . . And besides . . . our informant said . . .'

Blinking suddenly, Danny looked him right in the eyes and stopped him in mid sentence. 'What informant? Anyone could have seen where they hide their keys . . .' He ran his hands through his hair impatiently, and again went to fiddle with the earring that wasn't there.

'The odd one or two might have had their keys seen being used maybe, if they were near the front doors, I'll grant you that son . . . and hiding keys outside anywhere in this day and age is somewhat foolhardy; but all of them? Bit more of a coincidence, wouldn't you agree?'

Danny shrugged. 'Dunno . . . but we didn't do it sergeant . . . I'm telling you.'

'Our informant seemed perfectly sure of your motives . . . she even told us what they were . . . same as your mate did . . . though he gave it to us in a lot more detail . . .'

'She . . . ? She who? What motives?'

'They both told us about your mum and your old man. It was your mate said he beats her up though. Your girlfriend . . .' he smiled slightly as Danny's eyes burned black with anger; 'or is it *ex* girlfriend? Told us she'd heard he drinks his way through all his giro and your mum's wages, and that it's left up to you to make sure you and your mum can eat occasionally . . .'

'I earn enough for that without thieving!' he said shortly.

'Must be tough though . . .'

Danny looked into the sergeant's eyes once more, his own eyes black and menacing, and he almost whispered. 'That's our business, not yours . . . or Hannah Derby's. We manage, I said . . .'

Tidbury sighed, knowing they were getting nowhere fast and needing a break.

'Well, I think that's enough for now son . . .' he said, standing up and pointedly glancing at his wrist watch. 'Don't leave the country though Danny boy . . . we'll want to speak to you again . . .' He opened the door of the interview room and held it back for Danny to leave.

'About bloody time too!' He said, standing up and swallowing his barely suppressed anger.

Leaving the room though, he stopped briefly and turned back towards the sergeant.

'Hannah Derby is not, never has been, and never will be, my girlfriend . . . . And I ain't no bleedin' thief neither!'

Chapter seven

Despite all her family problems Lizzie Fidler had settled in well working at the Hart, arriving first thing in the morning to prepare meat and vegetables, or curry on Tuesdays, make up the baguette fillings for lunch, and helping behind the bar at lunchtimes only when the balance of need swung in that direction. There was another girl that came in to help Flynn behind the bar in the evenings so Lizzie tended to be just in the kitchen then, where she was happiest: rarely coming into the pub, always refusing the offer of anything to drink other than tea or coffee, or fruit juice, and calling Donna or Flynn to serve meals when they were ready. She was still awfully quiet and withdrawn despite Flynn's constant attempts to praise and encourage her, and Donna's attempts at friendly conversation were always met with polite but distant responses.

She was a hard worker, but it was her relationship with her husband that really worried Flynn, and it was clear that she visibly avoided going in the bar during his nightly visits. The man had a serious drink problem, which she was obviously embarrassed about, and once he'd had a few he seemed to delight in drawing attention to her by making barbed comments about either her appearance or her cooking to anyone who would listen. He had also taken to loudly voicing his resentment that she often stayed well after her official finish time, even though she'd said it was in order to leave everything clean and tidy in the kitchen before the next day in case the brewery inspector made an impromptu visit. She worked shifts from eleven until two and then again from six until ten, and had Mondays off, when the kitchen was closed. On Monday mornings the industrious Lizzie supported her liability of a husband, who didn't seem to be working at all, by cleaning the church; scrubbing at the floors and polishing the pews, and tidying up after the Sunday service activities. On Monday afternoons she cleaned the Rectory and the Taylor's house by the lake, but if anyone was home at either she rarely spoke unless spoken to, and often worked much longer than her allotted two hours at Clearwater House, delighting in the stunning art works hanging all around, and in particular, seemed taken with a huge portrait on the wall of the dining room that

Paul had done of his wife with such obvious love that it just hypnotized her.

It was the most beautiful portrait she'd ever seen; not that she'd seen many real oil paintings in her life of course. If alone in the house, she often just sat at the table and gazed up at it open mouthed, finding it so hard to believe that a husband could be so lovingly observant that he had caught every hair on her head, every eyelash, and even the dimple in her chin to such perfection.

Flynn began to wonder if she ever spent any time at home, she seemed so reluctant, but the first time it began to dawn on him as to why that was, apart from the obvious reason, was after she arrived for work one morning with a poorly disguised black eye. Donna caught the look on his face and he'd caught the look on hers: so he wasn't imagining it then.

She'd been embarrassed of course, and explained it away with an unconvincing laugh as having walked into a cupboard door she'd left open in her kitchen. But the alarm bells were ringing in Flynn's head by then and after that he'd kept a closer eye on her. It didn't happen all that often of course, well not visibly anyway, but it did happen, he was now quite sure of it. He'd noticed that she avoided wearing short sleeves and low cut tops anyway, but when she once took off her cardigan while cleaning the ovens he'd noticed bruises of varying shades, and therefore ages, on her upper arms, as if she'd been forcibly held, and once she'd arrived with a large bruise on one side of her face that she'd again tried to cover with poorly applied cheap makeup.

They were getting on well by then but when Flynn had gently asked her about it she'd glossed over it and told him he was seeing things that weren't there. Something had fallen off the top of her wardrobe . . . she was clumsy, that's all. Ask Danny, she'd said.

'I'm just clumsy . . . .'

Donna tried too. She'd actually recognised the signs before Flynn, and had talked to Lizzie, bravely sharing her own childhood experiences with an abusive alcoholic father. For one tense and seemingly endless moment as she quietly offered Lizzie an innocent looking chapstick for her handbag that had a cleverly disguised domestic abuse helpline phone number on it, it looked as if she might finally have got through her defences.

But just as Lizzie had reached out to take it, the door to the public bar had opened and Len had appeared, breaking the spell with one intense stare, and sending Lizzie scuttling back to the kitchen, away from him as fast as her shaking legs would carry her.

The chapstick had rolled off the table and disappeared under the bar.

It didn't take an Einstein for the people of Frincham to see what a waste of space Len Fidler was. Each night he would enter the bar soon after seven; and the drunker he got the more he picked on his poor wife by taking every opportunity to criticise and make jokes at her expense. He would always stay until closing time, spending at least the last hour nagging at her to leave with him and go home.

Sometimes he arrived with Danny but usually he was alone, as Danny obviously objected to paying for all his drinks for him, and the one or two locals that had tried to befriend him had soon discovered that he had a tendency to enjoy their generosity, but then vaporise when it was his round.

Unless of course Lizzie had just been paid, in which case he was, briefly, generosity personified.

Flynn found himself disliking Len intensely, and he wondered where the money was coming from for all the whisky chasers he always ordered with his pints of beer. As far as Lizzie would actually say, Len was still unemployed, so Danny was the only family member apart from his mother who was working, and window cleaning couldn't be that lucrative, even if he had nabbed Stanton Court . . . . and he also knew that recent events had affected their business irretrievably now anyway . . .

When he saw another pattern emerging though, Flynn decided he needed to act.

On the last four Thursdays, payday surprisingly, the till had been exactly twenty pounds short. He'd taken to cashing up after her lunchtime shift on Thursdays as well now, so he knew for sure that it was at lunchtimes that the money was going missing. He also knew it had to be Lizzie that was taking it.

On the following Thursday, and just before closing time with no remaining customers, in order to be certain, he marked the top twenty pound note in the till drawer, and the top two tens, with a dot of purple marker pen just to the left of the serial number. He then went down to the cellar to check all the barrels as usual. After Lizzie had gone home, with her pay packet, he opened the till and immediately noticed that the two marked tens had gone.

That evening he waited to see if either Len or Danny paid for their first drink with a marked ten. Len was alone that night, and he didn't. Much to Flynn's disappointment he paid for it, and for several other people's, from a surprisingly full wallet for an unemployed man, with a twenty. In fact in the brief glance of the inside of Len's wallet that he'd had, it looked as if it was all twenties in there, and he'd paid Lizzie in twenties just that morning.

On his way back from Newbury the following morning, Flynn saw Lizzie go into the Grocers in the Square. Intent on following her, he pulled over to the parking bay and went in to buy some milk and a newspaper. The shop was otherwise empty as he secretly watched her hand over a ten pound note for her single purchase at the till, take her change, and leave the shop; the door opening with a loud ping before closing behind her. When he'd then come out from behind the cheese counter and paid for his own shopping with a twenty pound note, he'd been given the top ten pound note from the till in his change. It was marked. His pulse racing, he knew he'd finally got the proof he needed, and decided to confront Lizzie when she came in again at lunchtime.

When she arrived, he asked to see her quietly and sat her down in the room out the back of the kitchen that they used as a sort of storage room; its floor space mostly taken up with boxes of crisps and cards of packets of nuts, but there was a small table and two chairs in the corner. He came straight to the point, and to her credit she admitted stealing the money immediately, looking otherwise reticent as usual, but then her eyes betrayed her and she began to shake uncontrollably.

'Flynn I'm . . . I'm so sorry . . . I never meant to . . . It's just that I can't manage . . . Danny tries to help but . . . it's so hard now his business and most of his customers have . . . you know . . . and Len doesn't like it when I can't . . . I'll . . . go . . . .' She stood up and the chair scraped against the floor tiles.

Flynn bit the bullet.

'Lizzie,' he said, placing his hand on her arm so she sat back down. She winced at his touch and he caught his breath. 'Is he taking your wages off you too?'

Her brows knitted slightly at the thought of what else she knew he suspected, but she didn't move.

'I know he's hurting you . . . so please don't keep trying to deny it . . .' he said quietly. 'You know, you can trust me . . .'

Seeing he'd got her undivided attention he reached down into a box on the floor and drew out the reason for his trip to Newbury this morning: a mobile phone.

'. . . I heard he won't let you have one of these . . . so I . . . I got you one . . . and I've set it all up on my contract . . . so it's ready for you to use and it won't cost you a penny. I want you to be safe Lizzie . . . I . . . I've put my own number in the memory for you, just as 'work' . . . look, it's just here, see? Then you know you can call me any time . . . you know that you can . . . don't you?'

She stood up suddenly, as if to defend herself but, seeing him for the lifeline he potentially was, she nodded quickly as she grabbed the phone from his outstretched hand, and burst into tears; her free hand covering her face as she desperately tried to stop.

'I . . . needed to buy . . . tampons . . .' she sobbed, as the grubby and makeshift bandage on her left wrist that had been hidden by her coat sleeve became visible, and once again he shook his head slowly at the state of her.

Instead of sacking her on the spot like he knew he should, he found himself feeling hot and angry, and his heart was beating painfully. He experienced, and not for the first time, a surge of impulse to want to protect her; wanting to wrap her up in cotton wool . . . and then go round there and break the bastard's neck with the thick end of a pool cue.

Once she'd let her guard down Lizzie found she just couldn't stop, and again Flynn heard something in her gulping cry that tugged at his heartstrings.

Then, like footfalls echoing in a memory somewhere deep inside him, he knew.

Pulling her into his arms, his eyes wide with shock, he shook his head with a gasp of disbelief, as his mouth fell open, and he swallowed hard.

*　　*　　*

Lizzie Fidler she may be now; but she'd always be Beth Edwards to him . . . Beth Edwards; the only girl he'd ever loved.

She'd been just sixteen years old when she'd disappeared, and he'd been seventeen and friends with her older brother Kevin at school. Their brief relationship had been a bit on the sly because of that.

Her father was a brute he remembered, and it was some time after Beth and the rest of her family had disappeared that he'd found out from the newspapers that on one awful night he'd murdered her mother with a kitchen knife, so Beth and Kevin had been moved to safety, and God only knows where.

He'd heard on the grapevine that they'd been split up; given new identities and new homes.

So he had no way of finding her, and no way of knowing if she even wanted him to try after the last thing she'd said to him the day before she'd disappeared was so cruel. They'd argued over something that, at the time, seemed so important, but now seemed so silly and immature.

He closed his eyes as he remembered how they'd spent a secret day on a coach trip to Bournemouth that day, and that he'd written *Je t'aime* in the sand in his best schoolboy romantic French. But she'd blushed crimson and pretended she didn't understand what he'd written, and they'd ended up having a silly argument, mostly, he shuddered to think now, because he'd been immature and embarrassed in front of so many other people on the beach that day. Probably equally embarrassed, the last thing she'd said to him as they'd parted company at the bus station was 'drop dead!' . . . and she'd never contacted him again either.

Now though, so many long years later, here she was, here in his arms; a tattered and broken shell of the shining girl she'd once been; and with a sickening irony—looking just like her mother before her. The only thing remotely similar to the girl she'd once been, was the gulping sound she made when she cried.

He allowed her to sink her head onto his chest and sob; 'Where were you when I met him, Flynn . . . ?' with the phone still clasped in her hand; and felt himself falling helplessly, all over again.

'Beth, it's me . . . Paddy . . .' his heart whispered.

But his mouth stayed silent.

And for her to be safe, silent it would have to stay.

Chapter eight

Watson's 5,000 page planning application went in. Sarah Palmer leapt straight into action with all the members of her previous protest committee, but they soon found that it was deliberately almost impossible for them to decipher the application, with its countless reference and cross referenced reports to try and figure out but, undeterred by this, the protests were well underway.

At that stage it was fair to say that not everyone was against the plans, especially those with disabilities, or mothers with pushchairs, who all found it difficult to get around the small village shops and preferred Newbury's wide aisled supermarkets. So to those, the idea of one closer to home was a major plus. The protestors however, just considered that those people had donned rose tinted glasses, and just needed to be won over because they hadn't really considered the environmental cost of the plans at all.

A petition had gone all round the surrounding villages, and Paul Taylor had been persuaded to allow the press to talk to him for once, in order to raise awareness by getting their story in the nationals, and his own legal people had been put on the case to decipher the application, for which he was paying. Letters of objection had been sent to the council by the hundreds too.

On one of the proposals though, all the residents were as one against. As with the previous housing application, access to the proposed supermarket had to be addressed. It was impossible to simply widen the road on the approach due to the position of the churchyard on one side and a grade 2 listed Elizabethan cottage on the other. It was therefore proposed to build a completely new road, cutting across undulating chalk hills and flood meadows on Sir Christopher's land. Everyone locally knew if the road was constructed in that location, nobody would want to go the extra three miles round to get to the site. So without doubt, Frincham would become a rat run, or shortcut, to the dreaded supermarket.

Once the word was out, the publicity and fundraising committees became feverishly active, and a tree camp sprung up in the disputed woods overnight. Students were arriving like bees round a honey pot from all over the country.

They were headed up by a very tall gangly youth called Nigel with a speech impediment, Quaker style sideburns, and a ring through his left nostril, whose new mission in life was to protect the endangered ancient woodland on Sir Christopher's land. Nigel's girlfriend was a rather floaty woman called Misty, at least ten years his senior, and draped in all sorts of bangles and beads. She had her long red hair tied in plaits around her head and wore layers and layers of tie died, rag bag clothing with Doctor Marten lace up boots.

The protestors all became well known in the village as they tramped this way and that, and Danny and Nigel quickly became friends, after Danny had arrived up at the camp one morning, anxious to get involved, but in truth just to wind up Hannah. The sound of their drums and whistles became part of the countryside, and the disputed trees became adorned with an assortment of improvised rope walkways high up in their canopies, along with bed blankets, old duvets, blue plastic tarpaulins, balloons, and tingling wind chimes. A network of tunnels was also dug into the native chalk by the students, in order to render it impossible to bring in heavy machinery to bring the trees down for fear of burying people alive. They were well practiced at this and were awfully good at tunnels, making them impossibly narrow in places so that even the skinniest of them had to squirm through, and any better fed security guards wouldn't stand a chance of getting to them.

So very soon they had dug in and made themselves quite at home from the frequent rain showers. Local people began to bring them food parcels and blankets, and the chalk they'd excavated became useful for scrawling messages on the roads up to the camp.

Pretty soon after their arrival Sir Christopher even had to move his Highland cows off the chalk hills nearest the camp to stop the protesters stealing milk for their children, their animals, and their copious amounts of tea.

One of the protestors, an instantly memorable graduate with a Botany degree, thought he might have found an early answer to their problem. Tindy, a very tall and slender African student with the incredibly handsome facial features of his tribe with his ebony skin, high cheekbones and hypnotic eyes, also had a mass of chattering shell beads attached to the ends of an absolute mass of rich black hair braids.

He and his English Rose of a well spoken girlfriend called DeeDee, had measured one of the oak trees, thinking it worthy of a TPO, or Tree Preservation Order, from the local council. The magnificently knarled and bulbous tree with a great hole through the base of its trunk that would have made it look like the one the white rabbit had disappeared into in Alice in Wonderland if it had only had a door in it, measured almost twelve metres around its girth; therefore making it well over five hundred years old.

Hope flourished when a very official looking man in a suit and green Wellington boots from the local council duly arrived on the site with a tape measure and a clip board and agreed that it was indeed worthy of protection. But their hopes had been dashed when he pointed out that whilst a TPO could be implemented within hours in order to protect the tree, the bad news was that making a TPO in the first place is merely a 'discretionary power', which means the council does not have to do it. He said that there was no legal reason why a council has to make an order at all, but once one has been made, they have a duty to enforce it, and that costs money considering that TPO's do not offer absolute protection for trees in the first place.

'I'm sorry to disappoint you all,' he said, 'but applications can still be made to remove a tree, even with an order on it, for lots of reasons. And what's more, TPO's can be terminated at any time if the council decides that the reason for doing so is necessary, like if works on dying, dead, dangerous or nuisance trees are needed, and this one's seen better days . . . so if Watson's bring in the Forestry Commission and they did it under a felling licence it would be allowed too. And in previous cases I've been involved in, believe me they go to great lengths to make sure their detailed planning permission is sufficient to override any existing TPO.'

After that he'd packed up and gone, so it was back to the drawing board for Tindy, Nigel, and the rest of the protestors.

*   *   *

The local press and TV station were full of the protests, and as time went on and the camp became established it was visited by numerous people, including one or two 'B list' celebrities, keen to be seen as environmentally aware or, in some cases, just keen to be seen.

And the thefts by the colloquially tagged 'Frincham Phantom' were briefly sidetracked by unfolding events.

Danny turned legally eighteen when the protests were in full flow, and celebrated the auspicious occasion by arriving at the Hart that evening with Nigel and Tindy for his first legal drink, handed over traditionally free but slightly dubiously after the previous incident, by Flynn. Tindy, at the age of almost twenty two, had wholly embraced the student lifestyle when he arrived in the UK and was now well practiced in the art of real ale drinking, and Nigel was also a student after all, so Danny quite quickly found it a bit of a struggle to keep up with them. Flynn kept a watchful eye on him as their table filled with glasses and Danny sunk lower in his chair, but his father seemed quite proud of him and grasped the opportunity of free drinks for himself from the kind hearted locals on the occasion of his son's Coming of Age.

It was when Flynn finally called Time at 11pm that he noticed the RSPCA collecting tin was missing from the bar, and set about reporting the theft to the police. Len had gone, having had no luck and presumably run out of money, and Danny was totally plastered and fast asleep; his face having lost all its habitual moodiness in its innocent slumber. Lizzie watched through the kitchen hatch as Nigel and Tindy hoisted him onto their shoulders and dragged him, limp and lifeless, out of the door; Nigel declaring over his shoulder towards her that they would take him back to the camp for the night, and that she '*shoon worry we'll see 'es alright . . .*'

Flynn locked the doors behind them and turned to face Lizzie with an expression that hopefully conveyed a sort of '*they always do that on the first night of legal drinking but it doesn't make him an alcoholic like his father,*' look. Lizzie smiled slightly and gave him a sort of half nod, and turned away with a resigned sigh, preferring to discuss the missing money tin than face the crouching demon that was the real problem tonight. That if Danny stayed at the camp, she'd have to face her drunken husband on her own.

Talk of the missing tin soon exhausted, and unable to put it off any longer, she left the pub just after midnight and, refusing Flynn's usual offer of a lift, Lizzie made her way home as if her feet were encased in concrete. Her head beginning its all too familiar tense throbbing, she reached up to the back of her head and pulled out her tight ponytail to ease the tension on her scalp, wincing as the elastic band tugged at the sensitive hairs growing in the nape of her neck; and ran her fingers through her loose hair gratefully.

Just after one she turned the key in the front door and let herself quietly in, praying that he'd gone to bed already and be fast asleep . . . and harmless. The house was in complete darkness so the signs were good, and Lizzie felt her thumping heart gradually calming as she made her way by the light of the moon through the still open sitting room curtains, and into the kitchen.

Removing her jacket to hang it loosely over the back of a chair, she began her nightly soundless ritual of tidying away his discarded empties, clearing his vomit if he'd missed the sink, and checking he'd locked up; before settling down on the sofa to sleep so as not to wake him, as usual.

No vomit tonight, which was a blessing at least.

And nothing worse to clear up, either . . .

Calmer mow, and Idly picking up some post from the kitchen table, she turned to go back into the sitting room but, stopping quite dead in her tracks, a strangled a gasp caught in her constricted throat. Len was standing in the darkness, blocking the partition doorway, with his eyes wildly glinting in the innocent light of the full moon.

*   *   *

'You're late,' he said.

Lizzie swallowed hard and chose not to wind him up by saying he'd made her jump. Instead, she forced a brittle smile and kissed him on his cold, unresponsive lips.

'Oh, you know I sometimes can't leave on time, Len,' she said, she hoped, confidently. 'We were absolutely rushed off our feet tonight . . . . and someone stole the RSPCA collecting tin off the bar so Flynn had to report it to the police . . .' Biting her lip she walked past him and, with a shaking hand, switched on the kitchen light for some comforting support. The sudden glare of light from the bare bulb made both of them blink momentarily.

'You weren't that busy when I was in there,' he said quietly. 'Not busy at all then. You had plenty of time to chat with your fancy man Flynn though . . . I saw you.'

Lizzie swallowed; her throat as dry as dust. 'We . . . got busy after you'd gone. A . . . a whole load of people came in . . . after you left.'

He sneered at her as she spoke quickly, obviously trying to head off his all too predictable temper.

'Len I told you, he's just my boss . . . it would be rude if I didn't talk to him when . . . when he talks to me . . . and the tin had gone and . . .'

'So you say,' he said, his eyes darting involuntarily to the top of the fridge, where the stolen collecting tin sat brazenly. She hadn't seen it yet, obviously. 'But there's no point you making excuses Lizzie, I've seen the way you look at him . . .'

'I . . . don't Len . . . honestly . . .'

Eyes fixed on her, his head tilted slightly to one side; thinly veiled menace on his innocent face.

'Your hair is different. What have you done to your hair Lizzie?' he lifted some of it in his fingers, twisted it round them, pulling it tight until she flinched, and then let it fall.

'Nothing I . . . it's just loose Len, I took the band out on the way home . . . that's all . . . I have a bit of a headache . . . and my hair was tight . . . so I . . . .'

'You wore it loose for your fancy man . . . that's what you mean . . . Likes it loose doesn't he, your Flynn . . .'

Her hands began to shake so she clasped them together to hide it from him. 'No he . . . .' she swallowed. 'I didn't Len . . . I told you he's not my . . .'

'Shut your mouth woman!' he spat suddenly, the quietly spoken pretence over. 'You can't hide it from me . . . I can see it in your eyes . . .' he pushed his face close to hers; his breath foul smelling, his teeth bared, and his fists now clenched. 'He let it down before he had you tonight after closing time! Admit it!'

'No! Len I *swear* . . .' Lizzie gasped. Then, as she closed her eyes she took one resigned deep breath inwards, and awaited the inevitable.

With her eyes closed she wasn't ready to react when he pushed her, and she fell sideways heavily against the cooker, hitting the side of her head on the corner edge of the grill with a dull thump. Dazed and bleeding from the resultant cut just above her right eye, she tried to stand but he kicked her back down again, placing his foot, still in its outdoor shoe, against her throat.

'You're a common slut *Elizabeth Edwards!* A common slut that doesn't deserve to have my bleedin' name! You'll have sex with anyone that comes anywhere near you!'

He sniffed down towards her and pulled a face; his lip curling. 'I can smell it . . . and you love it don't you? You always did . . . and I fell for it and was the sorry fool that went and married you! Used goods . . . that's what you were Lizzie, used goods . . . you and your bleedin' brat! And where is *she* now then eh? Even she couldn't stand you once she was old enough to see what a *whore* you are could she? You just won't learn will you?'

Lizzie whimpered and tried to shut down her mind to what was happening to her by singing the song in her head she always sang when he lost his temper and it started; the song she used to sing to her baby daughter before she'd become so broke and desperate she'd married the first man that had asked her. And after all they'd been through Anna grew up and ran away before he beat her up too.

Or worse.

Red and yellow and pink and green . . . orange and purple and blue . . . I can sing a rainbow, sing a rainbow . . . sing a rainbow too . . .

Quite suddenly for a drunken man, he grabbed her whole head of hair in both of his hands; pulling her across the kitchen as she cried out in pain, trying to help herself by pulling her hair back towards her scalp and stand up. Her legs scrabbling helplessly for some kind of grip, he pulled her past the table as she collided painfully with the chair she'd just put her coat on; sending both tumbling noisily to the floor.

Reaching the stubbornly opening cutlery drawer, he tugged at it with such force that the whole of its contents went crashing downwards.

One of the sharp knives she kept in the drawer fell away from the rest, as if in slow motion, spiraling itself over and over as it glinted in the light, before landing point downwards, impaling itself in the back of her hand. But its own momentum brought it back out from the resultant wound, to fall and hit the floor, bloodily.

She instinctively put her injured hand up to her mouth, sobbing as she tried to stop the bleeding by sucking at it.

Len groped around on the floor, cursing angrily until he found what he was looking for.

'I'm going to die' she thought desperately. *'Like I saw my mother die . . . he's going to cut my throat and I'm going to die . . .'*

Heaving for one more angry breath he grabbed harder at her hair with one hand, while he kicked and tugged her into the right position. Then he began to cut at her hair randomly, and painfully, with a pair of blunt kitchen scissors.

Red and . . . yellow . . . and pink and green . . .

'Likes your beautiful hair does he, your Flynn? Well let's see what thinks now Lizzie eh? He won't be eyeing you up any more!'

He elbowed her hard across the face as the open blades of the scissors caught her again; turning the cut above her right eye into an open ugly gash.

Orange and purple and blue . . .

Lizzie's hair cascaded to the floor all around her in desperate tresses until, frenzy over, it was all gone.

Her head was naked and cold, her blouse torn open, and her shabby, ill fitting bra was exposed. She was bleeding down the right side of her stricken face and onto the floor, and both of her ears were bleeding where he'd caught them with the scissors.

She felt damp underneath her bottom and wondered why for the briefest of seconds; and as she clasped the edges of her blouse back together, she was so shocked she couldn't even cry.

Taking this as defiance he slapped her hands away, forcing a dirty hand into one cup of her bra; grasping at her full breast clumsily, and tugging it free of the cup. Her chin went up as she closed her eyes, to shut out the look of pure evil on his face. Fighting hard not to shudder and anger him more; with a jolt she realised she was still wetting herself. Terror was rendering her powerless to control the warm sensation of her own urine trickling shamefully between her thighs.

Misreading her closed eyes as sexual excitement, he suddenly let her go. He picked up, then dropped a handful of her fallen hair into her lap as she lay helplessly against the sink cupboard, and smirked at the dark yellow puddle that had now appeared on the floor beside her. Then he wiped his hand against his sweaty shirt with a sneer of disgust, and turned away.

He left her there, pulling the torn cup of her bra back over her exposed breast with the bile rising in her throat, and beginning to retch.

Going calmly up the stairs, he closed their bedroom door with a slam, as Lizzie whimpered in terror once more; and vomited.

It was over.

Her body now curled into the foetal position with her head on the floor she pulled her blouse across herself tightly. Oblivious to the blood still oozing from the gash above her eye: oblivious to everything but her eyes focused on the upturned cutlery drawer, she eventually broke the eerie silence of that terrible scene and whispered . . .

'Listen with your eyes . . . Listen with your eyes . . . and sing everything you see . . . You can sing a rainbow . . . sing a rainbow . . . sing along with me . . . .'

Chapter nine

Lizzie did not appear for work the following morning, nor did she ring Flynn to explain why, and he knew something was very wrong once he'd found that the phone he'd secretly given her was not being answered either, despite her promise to keep it with her at all times.

He called Donna to come in early, and as soon as she arrived he set off for the estate with Belinda in his car for visible, if not tried and tested backup.

Pulling up outside Lizzie's house in Hyacinth Close, he looked up the still rather overgrown garden path towards the front door for signs of life. Anticipating a cool reception from Len, Flynn let Belinda out of the back of the van, clipped on her chain and checked his jacket pocket while she had an inquisitive sniff around, to make sure that what he'd put in there was still there: not that he'd set eyes on it in a very long time.

He rang the completely redundant doorbell and, hearing no sound omit from it, thumped loudly at the door with his clenched fist; but the door just rattled hollowly on its hinges and there was no reply. Looking through the sitting room window with cupped hands to shield the backlit sun, and then bending at the front door to peer through the letter box, Flynn was almost knocked backwards by the stench of stale booze, cigarettes, body odour, and goodness only knows what else. To his increasing unease the view through the hall to the kitchen still showed the signs of last night's incident. A chair lay forlornly on its side, and it looked like there was cutlery all over the floor, but his heart leapt into his throat when he saw the blood . . . and what looked horribly like vomit and . . . cut hair: Lizzie's hair. He hammered on the door again, angrily this time, and Belinda began to whimper beside him, knowing by now that something was wrong.

The gate hinges squeaked behind him and he turned around sharply.

Len Fidler had come back, carrying four easily identifiable beer cans in a carrier bag from the grocers in the square, and looking ten times worse than Flynn had ever seen him; even by Len's standards.

'. . . Come for her stuff, have you . . . 'cos she's too scared?' Len drew deeply on his half finished cigarette and blew the smoke directly at him, provocatively, as he approached.

'Where is she and what . . . do you mean come for her stuff? What have you done to her Len?'

Flynn indicated towards the house and what he'd seen, and his grip tensed against Belinda's chain. Now quivering with rage, he ignored the cigarette smoke that Len had just blown into his face. Feeling those vibrations through the chain, Belinda began a completely out of character, low pitched, and guttural growl beside him.

Caught out by Flynn's obvious innocence as to Lizzie's whereabouts and the menacing growl coming from his previously soppy dog, Len just glared at him.

'Dunno what you mean . . .' he muttered, taking a step towards his front door but thinking better of it as he saw Belinda's head drop, and her hackles begin to rise. 'She got nuthin' she didn't deserve!' Sensing he was rapidly losing control of the situation, he continued; 'I know what's been going on between you . . . there's no point denying it . . . Her coming in late every night . . . gettin' out of your van . . . hair all over the place . . . way after closing time . . . I'm not a bloody fool . . .'

'You are a bloody fool if you think that . . . I've not laid a finger on her . . . unlike you, you . . . bloody coward . . .' Flynn's fingers loosed on the leather handle of the chain for a second, and Len took an involuntary step backwards.

'What happened in there last night?' Flynn indicated to the front door again with his head, 'I saw it through the window . . . There's blood and . . . hair. Where is she? What have you done to her?'

There was a slight pause as Len tried to weigh up his options in his muddled head.

'Well if you haven't got her I dunno where she is . . .' he shrugged, doing his best to feign disinterest. 'She's gone off somewhere . . . But when I find out where, I'll . . .'

'Not if I have anything to do with it, you won't!' Tugging at the frozen to the spot and growling Belinda, Flynn pushed past him. 'Get out of my way Len Fidler . . . you're nothing but a cowardly drunken thug . . . And you might think you can get away with treating Be.' He corrected himself suddenly; '. . . Lizzie . . . like a punch bag . . . but you don't scare me . . . not even a little bit! I'm Irish . . . born and bred a Derryman . . . and I've witnessed things . . . and done things . . . in my time'd make what's left of *your* pathetic hair curl . . . !'

Flynn stalked angrily back to his van, turning back briefly only to add, 'And if she's really gone . . . then all I can say is . . . it's about bloody time! And I know she's too scared of you to do it . . . so *I'm* reporting you for assault with intent . . . *and* her as missing to the police . . . and *I'll* stand up in court and face ya even if she won't. I've seen enough through that window t'send ya down for it . . . . And don't you bother coming in The Hart to get your fix again either . . . I can do without your business . . . I'd sooner starve!'

*   *   *

Once back at the pub Flynn unclipped Belinda's chain and rubbed at her ears lovingly in gratitude before he made his way back behind the bar. Going through to the storeroom as she followed to lap gratefully from her huge water bowl, he took the phone from its cradle on the wall and as it dialled through to the police, he slipped his free hand into his pocket and removed the menacing looking brass knuckleduster he'd taken with him for protection. He fingered it gently as he turned it over in his fingers. That thing hadn't seen the light of day in more than thirty five years . . . and his mind went briefly back in time to the day his older brother had picked it up from the pavement on the way home from school, after yet another street riot.

He'd never used it in anger of course, despite his threats to Len Fidler, but his older brother had, and paid for it with his own life during The Troubles. Somehow it always calmed Flynn to know he still had it; if only to remind him that nothing he faced nowadays could compare to the horrors he'd witnessed as a young lad in Londonderry.

Danny arrived home from the camp a little sheepishly the following morning. Letting himself inside with a gargantuan hangover and a profound feeling of guilt at leaving his mum to face Len alone, and at night, he discovered the kitchen a complete mess that Len hadn't even attempted to clear up; such had been the speed of his departure.

To his absolute horror there was more than enough to show everything that had happened to his mother there. One of her shoes was wedged between a chair and the table as if it had been wrenched off, and he found her bag on the hall table exactly where she'd left it, containing nothing but her purse (empty of all but shabby and aged till receipts), an unfamiliar phone silently flashing several missed calls and texts; all from someone called 'work', and the red elastic band she always wore in her hair sat screwed up in the bottom of the bag with several more of her blonde hairs trapped within it. In fact, with increasing concern going through all of her meager belongings upstairs, Danny found no signs that, if she had gone of her own accord, she had taken anything with her at all . . . nothing. Not even a change of underwear.

His father had gone, his mother was possibly with him . . . And he didn't know whether she was dead or alive.

Chapter ten

Lizzie had remained stunned and silent on the kitchen floor for almost an hour until she heard Len snoring through the thin ceiling above her exposed and bleeding head. Breathing with the shallowness of an injured animal afraid of revealing its hiding place to a lurking predator, her body still shaking convulsively, she eventually got herself up with the aid of the fallen chair and pulled weakly at a screwed up and malodorous dishcloth from the draining board. Dabbing it carefully at her gashed eye, she then wrapped it around her injured hand, and carefully, noiselessly, turned the key in the back door. Her hand on the doorknob, her first thought was to call Flynn but, too frightened to risk going back through the house to get the mobile phone from her bag on the hall table, as she paused a moment to rub at a sharp pain in her hip, she discovered that she'd been lying on her jacket from the back of the fallen chair; and relief flooded her as she realised she'd been lying on some keys in her pocket. Screwing up her nose at what was all over it; she groped for the keys and dropped the jacket back on the floor. Then she opened the door to a gap no wider than she was and, barefoot, slipped quietly out.

The weather had worsened since she got home, as if God himself was showing his anger at what had just happened in that house. Rain and wind lashed onto her unprotected head from the heavens, seemingly without mercy, and fuelling her mistaken belief that she had driven Len to do it, as usual. But even as her vision became blurred in her distress, her bare feet cut and bleeding, she carried on, now convinced of her destination. Stumbling frequently, and leaping into the undergrowth to avoid the occasional car, she made her desperate way back towards the village.

Having used her keys to get into the church and re locking the south door safely behind her; not really knowing how long she had taken to get there, she lay down finally; utterly exhausted. Letting her eyelids succumb to gravity she fell into a deep sleep curled up on two long altar kneelers in the Sanctuary, lying just in front of the Altar, and using the richly embroidered Altar frontal as a blanket against the type of cold that only unheated churches can know.

She awakened the following morning to the level of birdsong in the churchyard that always follows a storm, and the warmth of refracted sunlight poring through the enormous stained glass windows of the Chancel.

As she lay there in the comforting silence of this ancient church where centuries of Frincham's population had declared their love, named their children, said goodbye to those they loved, and followed their own individual paths to faith, she suddenly heard the unmistakable squeak of the south door hinges. Fearing that Len had found her, she caught her breath and cowered beneath her improvised blanket, too scared at first even to breathe.

Relief quickly filled her lungs when she realised it was Rector Hector making his way up the aisle this morning. Whistling *'All things bright and beautiful'* cheerfully to himself as his left hand hopped lightly from pew head to pew head in rhythm, he skipped up the step into the Chancel and paused to bow before the Altar before heading on his usual route into the Vestry.

He jumped visibly at the sight of the bare Altar that met his eyes, at first fearing another theft, and then at the sight of someone cowering on the floor, under the bloodstained frontal. Thinking it was the thief, or a vagrant, his fingers clasped more tightly around his bunch of keys in acknowledgement that he'd just used them to unlock the door.

Then she said his name, as her butchered head, and then her shoulders, slowly appeared from under the frontal. He gasped, and only realised who she was by the sound of her timid voice, gently echoing in the vaulted ceilings of this century's old and hallowed place of sanctuary.

'Lizzie!' he exclaimed, dashing through the gates to her side, and falling onto his knees before taking her, finally audibly sobbing, into his arms. She was still damp and shivering; the skin under his palm on the back of her neck was clammy, and his nose involuntarily wrinkled at the strong smell of vomit and urine that hit his nostrils. 'Lizzie my dear girl . . . . my dear girl . . .' he said, in the deep and resonantly smooth voice that instantly filled her with reassurance, as it always did. 'You're safe now . . . you're safe here . . . I've got you . . . I've got you . . .'

*　　*　　*

Dizzy had accompanied her in the ambulance to the hospital in Reading, and sat with her, holding her hand as the police gently took her through what had happened. Finally summoning up enough courage to press charges against her husband, a patrol car was immediately dispatched round to her house, where they had found not Len, but an utterly distraught Danny, trying his best to tidy up. Able to tell him she was alive went some way to easing his pain, but they almost drove him insane when they would not let him see her at this stage, because with Len on the run, she was under police protection for her own safety.

From the moment Lizzie left the hospital she was placed under the professional care of the Berkshire Women's Refuge, and the police search for Len began in earnest.

The best sighting of him had been from Amy Palmer, while she was out putting the wall eyed Jethro over some point to point jumps, which had been at around 7am. She'd particularly remembered because he'd been talking to himself, and had sneezed so loudly that he'd made Jethro spook off towards the woods, giving her problems for a few seconds. Len had been heading purposefully out of the village and was carrying a large black holdall, she'd told them, which had appeared to be pretty heavy too; by the way he kept swapping it from arm to arm.

Since Anna had fled all those years ago, Danny had seen it as his own responsibility to protect his mum, and all because he'd got drunk on his birthday she was now broken, and refusing to speak to anyone, including him, it seemed.

After absorbing the facts and the days passed with no news, Danny gradually sank deeper into the depths of anger, guilt and despair. He had no idea where she was and his father, the evil bastard, was still missing, much as he would dearly love to get hold of him.

He drifted between the house and the protest camp, but despite DeeDee's efforts to be supportive, his heart was no longer in it. He'd only got involved in the protests to wind up Hannah, so after what she'd just done to him it was all wasted effort anyway.

All alone to deal with his traumas and his self imposed guilt, his behaviour became more and more sullen and erratic, and Hannah Derby, and her adolescent games, became the unfortunate focus of his hatred.

* * *

Hannah and Beau were riding out alone this morning because Amy and her family had gone away for the weekend. Her own father had been away for almost a week too, seeing to his business interests in Seattle, and Hannah was enjoying her solitude enormously, blissfully unaware of the seething hatred she'd unleashed in Danny Fidler by talking to the police. She'd ridden down to the Taylor's and seen to Jethro, and was now making her way out on the Stanton Court Road and back towards home to spend the rest of the day playing her music far too loud, and doing precisely what she wanted for a change.

Danny meanwhile had heard that Mad Dave Willis from the estate had got himself a car now, and when he screeched to halt beside Danny walking along the Yattley Road that same Saturday morning, Danny leapt at the chance of an adrenaline rush to go with him while he put it through its paces.

Dave had two other teenagers from the estate in the car with him this morning. Fidge, named for his inability to ever sit still, and Shultzy, who preferred that to his real name; Herman, were soon tearing along the quiet lane with the sound system blaring, and before long they were roaring noisily through the village square. Dave put his foot down the second he saw the national speed limit sign once through it, and headed off down the Stanton Court Road, and just around the tight bend Danny saw a horse and rider trotting purposefully along the verge ahead of them, and caught his breath.

'Oh look . . . It's lady muck!' He sneered.

'Snooty cow . . .' said Dave. 'She makes me sick . . .'

'Thinks she's so high and mighty that one . . .' Shultzy yelled over the music from the back of the car.

Dave let out a defiant whoop as he changed down a gear and began to accelerate towards her.

'Uh . . . Dave . . .' said Danny shakily, 'I don't think this is . . . .'

'Let's give her a real gee up!' shouted Fidge.

Hearing the car roaring along the narrow lane Hannah looked behind her and nudged her left leg at Beau's flank to move over in the normal way, to let them go past. But instead of passing her, the car stopped just long enough for Shultzy to lean out of the open rear window and taunt her.

Instantly sensing her fear through the tenseness of the reins on his tender mouth, and startled by the loud music coming from the car, the highly strung Beau suddenly took off with a terrified snort, and bolted.

Danny's heart missed a beat.

Hannah was a very experienced rider and held on tight, but she knew there was no steering Beau as he tore on at full gallop along the grass verge, with her ducking to avoid the low tree branches and praying that he wouldn't trip over something and send them both tumbling down. Her expertise made this look effortless so Dave was enjoying himself now and continued to speed alongside her, terrifying both her and her horse even more. Then Beau suddenly saw an escape route and veered off the road into an open field; losing his balance briefly as he skidded in some slippery mud near the entrance. Hannah held on for dear life, managing to stay in the saddle, but she was really struggling to keep control of him now. Dave overshot the entrance at first, but tugged the car indignantly into reverse and, in a screech of practically illegal tyres, followed her into the field: normally a safe haven for the local dog owners, and narrowly avoiding a loose dog whose horrified owner was racing across the field to retrieve it.

'Give it up mate!' shouted Danny, now beginning to get really scared. 'She'll get 'urt!'

But Fidge and Shultzy were cheering Dave on as the car bumped itself across the uneven field with the music still blaring, and with neither of the boys in the back of the car wearing seatbelts, they were laughing at the way they were getting thrown around in the car.

Still looking for a means of escape, Beau effortlessly jumped a wide ditch at the far side of the field but stumbled again in the soft earth on the other side, before pulling himself up and leaping a barbed wire fence awkwardly. Squealing in pain as a barb caught and tore through her left boot into her calf muscle on the way over; Hannah's foot had been wrenched from the stirrup as Beau took off at a gallop again.

Swearing profusely, Dave watched as the horse tore up a steep incline into the distance, with Hannah now visibly hurt and really struggling to stay on board.

Obviously unable to cross the ditch in his car, he was about to turn around and go back towards the road to head her off when, from the front passenger seat Danny's eyes widened in horror as he saw Beau, now on the crest of the hill, suddenly rear up onto his back legs before depositing Hannah heavily onto the ground beside him; her right leg still trapped in her remaining stirrup. Then, as the horse bolted in terror once more, he saw Hannah's lifeless body suddenly and horrifically snatch from the ground with him, before both of them disappeared from view.

'She's off!' Danny shouted, in a voice that sounded totally unlike his own. 'Stop the bloody car, Dave . . . I said she's off!'

The car engine came wheezily to a halt and Dave swallowed nervously as he saw the same thing and, reaching over to turn off the music, began to panic.

'So are we mate!' he said shakily. 'I'm not hangin' around if she's hurt! I ain't got no licence or insurance!'

'No . . . stop!' Danny yelled, as he realised what he'd just said. 'Dave you can't! You can't! Shultzy . . . tell him!'

He grabbed at the steering wheel as Dave rammed the gearstick into reverse and then set off in the opposite direction; revving the engine crazily as the car bumped over the uneven ground. The mood had totally changed and the two in the back seat had gone totally quiet now.

'Ge' off me!' Dave shouted, punching Danny's arm away.

'Dave, stop!' Danny screamed again. 'Let me get out . . . let *me* out! For God's sake! I'll go! I'll take the blame! We can't just leave her!'

With Dave intent on getting away Danny gave up on the steering wheel and instead scrabbled with shaking hands at his door handle. Finally managing to wrench it open, he fell as much as he jumped from the still moving car, landing heavily on his left shoulder and falling, tumbling over and over as the car sped onwards, leaving him there, without a care for whether he was hurt or not; it's passenger door hanging half off from hitting the ground so hard, back towards the road.

'Dave . . . . Shultzy! Come back! Fidge . . . ! Ah for God's sake . . . !' He called after them desperately as the woman in the field, still trying to catch her terrified dog, continued to watch on in horror at the unfolding scene.

Picking himself up, still cursing, Danny rubbed at his painful shoulder and staggered around for a few seconds in order to think. His breath coming in short, adrenaline boosted gasps, he turned and ran back across the field, scrambling over the deep ditch that Beau had cleared, and up the other side, swearing again as he stung himself badly on the mass of nettles and assorted other nasty prickly stuff growing in the bottom of the ditch, and warily clambered through the barbed wire fence that had caught Hannah's leg on the opposite side.

Running as if his life depended on it now, he made it to the top of the hill and looked around him; but to his horror there was no sign of either Hannah or her horse. They had completely disappeared from view. Scanning the field in a complete panic now, he tore his hands through his hair as he tried to use his spinning head.

Look for tracks.

Running down the other side of the hill with his arms flailing madly to keep his balance, he came to a breathless halt again and looked down into the soft mud by the gateway to the adjoining field. But there were no recent hoof prints there; just boot marks from the dozens of walkers that used the public footpaths across these fields. Turning around, he looked over towards a thickly wooded copse, coughed and spat, and made for it at a run.

Stopping at the edge of the copse, he peered into the pine scented, echoing darkness.

'Hannah! Hannah!' he called.

Nothing.

'She must have gone in here . . .' he said to himself, gasping breathlessly, and running his hands through his hair once more. Stumbling into the undergrowth and tripping on tree roots in the starkly contrasting dark to the daylight outside he continued to call, but the only sounds were the cries of startled wildlife, disturbed of their peace once more.

'Hannah . . . ! Hannah where are you?' he called desperately.

Running onwards, he saw something on the ground just up ahead of him, and ran over to it.

It was Hannah's riding crop.

Picking it up, sure he was on the right path now, he looked down at the ground around it anxiously, swallowing as he saw hoof prints, smears of fresh blood, and sinister drag marks in the soft mud to the side of the track. Beau had slowed down because the hoof prints were no longer heavy or deep enough to be a gallop. That was one thing anyway.

He set off into the blackness once again to follow the tracks amongst the broken and flattened ferns, until he came to a fork in the narrow woodland path, and looked up involuntarily sharply as the sunshine penetrating through a gap in the pine trees dazzled him, catching something; causing a bright and distinctly metallic glint. Then he stopped dead in his tracks and stared.

Beau was just ahead of him, standing perfectly still beside a huge tree, and watching him approach with both of his ears back but occasionally twisting around in alarm.

Nostrils still flaring, the horse stamped one front foot defensively and whickered.

Danny stood perfectly still, frozen in horror as he realised what he was seeing.

Hannah was still attached by her trapped ankle to the stirrup that had just glinted in the sunshine, and was lying to the side of her horse, face downwards in the crushed undergrowth, her body unnaturally twisted, and horribly still. Moving very slowly and with a slightly sideways gait to avoid making any sudden movements that might set Beau off again, fearing the very worst, Danny began to talk to him very gently with one arm out in front of his body in a calming gesture, keeping one eye fixed on him and the other on Hannah. As he approached Beau tossed his head and stamped his foot again, whickering nervously, knowing that something was very wrong with Hannah, and quivering and unsure after his fright as to what was happening now.

Danny stooped down to the side of the path, keeping his eyes fixed on the horse, and pulled very slowly at some long grass. Standing even more slowly and with his heart still pounding painfully Danny continued to edge his way forward, offering Beau the grass in a gesture of peace. After an agonising few seconds he managed to get close enough for the horse to stretch out his neck and sniff at it, allowing Danny to reach up and take an extremely tentative hold of his bridle.

Letting out a slow breath in relief he tethered him by his reins to the tree, gently stroking down his powerful jaw with calming sounds and trying to reassure him.

Then he bent down shakily to look at Hannah.

Totally out of it, her helmet and chinstrap were still visibly in place and had protected her head, but as he gently turned her over, her face was a mass of cuts and was still bleeding.

Her left arm was visibly broken; the bone just blow her elbow exposed and visible beneath her torn shirt, and the leg that was still trapped in the stirrup was hideously twisted out of its normal shape.

Danny gently freed her foot by manouvering the stirrup, keeping her foot very still, assured that she would not feel the pain of it but watching for signs that she could, and brought her freed leg very gently down to the ground. Now that she was free of the horse he knelt down next to her and tried to see what on earth he could do next.

He licked the back of one of his shaking hands hurriedly and wiped the side of his face with it, and then allowed his damp cheek to rest close to her mouth. Closing his eyes in a silent prayer of thanks he felt her shallow warm breath against his damp skin.

She was still breathing.

Slightly encouraged, he stood up again and reached into his back pocket for his phone, praying that he'd get a signal in the densely wooded glade.

It wasn't there.

Fumbling around in his jacket pockets he discovered it wasn't on him anywhere. Cursing, he realised he must have lost it in the race to find her. He looked back the way he had come in the vain hope of seeing it lying miraculously close somewhere; running one hand through his hair desperately.

As gently as he could he slipped his hands into each of Hannah's jacket pockets in search of a phone but only managed to find a half empty packet of polo mints, a carefully folded white handkerchief with an elastic band round it, and her house keys. Unraveling the handkerchief in a moment of automated curiosity he blinked in surprise: he'd found his missing earring.

Turning it over in his fingers, he bit at his bottom lip and stole the briefest moment of triumph, looked from Hannah to the horse, and then back at Hannah.

Taking the only course of action he could he tugged off his jacket, covered her as best he could to stop her from getting too cold, stole a feather-light tender kiss from her unconscious lips, and released Beau from the tree.

Chapter eleven

Danny's equestrian experience had been limited to a donkey on the beach in Southsea when he was about four, and he had never been on a horse in his life. In fact they terrified him close up because they were unpredictable, had very sharp teeth, and only toffs like the Derby's and the Palmers rode them to show off anyway.

Drawing Beau forward by his reins, safely at arms length, away from his teeth and away from the unconscious Hannah, he pulled himself up and over the saddle in a way that was effective but would not win any prizes for proficiency as Beau danced nervously on the spot. His ears went back with the whites of his eyes showing in alarm at the thought of more upset and a strange rider on his back but, gathering up the reins as if they were made of spaghetti and doing his best to get his long legs into stirrups set for the much shorter Hannah, Danny held on for dear life as Beau suddenly took off down the track and out of the copse, into the open field once more.

Totally unable to steer him, Danny had no choice but to give him his head and hoped for the best; that Beau would go somewhere sensible, even it was Stanton Court and he'd have to explain himself to her father; but at least he could get some help.

Heading down the hill at full gallop and back towards the road Danny realised with horror that Beau was heading for the dreaded ditch again. Closing his eyes, he waited for the two of them to part company and for the ground to come up and hit him, but amazingly Beau took off with a grunt and cleared the ditch like the thoroughbred he truly was.

Miraculously still on board but minus both stirrups now, Danny found it a lot easier to stay on board with his legs loose, and felt a bit more confident by the time they finally made it to the road and Beau slowed to a walk. He even managed to convey to him that he wanted to go back towards the closer village square, and patted his neck with encouragement as the horse did as he was asked. But in reply to this vote of confidence Beau broke into an enthusiastic trot that sent poor Danny bouncing about, both alarmingly and painfully, with no stirrups to help him.

Up the lane they went at near trotting-race speed, Beau's metal shoes hammering against the road surface noisily, and the stirrups bouncing about and banging painfully into Danny's legs until he almost wept with relief as The Hart came into view ahead of them. Reaching the car park, Danny tugged at Beau's left rein to steer him across the gravel towards the door, calling out for help as they did so, and yanked him to an indignant stop as Flynn and Donna came rushing out to see what all the commotion was.

'Ambulance!' Danny yelled. 'Flynn . . . Call an ambulance . . . It's Hannah! She's hurt . . . It's Hannah!'

'Danny what . . . what is it? That's Beau isn't it . . . ? Why is his leg bleeding? . . . What's happened?' Flynn looked incredulous as he dried his hands on a bar towel.

'Hannah's had an accident!' Danny was in tears now. 'Flynn, please!'

Flynn leapt into immediate action. 'Donna, grab Beau and tether him to the dog ring . . . And then get him some water . . . You'd better get on your phone to Ben Robinson at the Vet's about his leg too . . . he's obviously cut it. I'll call for an ambulance. Danny! Leave him . . . he's all right! Come with me . . .' He grabbed at Danny's arm as the boy bent to look at the bleeding leg. 'I said leave him! You'll need to tell them where . . .'

* * *

Danny had led the Paramedics to the copse where Hannah still lay completely motionless. His own, and Mad Dave's, part in the saga was not mentioned of course, but the witness from the field, who knew all the occupants of the car by sight, and now by name after Danny had shouted after them, had immediately reported the incident to the police . . . who did know them all, very well, and she had also handed in Danny's phone that she'd wrestled from her dog's mouth when she finally caught him too.

Danny went instantly from hero to zero once more, as he, Dave, Fidge and Shultzy were picked up one by one and taken to Newbury police station to be questioned.

As Dave had been the driver of the car, with no license or insurance, he was the one who was faced with an assortment of charges including dangerous driving with intent to endanger life, and leaving the scene of an accident; and found himself praying to the God he'd always doubted the existence of for the first time in his life, that the charges did not become any more serious.

Danny had been greeted with a; 'You just can't keep out of trouble, can you Danny boy?' from Sergeant Tidbury, and had run from the police station as soon as they let him out, jumping on a Reading bus at the stop just outside as it began to pull away.

An hour later he walked out of the lift at the ICU in the Royal Berkshire Hospital just as Hannah was being wheeled past him on a trolley.

Melting into the paintwork by pretending to read a leaflet he watched as the porters and the accompanying nurse took her to a bay and pulled the curtains quickly around her bed. Once he'd seen the porters leave and the nurse walked back to the desk to answer a phone he sneaked past her while she was distracted and, checking once more that nobody had seen him, slipped quietly through the curtains. Now shaking with emotion he caught his breath and swallowed hard. He knew she was in a coma because it was all around the village; just like the smallest of secrets always is. He also knew that the operation to deal with her injuries, both external and internal, had lasted for almost seven hours. She looked pale and so very young against her pillows as he took her hand in his and kissed it tenderly, imagining her elegant long fingers responding, wrapping around his like a glove.

The cuts on her face cleaned up now, she at least looked like Hannah again; much softer without her haughty expression certainly, and severely battered and bruised, but still Hannah. From what he could make out under the blankets her body was almost totally encased in either plaster or bandages though, and a collection of tubes and beeping monitors charted her progress from the head of the bed.

He let go of her hand briefly to lift a plastic chair a little closer to her bed and sat down.

Minutes past.

'Hey you . . .' he whispered eventually, trying to force a smile but jumping at the sound of his own voice in the silence of the bay. 'There you are! I've been looking for you everywhere!' He caught his breath and choked slightly. Turning his head to check if he'd been heard by the nurse he sat quietly for a few more minutes, kissing the back of her hand and pressing it to the side of his face as he quietly rocked back and forth in the chair. Finally taking a breath, he let it out slowly before speaking again. 'This isn't how it was supposed to end up . . . any of it . . .' he said quietly. 'I know I'm an idiot . . . I've been a complete prat . . . as per usual . . . but only 'cos you wind me up so much, you really do . . .' he shook her hand in mock anger but kept hold of it in both of his. Adjusting his chair noiselessly so that he could lean closer to whisper, he cleared his throat. 'I don't know . . . how . . . to be the sort of person who . . . really deserves someone like you . . . but you could help me, if you want to. It's just . . . I'm . . . used to people thinking the worst of me . . . they always have, so it's what I expect . . . and so it's what I do, see? I hurt them before they hurt me . . . . But you're different . . . I know that now.' A single tear crept unheeded down his colourless face. 'I've never met anyone like you before. You're so lovely Han . . . When you're not turning your nose up at me . . . but I can see it in your eyes you're only trying not to want me 'cos you know your dad won't like it . . . and your face goes all pink and stuff . . . but it's too late now because the truth is . . . *I* think . . . you're the most beautiful girl I've ever seen in my life and . . . I just wanted to say . . . I'm s . . . sorry . . . I never meant for any of this to ha . . .' He swallowed again and gently moved a strand of loose hair from her eyes, 'and I really need you in my life Hannah . . . if you want me. I need you to wake up and get better so I can . . . tell you . . . So I can tell you . . .'

Dr Jemmie Ryan switched her gaze from the adjoining curtain back to the pages of the bed chart for the patient in the adjoining bay, and rubbed absently at her pregnant stomach as her baby kicked again. Danny Fidler was a tricky character to be sure, but this was quite an unexpected development. Peeping through the curtain unseen again a few moments later, Danny's head was now drooping down towards his chin. His hair, the replaced gold hoop earring glinting through it, was hiding most of his face, and his hand still held hers tightly as they both slept. Jemmie allowed herself a little smile.

The Montagues and the Capulets . . . This was going to be interesting.

Chapter twelve

Lizzie opened her eyes and once more checked the beating of her own heart to remind herself she was still safe. She'd been secretly staying in the Rectory for almost two weeks now, with still no word or sign of Len, and the Hardy-Mitchells had made the difficult decision to withhold the information about Danny's involvements with the police from her in case she put the love for her son over her own safety and broke her cover.

She could not fathom the generosity of this family. Hector and Dizzy were being so kind to her, and their girls were so sweet, bringing her regular, precariously balanced half cups of tea (with the rest in the saucer), accompanied by the hobnob biscuits that were such a treat in the Hardy-Mitchell household and that, she knew full well, she was being given at the selfless expense of someone else's share. Their girls were old enough to understand too that Lizzie was still in danger, and had kept the fact that she was hiding in the Rectory a total secret from all their friends, viewing it as all rather like being in a story, or in a crime drama on the television; not that they were permitted to watch them of course.

Lizzie was lying in the sitting room in an overlarge and shabby winged chair of sun faded chintz, and had been asleep for about an hour and a half with her feet up on a matching footstool, with a much used and rather thin crocheted blanket over her legs.

She seemed to spend most of her time asleep these days. Must be the pills the doctor had given her.

She yawned and stretched, scratched at her itchy scalp, felt gingerly at the stitches above her right eye, and listened for sounds of the family.

The children were home from school because she could see Batty and Tesco through the French windows feeding the guinea pigs, and the sound of the desk chair scraping against the floorboards in the bedroom above her head indicated that the studious Looby-Loo was already starting her homework.

In the quiet days since she'd been brought here from the care of the Women's Refuge she'd become so sensitive to every sound, every spider scurrying across a rug in this house. Just then she heard Hector sneeze loudly in his study on the other side of the wall, and she heard Dizzy shout 'Bless you!' from the kitchen; but then her brows suddenly knitted together painfully and her hand went up to her stitches once more. There was another voice today. She strained her ears to hear, her breath held, as the sounds of light laughter filtered through the door.

Maybe it wasn't the police then; maybe they hadn't found Len.

She breathed again.

She heard the sound of the kettle being filled at the sink and plugged in at the adjoining wall, still trying hard to identify the other voice; a woman's voice.

The door creaked open noisily beside her, and Dizzy's head appeared around it.

'Oh Lizzie, lovely, you're awake. Would you like some tea? We're just making some . . .'

'Who's here?' she said guardedly, nodding in response to the offer of tea.

'Don't worry darling it's just Jules . . . Jules Taylor. Why don't you come out and join us in the kitchen?'

Lizzie's hand involuntarily went to her butchered scalp and she shook her head, so Dizzy came fully in to the room, stooping to take a hold of her hands.

'Lizzie, sweetheart, you'll have to learn to face people again, you know that. You can't avoid life by not facing it you know . . . . And the more you face up to it, the braver you'll get. You can trust Jules whole heartedly . . . she's my best friend . . . I've known her for years . . . and I know that she won't tell a soul you're here . . . honestly.'

'I know . . .' Lizzie whispered, 'but I feel such a . . . it's just . . . seeing people . . . anyone . . . seeing me . . . like this . . .'

'Hector uses an expression all the time when anyone he meets has to face something either new or very difficult . . . You only have to do it the first time once . . .' Dizzy said gently. 'Then each time you do it you'll feel a bit stronger. Trust me. Come on . . . .' She stood upright again and picked up the headscarf that Lizzie had been using from the back of her chair, tied it around her butchered scalp neatly for her, and then Lizzie allowed herself to be led into the kitchen where Jules was busy making the tea.

Jules smiled at her in welcome, as if she had noticed nothing whatsoever out of the ordinary.

'Hello Lizzie . . . Milk and sugar is it?'

'Thank you.' Lizzie nodded, then sat down and cleared her throat nervously, as if the sound of her own voice had just surprised her.

Jules sat down next to her and turned her chair slightly. 'So . . .' she ventured carefully, 'How are you doing?'

Lizzie smiled sadly as she blew on, and then sipped at her tea. 'You don't want to hear my troubles Mrs Taylor . . .'

'This table has had more than its fair share of tales of woe since we've been here . . .' Dizzy paused behind Lizzie's chair and bent down to plant a soft kiss on her head before sitting down opposite her.

'. . . And quite a lot of it from me and my marital dilemmas!' Jules turned to Dizzy and smiled.

Lizzie blinked herself out of her own private thoughts and turned to face her. 'You?' she said incredulously, 'I'm sorry but . . . you? I find that a bit hard to believe . . . You and Mr Taylor are obviously so . . . happy together . . . anyone can see that. It's like you only just met sometimes . . . I can't believe he'd ever . . . Well he would never . . . You're not saying . . . he . . . Has he?'

'Hit me?' she said gently, 'No Lizzie he's never hit me but . . . well . . .'

She looked across at Dizzy for moral support, and then looked at the table.

'He has . . . hurt me though . . . very deeply . . . in the past. He turned into quite another man from the one I married too . . . and we . . . well we broke up . . . We got divorced actually . . .'

'Divorced? But . . . what . . . what happened?' Lizzie's eyes were wide but she checked herself. 'Sorry . . . it's not my business . . . is it . . .'

Jules shifted position slightly, her eyes cast downward momentarily. 'No, it's fine, really. It's all

water under the bridge now anyway. He had a very . . .
public . . . affair . . . it was all over the papers . . .'

'Oh . . . yes . . . I think I remember that now . . .'

Jules nodded and pulled a face. 'Quite . . . and . . .
you'll remember then that he left me . . . for a younger
woman . . . it was almost four years ago now . . . so . . .
I had to learn . . . to pick myself up off the floor and
start again . . . on my own . . . And it was hard, believe
me it was hard . . .'

Lizzie took another sip of her tea and shook her
head slightly in disbelief.

'I know that you'll think I'm different because in our
case we eventually got back together . . . But I honestly
never knew at that time if that would ever happen . . .
or even if I wanted it to after the way he treated me.
So I had to learn . . . how to be me again . . . And yes,
we did get back together eventually, obviously . . . but
after a lot of soul searching and a lot of hard to come by
forgiveness, believe me . . .' She took a sip of her own
tea and winked at Dizzy. 'It's different between us now
though, but in a positive way, because of all that. I'm
more independent . . . I can think for myself and make
decisions on my own if I have to . . . I have my own job,
my own money, which I love, and I'm not prepared to
give it up unless *I* want to, no matter what other people
might think about my having a rich husband and not
needing to work for a living . . . It's not about that, for
me. And I'm not afraid to say if I don't agree with him

sometimes . . . I'm . . . well, we're both more, of an equal partnership.'

'Len changed . . . he wasn't always . . . like he is now . . .' Lizzie mumbled. She used the sleeve of her cardigan to wipe at her eyes, and then looked at both of them uncertainly.

Dizzy gently touched Jules' foot under the table with her own.

'When he was young and we first . . . met . . . he was such a charmer . . .' She almost smiled at the recollection, but her lower lip was trembling. 'He changed . . . when he . . . started to drink more . . . and then he lost his job . . . at the post office . . . for opening mail that had money inside . . . birthday cards and that . . . and then he got charged and . . . either didn't want or couldn't get another job then . . . and things just went downhill from there. We couldn't pay the rent on our flat so we got evicted . . . and by then he was so depressed he spent what little money we did have on drinking more and more. We got moved into a tiny council house in Newbury, and we had Danny by then as well . . . and once he'd got his own child he . . . started to be really awful to Anna and . . . when I tried to stick up for her one time, he felt I'd shown him up . . . undermined him or something . . . He rounded on me and . . . punched me in the face and . . . split my lip . . . and because it wouldn't stop bleeding . . . I had to lie at the hospital and say . . . say I'd fallen down the stairs or . . . something. He threatened Anna that if she told them the truth he'd bring a big vicious dog home from the pub to bite her . . .'

She sipped her tea again and rested the mug back on the much abused, scrubbed pine table.

Dizzy's brows knitted together as she looked once more at Jules, who shook her head and shrugged slightly.

'He was sorry of course,' she continued quietly, '. . . and some of the time he could be . . . lovely to me . . . to all of us . . . as well . . . He was like . . . who was it . . . that Jekyll and Hyde . . .'

'It must have been awful for you . . . living in fear like that all the time . . . .' Jules said quietly.

She nodded. 'He used to say it was the drink and not him . . . tried to tell me his dad drank too and that it's hereditary . . . but either way it gradually got worse and worse over the years . . . and it was always like it was my fault for winding him up . . . never his fault.' She shifted position in her chair slightly as she gained in confidence to continue her sorry tale.

'You know, people ask me sometimes why I still stayed with him once he started beating me more and more . . .'

'Why did you?' Dizzy took hold of her hand and held on to it, stroking the back of it with her free hand very gently.

'My kids . . .' she said simply. 'Where could we go? They were too big for a hostel by then . . . and I didn't want them to end up in care . . . like I did, I suppose. And then when Anna got to the age when her . . . you know . . . her . . . breasts . . . started to show, he started making . . .' She shuddered involuntarily; 'crude . . . comments and suggestions . . . and one night he came home from the pub really drunk and forced his way into her bedroom . . .'

'Anna?' Dizzy interrupted suddenly, unable to bear her curiosity any longer.

'She's my daughter. I . . . had her before I knew him . . . Her father . . . well that relationship never worked out. She ran away that night so he won't let me . . . let me talk about her anymore . . . . When I found myself homeless with a baby I had nobody to turn to . . . My older brother Kevin emigrated to Australia, see? So I didn't have anyone I could go to. When I met Len I was living in a hostel in Reading that Social Services put me in with her and . . . and I married him when she was four.'

'And when he got into Anna's room . . . Did he . . . hurt her?' Jules held her breath.

'No . . . he didn't. I stopped him . . . and that's when she ran out of the house. It was good for her but . . . then he just . . . took it out on . . . me instead.'

'And where was Danny . . . when this was all going on Lizzie?'

137

'He was asleep . . . I made sure . . . I made sure I didn't . . . I made sure I didn't . . . wake him up . . . 'Cos it would have frightened him so . . .' She shifted uncomfortably in her chair at the recollection of that terrible night.

'And then the next morning he came in and told me Anna and all her clothes and stuff had gone . . . and I haven't . . . I haven't seen her since.'

'Have you not tried to find her? How old is she now?' Dizzy pulled a slightly fluffy tissue from her sleeve and handed to her. 'Don't worry, it's clean . . .'

'She's almost twenty four . . .' Lizzie wept. 'I haven't been able even to try and find her . . . anyway she's safer . . . wherever she is . . . I know it's better for her this way . . . it's my way of still protecting her from . . . him . . . as much as I would love to see her . . . see how she is . . . But that's also why . . . why I have to stay you see . . . I know sometimes people like me say they stay because they . . . but I don't . . . I don't . . . I didn't . . . love him you see. I'm not sure I ever did . . . even before . . . all this. It's just that I left word with the neighbour I know she'd go to, when we moved here . . . so she would still know where to find me if . . . she ever . . . needed me . . . you see?'

'That's one of the hardest things about being a parent Lizzie . . .' said Jules, '. . . accepting that we can't always protect our children from being hurt by the cards they are dealt at whatever age they are. We can take all the precautions in the world and worry ourselves silly about where they are and what they're doing . . . But each child comes into this world with a life to live, no matter how scary it gets. We give our children life . . . but sometimes we forget that they're the ones who have to live it . . . We can't live it for them . . . She's an adult now Lizzie . . . wherever she is . . . and she'll be making her own way . . .'

'That's right . . . .' said Hector, coming into the kitchen and laying his hand on Lizzie's left shoulder. 'Anna is out there somewhere . . . living her life . . . safe and well . . . and has probably got herself a fine young man to take care of her by now. She may even have made you a grandmother . . .' He tilted his head to one side and tried to encourage a little smile. Lizzie reached back and patted his hand with hers. 'But you know you're perfectly safe here with us too Lizzie, and Frincham is a small enough place that if she did get in trouble and come looking for you, we'd get to hear of it and tell you . . .'

'I know you would, thank you,' Lizzie nodded, patting his hand again. 'If I could just know he'd moved on though . . . it would make me so much more able to relax and get out of your hair here but, I just feel . . . I just get the feeling, more than that really, that he's still around . . .'

'Why do you feel that, do you think Lizzie?'

'I just know it . . .' she said regretfully. 'There's more to this than him being scared about what he's done to me I reckon. He's up to something more. And he thinks I know it, and that's why he'd want me to feel threatened you see . . . so I won't tell anyone. He's holed up somewhere. I feel it.'

'I said before, this is a small place . . .' said Hector gently. 'If he were still around, somebody would have seen him. He's gone, Lizzie. We can be sure of that.'

Chapter thirteen

Not a million miles away that night, a young woman moved restlessly in her troubled sleep.

She had been sixteen years old when she fled her home that cold, hostile November night. But she had long been unwilling to be alone in a room with him; his very presence had sent shivers into her young soul. His eyes; bloodshot slits in his veined and swollen drinker's face watched her like a hawk in everything she did, and since her adolescence his comments were becoming more and more thinly disguised lust, and very crude. On that particular night she had come in quite late from a night out with her best friend, a girl called Stacey Chamberlain. Her older brother Phillip and one of his school friends had made up the foursome for a double date. They'd all been to the cinema and for a pizza afterwards, and she'd come into the house still bright eyed and buzzing because she'd fancied Phillip for ages and the date had gone really well.

She'd thought that everyone had gone to bed by then because the house was totally quiet, so she'd slipped off her shoes on the front door mat and padded quietly up the stairs to her room, closing the door carefully behind her so as not to wake anyone. She was just in the process of undressing for bed when she thought she heard the front door open again; she paused with her jeans halfway down her legs to listen. She'd heard the loud thump as he tripped, presumably over her shoes on the door mat. Then came the familiar low cursing before she heard him say her name, and she shuddered.

Her eyes wide and her heart beginning to pound, she quickly pulled up her jeans and was bending to the floor for her sweater when her bedroom door burst open and hit the side of the wardrobe with a bang, sending the collection of bottles and hair products she kept on her dressing table tumbling in all directions. Before she knew what was happening he had pushed her onto her bed and was glowering down into her face, inches away from her. In one hand he held one of her offending shoes and was angrily waving it in her face. He mumbled something incoherently about her trying to break his neck and raised the back of his free hand as if he were about to strike her. She flinched, but then he stopped. Lying flat on her back,

Anna, struck dumb with terror, was breathing heavily; her pert young breasts rising and falling rapidly, and he could see her heart visibly pounding. Her jeans were up but still unzipped, and though she had vainly draped her sweater across her body in an attempt to shield herself from his penetrating eyes, she was only wearing her pink and black cotton bra with the playboy bunny logo on one of the cups. It was her favourite bra, and she was wearing the panties to match that night too. He stood slowly and looked at her as if through very different eyes. She read his thoughts and swallowed harder than she ever had in her young life.

He turned away from her to peer through the door onto the landing, cocking his head to listen for sounds of life from either of the other two bedrooms. Satisfied at the silence and closing the door; turning back towards her, he smiled a crooked, evil looking smile.

'Look at you, you little whore . . . .' he slurred.

She swallowed again and tried to find her voice. 'If you come one step nearer to me . . . I'll scream so loud I'll wake the whole street!' she said, but her throat was dry as dust and the only sound that actually reached his ears was, 'wake the whole street . . .'

'Oh we will my girl . . . we will . . .' he sniggered, struggling out of his heavy jacket and kicking off his shoes. 'You want it . . . you know you do . . .'

In absolute horror she realised that he was undressing clumsily. He was a still a big, heavy set man then, and he was standing solidly between her and the door, completely blocking her only means of escape. Looking vainly around for some sort of weapon to try and protect herself, she picked up her hairbrush from the bedside table and brandished it at him, but he just laughed and knocked it away from her with one sideswipe of his hand. Standing over her in just his Y fronts and his socks, he caught hold of her jeans and began to try wrenching them downwards.

She had wriggled and bucked. She screamed for her life before his hand went across her mouth to stop her. She tried to bite him but his hold was too tight. He had clambered on to her bed by then and was still fumbling with her jeans. He'd got them down and was drunkenly trying to get them over her ankles, when she suddenly realised that by him doing so, she had one free leg under him and almost involuntarily brought her knee up hard into his lustful groin. Screaming in pain and rolling off her with his hands cupping his Y fronts in agony, she'd managed to get away from him and was fleeing for the door when it burst open into her; and she came face to stricken face with her mother.

'Anna . . . What . . . ?' She said, shaking her head with her eyes wide in disbelief. 'Len . . . what . . . what are you . . .' One hand went up into her hair, grasping at it in horror and the scene before her eyes. 'Anna . . . ?' She'd looked towards her daughter and tried to put an arm around her, but Anna rushed past her, pulling on her sweater and sobbing, down the stairs and out of the front door. She'd run, barefoot and utterly oblivious to the consequences she'd left her mother to deal with, until her lungs felt as if they would explode and she'd had to stop. She'd found herself outside the telephone box near the park and, reaching into her back pocket for her wallet, relieved beyond words to find it still there, she opened the door and called the only person she could think of: Stacey.

Dialling her number with a shaking hand, it had actually been Phillip had who had answered, and so it had been Phillip who raced to pick her up in his parent's car. She'd stayed the night in his room at their home, planning; curled up in his arms, like an enormous and comforting teddy bear.

In the early hours of the following morning, once he'd trusted that, one way or another, the coast would be clear, it had been Phillip also who, using the dustbin, had clambered onto the back shed roof, shimmied up the drainpipe to Anna's bedroom, now deserted, and slipped quietly through the window by reaching one long arm down from the open top one and freeing the stay. Following Anna's instructions, he'd swiftly packed everything he could lay his hands on into one after another from a roll of black bin bags, throwing them out of the window to the ground as he went. Taking one last look around and noting the time on her bedside clock as approaching 3.45am, he'd slipped skillfully back down the drain pipe, and loaded the bags into the boot of the car, before driving slowly away, so as not to raise the alarm.

Anna opened her eyes with the usual tears coursing down her cheeks and reached out in the darkness for the glass of water on her bedside table.

'Are you ok?' he said quietly, awakened by her movement.

'I'm fine love, go back to sleep . . .' she whispered.

She'd never gone home.

She could never go home.

Chapter fourteen

That night and also not a million miles away Len Fidler looked over at the Rectory in the darkness of a crescent moon from the top of the church cellar steps and, once sure that neither vicar was still up and around he moved, shadowlike, along the wall, letting himself quietly back into the south door with a key.

The Disciples, permanently illuminated by the emerald green glow of the fire exit sign above their Last Supper heads, stared critically down from their vantage point on the wall behind the font as he continued on his way up the carpeted stairs to the balcony. Looking around once more, in some sense afraid that one of the parables depicted in the stained glass windows might spring to accusatory life in the darkness, he took a long key from his pocket and opened the only door. Then, climbing the three steps up into the bell space, he closed the door carefully behind him, stepped over his crumpled sleeping area (made up from of the contents of several sacks of old Choir robes) and, pulling a recently stolen packet of biscuits from his pockets, ate hungrily.

He had been hiding here ever since Flynn's visit and his threats; his only company being the assortment of redundant rubbish that nobody in the church would actually bite the bullet and throw out. Confining his movements to the dead of night, he sat silent as the grave during church services, watchful of the Bert the Verger, and profoundly thankful that St Mary's team of ringers had long ago disbanded and that, thanks to some dodgy stonework on the bell tower, the bells had been out of bounds to visiting ringers for almost a year.

Len looked around his self imposed universe, licking his sticky fingers and wiping them down his now filthy trousers. In this short space of time he had become just another faceless tramp; swiftly passed by and ignored in the streets. Which at this moment in time it suited him just fine.

Standing again, he weaved himself through the ropes, moved over to the dusty and cobweb ridden but plain glass window, and looked down on the Rectory garden. The house was in total darkness now; the top of the front garden illuminated solely by a streetlight from the road.

Sure that he was safe to move around, he flicked on the torch he'd stolen from the vestry and shone it on the area of floor directly under his window. Bending low, he gently eased up the loose floorboard, easily pulling it free now that it was used to it. The floor space beneath the resultant hole was large, and big enough to hide the black bag containing the items he had stolen over the last few weeks.

It had been so easy. Danny and that dimwit friend of his had been so cocky about their customers' hidden house keys. All he'd had to do was observe them while they worked, and then each time they looked under a flowerpot, a stone or, in Jimmy Knapp's case, pulled a string through his letter box, he'd known that the house owner was out and simply repeated the exercise as soon as they'd gone. All he'd had to do was make sure bloody Lizzie didn't put two and two together when she'd seen him hanging around one morning; and that had been easy enough. He'd just told her he was helping Danny and Baz with the round because they had so much work on, now that they'd got Stanton Court. She'd been so pleased; hadn't even bothered to ask them if it was true.

Finding somewhere to hide his ill gotten gains had been child's play too. Lizzie had been given a whole bunch of keys to the church and its rich assortment of old doors by the old verger, and had even commented that she couldn't see why she'd been given the bell tower one she'd never even need because it was heavy and weighed the rest of the bunch down. So he'd taken that one off for her and kept it, and simply had the south door key copied in Newbury one day while she was working at the pub. Then, with a devious eye on any or all contingencies, he'd copied her set of pub keys while she'd been cleaning the church one day. It mattered nothing to him that his son would get the blame for the thefts. In his twisted mind he had just decided that Danny was getting too big for his boots anyway with his airs and graces about wanting to get on, and his designs on that stuck up little mare from Stanton Court that he thought wasn't noticeable to any fool that looked at him. Lizzie could see no wrong in him of course, and she was turning him into a real Mummy's boy, keeping him by her side and making sure she always knew where he was. It made him sick.

He couldn't stay here much longer, he knew that. Bert the Verger was already suspicious after he'd left his torch and a carrier bag of food rubbish by the door, ready to go out. But he'd been caught out that night when Bert came back into the church after playing dominoes at the pub, to set the church up for a funeral the following morning. He'd overheard Bert talking to Hector and Sir Christopher about it the following day after the collection got stolen, stating that he thought a vagrant had been sleeping in the church, and heard them down there as they searched around for further clues; but thankfully none of them had thought to look in the locked tower.

He reached down into the hole in the floor once more and brought up the bag that Amy had seen, and from it took a dark green money bag that he'd stolen from the vestry. Opening it, he extracted what remained of the funeral collection money and pulled a face: not enough to even buy a few cans from the weekly travelling shop, and no more funeral services this week; according to the discarded newsletter he'd picked up. There was nothing for it; he'd just have to break his cover and start selling off the rest of the stuff. Reaching into the bag again, he pulled out several items and studied them more closely in the light of the torch.

He'd seen a Boot Sale poster for the following Saturday on the church notice board, so now all he had to do was get these over to Yattley school where it was to take place. He knew just how to achieve this, and how he could get that smug Irishman at the same time. Carefully lowering bag inside the hole again, he replaced the floorboard along with the little tamper marker he'd rigged up, and settled down onto his improvised bed for another night.

*   *   *

The Grandfather clock with its deep and comfortingly bass tick-tock had just declared the hour to be midnight directly below her room and, temporarily trapped inside her own troubled dreams, she awoke with a start as the clock began to strike, her breath coming in short gasps; one hand leaping to her chest as if to check that her heart was really still beating. As she awakened fully and stared at the ceiling in the darkness she repeated her usual routine of reminding herself that she was safe, but she was worried. Something was nagging at her brain in these dreams, she was sure of it. She knew something more about Len.

The dream was always the same. Each time she had it, it was as if she was really there, but floating above the horrors in that terrifying and bloodied kitchen. She could see herself perfectly clearly, whimpering like an injured animal on the floor below, and she could see him; kicking at her and hacking at her hair. But then the same thing happened every time. As soon as he had left her in the room her eyes became those of the woman on the floor, staring at something right in front of her eyes. Obscured, or just out of reach . . . it just wouldn't show itself though. She remembered seeing that something quite clearly that night too . . . and, confusingly, it had something to do with the cutlery drawer, she was sure of it.

She sat up and took a gulp from the glass of water on her own bedside table, as her missing daughter just had; but had no loving partner to ask her if she was all right.

She turned over her pillow, punched at it impatiently, and tried to get back to sleep.

Chapter fifteen

Sergeant Tidbury watched from the front windows of the police station with his hands in his pockets as Danny Fidler left after yet more overnight questioning and ran to jump on the passing Reading bus. Then he pressed his entry code into the front desk door panel to take him back into the inner realms. As he made his way past the back of the reception however, the desk sergeant called him back.

'Luke? You're doing the Frincham thefts, right?'

'Right . . .' he said slowly, involuntarily glancing out of the window where the bus could clearly be seen disappearing into the distance. 'Why?'

'Got another one for you . . . Just came in. The Landlord of the White Hart pub; a Mr . . .' he checked his paperwork; 'Flynn . . . had his van stolen from the car park during the night last night. The alarm never went off and he swore he'd locked it up securely. He's still got his keys . . . .'

Tidbury took the sheet of paper from him and blew out a resigned sigh. Both Danny Fidler and his mate Baz had been kept in all night for further questioning when the van was as reported stolen.

He was beginning to think Danny might be telling the truth for once in his life. Or maybe Frincham really did have a phantom . . .

*   *   *

Later the next day, Lizzie's friend the old Grandfather clock in the sitting room now said 2.15pm, and she was trying hard to concentrate on an edition of *Through the Keyhole* that she was halfheartedly watching on the television, before the children came home from school. She crossed one foot comfortably over the other beneath her favourite blanket and took another sip of tea from a mug with a picture of a guinea pig on it; that she suspected must belong to Tesco. Doing her best to concentrate her mind on '*who lives in a house like this?*', she'd just been given the sneak shot of the house owner the panel didn't get to see, and smiled at the welcome distraction as Dizzy's head appeared around the sitting room door.

Sally Breach

'I'm off to get the girls, love. Hector is in his study working if you need him . . .' She looked at the TV screen dubiously and laughed. 'What *are* you watching?'

'Oh just *Through the Keyhole.*' Lizzie said absently. 'If the panel doesn't guess whose house they've been shown from the clues, the owner gets a big key in a box as a prize . . . but I don't even know who he is and I've just seen him . . .'

Dizzy smiled. 'And what on earth can they do with a huge key in a box?' she laughed, and snorted slightly. 'We've got enough huge keys in this house to make people think we've been in every series . . .'

Lizzie grinned as she went to take another sip of tea, but with a jolt suddenly stopped dead with the mug halfway to her lips. 'What did you say?'

Dizzy blinked. 'I said we've got enough huge church keys in this house to . . .'

Lizzie's eyes widened. Hands shaking, she put the mug carefully down on the little table beside her armchair.

Dizzy rushed fully into the room and stooped to take her hands as Lizzie became more and more agitated; alarmed that her breathing was becoming shallow and fast again.

'What I keep seeing . . . in the dream!' she gasped.

'I don't understand, darling . . . Calm down . . . it's all right . . . you're bound to have nightmares my love . . . but . . .'

Lizzie jumped up out of the chair, jogging the little table, spilling tea all over the floor as the mug tipped over. Grabbing at the loo roll she'd been using as a substitute for tissues she began frantically rubbing at the threadbare carpet and apologising tearfully; 'I'm so cl . . . clumsy . . . I'm sorry . . . I'm so sorry . . .'

Dizzy gently pulled her hands away from the wet patch and removed the soggy mess from her hands, placing the empty mug back on the table. 'Leave it darling . . . it doesn't matter . . . honestly . . . one more stain on this old carpet won't even notice . . .'

Lizzie looked doubtful as she stared at the dark stain and sniffed, rubbing her nose on the wristband of her cardigan fitfully.

'Come on now; tell me what's wrong . . . .'

Lizzie sat back on her heels, taking a deep breath inwards but still looking down to the floor. 'When I was on the floor in my kitchen that . . . night . . .' She stopped for a moment and shuddered involuntarily. 'I . . . saw something . . . . on the back of the cutlery drawer . . .'

'Something on the back of the . . . ?'

'It's really hard to . . . open . . . and he pulled it right out . . . to get the s . . . the scissors to cut my . . .' her hand went up to her scalp, 'a . . . and the whole thing fell . . . and I saw it when I was lying there . . . like it was hidden . . . it's too big for a pocket, see? But I couldn't . . . . make sense of it. I've been seeing it over and over in my dream . . . like I knew it must mean

157

something . . . and now I think I know what it is . . .'
She took hold of Dizzy's arms and looked her fully in
the face. 'It was that big bell tower key! He took it off
the bunch the verger gave me . . . and it was there . . .
taped to the back of the drawer!'

'But why on earth would . . . he want to hide
it . . . ?'

'Dizzy can't you see? It's him . . .'

'Him . . . what love?'

'It's all about keys . . . . all of it . . . .'

'Lizzie . . . darling . . . .'

'. . . Len wasn't working with Danny and Baz . . . .
He was following them . . . watching them . . . and
I saw him . . . . And what if he's been doing all the
thieving the police think *they* were doing . . . using the
house keys . . . . And . . . then maybe using the big key
to hide the stuff in the church . . .'

'Lizzie . . . are you . . . . quite . . . .'

'Please . . . Dizzy . . . . I knew he was up to something!
I saw him! He told me he was working with them on the
round . . . . but Danny's never even mentioned it . . . .
And I think we . . . should tell the police to at least take
a look up *there*!' Her arm shot out, her index finger
pointing straight towards the church; to the upper bell
tower window.

*　　*　　*

Tidbury backed out of the tower and down the steps to join Hector on the balcony, still talking into his phone. 'Yes sir, definitely. It's obvious he's been kipping down in there very recently too; there's all kinds of fresh food waste and stuff up here . . . and nothing's mouldy. He's got an excellent view of the Rectory and half the village up here to, sir. Been up here a while I'd say . . . The Rector said they found some rubbish and a torch over a fortnight ago but thought they'd had a vagrant in . . . .'

He paused a moment to listen to the unheard voice at the other end of the line.

'Yes I do . . . and money missing from collections too . . . The floor is a bit loose in places up here. I pulled a board up because there was a bit of old ribbon sticking out from under it. It was an old medal ribbon as it turned out . . . and there's a bag down there with some jewellery and a few bits and pieces in it . . . but it looks as if he's maybe taken the rest . . . if he hasn't sold it already . . . .

I'd say Mrs Fidler is right sir . . . . . . Young Danny and his mate were actually telling the truth, and we should have been looking at her old man . . .' The person at the other end said something else and Tidbury nodded his head. 'Yes sir, Mrs Fidler told us how . . . . . and from what I've just found up here I reckon she's right. He's been having a field day . . . letting himself in all over the village, sir. We've got the real Frincham Phantom hiding out up here . . . Now we just need to catch him . . . .'

Chapter sixteen

Meanwhile Flynn received a telephone call from the shop owner in nearby Hermitage, having taken down the telephone number of the pub from the side of his abandoned van; to say could he kindly come and get it because it was blocking her doorway.

In order to catch Len the police had decided to act as if all was undisturbed up in the bell tower so that he would hopefully return to his hideout at some point. Church services carried on as normal apart from the sudden addition of two plain clothes police officers to blend into the congregations posing as a couple, just in case, and once Tidbury and his team had received word that he'd been seen in the vicinity three days later, a plan was put into action. Two police officers moved into one of the bedrooms at the pub, almost opposite the front of the church, whilst two more moved into the old concrete gun emplacement on the river bank, affording an excellent view of the rear of the church, at the bottom of the Rectory garden.

Everyone settled in to see if Len returned to his roost that night; or just for the rest of the stolen items he'd got stashed in the floor, because of course, the bag was still there.

Tidbury knew that Len had been trying to sell off the stolen items at a boot sale in Yattley. Before he'd dumped it, Flynn's van had been reported as being seen by Jules Taylor working on a stall in the school playground. Len had fled once he'd seen her and thought he'd got away without being seen, but as a precaution he'd dumped the van outside the shop and taken the black holdall with him on foot back towards Frincham; entering the village only once safely under the cover of darkness.

Sure enough, just as Lizzie heard the grandfather clock strike one that night, the police officer on first watch in the pub nudged his colleague awake and pointed silently at the figure making its way in the shadow of the ancient walls towards the south door of the church. He paused there for a moment to rummage in his pocket, inserted the key, and entered.

'Target has just gone into the church sarge, over?' he said calmly into his radio.

'Received . . .' said Tidbury quietly, from his vantage point in the considerably less comfortable pill box. 'Stand by all units . . .'

A torch light beam flashed across the inside of the upper bell tower window as Lizzie caught her breath on her window seat. Unable to sleep, she had been sitting in the dark for over an hour behind the net curtain at her bedroom window, with its clear view of the church tower; all the time wondering if Len had known where she'd been hiding all along.

She gasped as four ghostlike figures made their way across from the church car park, silent and low as the ancient grave stones that provided their cover; to their positions along the walls, and waited.

Then the torch beam went off in the bell tower and all was darkness once more. He must have settled down for the night.

Slowly, the officers lying in wait made their way towards the back of the building and stood talking with their heads together quietly. Then her eyes were drawn involuntarily as another one appeared from some way behind them, at the top of the cellar steps, and began to run, still keeping low and using the gravestones for cover, towards the village hall car park.

Her brows knitted slightly as she wondered why that could be.

The other officers then dispersed to cover the remaining church doors, cutting off Len's entire means of escape. Lizzie's gaze scanned the village hall car park as best she could from her position, which wasn't great, but she could just see the recycling bins on the far side of it and almost missed what was unmistakably the front of Flynn's recently returned van, carefully parked beside them, so it couldn't be easily seen from the road. She warily scanned the area once more, continuing to watch as the plans to capture her husband unfolded below her.

Suddenly, her eyes were drawn back to the village hall car park, having heard the unmistakable sound of an engine starting up from that direction; or more specifically, from beside the recycling bins.

The officers hadn't taken any notice of it at all; probably assuming that it was just Flynn off out somewhere at this late hour, and still sure that Len was still inside the church.

And the ones over in the pub wouldn't be able to see round that far either . . .

She was down the stairs and out of the front door in an instant, and running, her bare feet being torn to ribbons on the sharp gravel path, and heading out to raise the alarm to the police in the pub before Len got away again. Flynn blinked in complete disbelief from his vantage point in the pub bedroom with the two officers on watch, as he saw Lizzie emerge from the Rectory front door wearing nothing but a white nightdress; tearing down the path screaming at the top of her lungs and pointing at the village hall. He shook his head momentarily that she had been hiding so close by, before leaping out of his chair and down the stairs as if he was on fire.

Then all hell broke loose.

Len Fidler was a drunk and a thug, but he was no fool. He had immediately known that his hideout had been discovered once he'd seen that the tamper marker at the edge of the loose floorboard was now down inside the hole, and he'd soon guessed the rest. He had made his escape via the church boiler house, accessible from inside the church only if you lift a heavy iron grating at the chancel step and grope your way along a narrow tunnel beneath the floor. From there he had carefully removed the hinges on the inside of the old and worm eaten oak door, using a handy screwdriver from the verger's tool box, and made his way carefully up the dank and slippery, lichen encrusted stone steps of the cellar, to the churchyard; unseen, or so he thought, and away.

Unable to believe his luck in spotting Flynn's van again, he threw the bag into the back and tore out of the car park to the road in a hail of flying gravel. Lizzie, running out into the road intent on raising the alarm, froze to the spot like a rabbit in the face of disaster from the oncoming, lightless, van.

Len, stunned for a split second, saw Lizzie in her white nightdress standing in the middle of the road and, in a moment sheer green eyed monster of jealousy madness, assuming she was making for her lover's bed at the pub, put his foot down and drove the van straight at her.

She watched him, as if in slow motion, as his black eyes fixed on her at last and, closing her own, awaited the inevitable.

This was going to be it then, like this.

And the last thing she would ever see in her pathetic life was those evil eyes.

Her last breath came as a single gasp of the drizzly night air: she was almost glad of it.

*   *   *

She heard, but did not feel the impact and was flying through the air as if lifted, and felt no pain. She felt herself land, heavily, on the grass to the side of the road, and she thought she heard her name-her old name; Beth, which didn't make any sense either, unless it was an angel calling her home of course.

The van's engine in a poor choice of gear roared through the darkness as surrounding bedroom lights

165

flicked indignantly on and windows opened. Len continued his way out of the village square as the sirens of the police cars announced themselves getting ever closer behind him.

If this was dying it wasn't so bad after all.

She lay there, silent and unsure whether she was almost alive or almost dead, in no pain, until the sound and the vibrations of crunching gravel invaded her consciousness. Then the familiar, but raised in alarm voices of Hector and Dizzy.

She felt gentle but urgent hands on her body. She heard their voices close to her; and then she heard them as if they were farther away. Both of them were talking to her but saying different things . . . it was as if they were talking to two of her, and as she lay there she was becoming more and more confused.

Slowly, she opened her eyes and met Dizzy's.

'Lizzie! Lizzie, are you all right?' She stroked one hand gently down the side of Lizzie's face, and then turned and called over to Hector. 'She's coming round Hector . . . ! What's happening now?'

Hector's voice sounded more distant. 'I've called for an ambulance . . . It's on its way!'

'Is it L. is it Len? Is he . . .'

'No darling it isn't Len. Len drove off after he tried to run you down . . . The police will have caught up with him by now . . . .'

'One of the . . . please God . . . not one of the girls . . . ?' she whispered.

'Shh . . . darling, lay still. No. No, the girls are fine . . . they're fine . . . I promise . . . . There's a police officer with them indoors . . . . The ambulance is coming. Everything is going to be all right, you'll see. You're being very brave . . .' she knelt forward and kissed the top of Lizzie's head.

'But . . . I don't think I need an ambulance . . .' she said quietly, sensing around her body for pain, but there was nothing much. 'I'm just a bit bruised . . . it was like I flew out of the way . . . I don't understand . . . Dizzy . . . ? What's going on?'

Dizzy took her hand. 'You didn't fly out of the way darling . . . It was Flynn. He ran out and pushed you clean off your feet . . . but then Len hit him with the van instead . . . and I'm afraid he's hurt . . .'

Lizzie was off the ground in seconds and stumbling across to where Hector sat crouched next to Flynn; lying ominously still in the road where he'd landed.

She screamed, falling to the ground at his other side. 'Flynn! Flynn . . .'

But he couldn't hear her. He lay still and silent, in a pool of blood from an ugly looking head wound that looked even worse because it was dripping into a puddle; as the rain began to fall more steadily.

*　　*　　*

The tenant farmer on the Stanton Court Estate was a man of almost seventy three summers called Ernie Jones, and together with his two burly sons, Matthew and Mark (their mother having sadly died before they'd been able to complete the full set of Gospel authors), they ran the fairly considerable Stanton View farm, with a mixture of arable crops and a bit of income from point to point events and shooting parties. They also kept a few rare breed sheep and cows, and a variety of fowl including ducks, turkeys and chickens, and the eggs from those were very popular locally.

As well as working on the farm Matthew was renowned locally as an experienced and passionate bird of prey enthusiast, and when he wasn't behind the wheel of a tractor he could often be seen with an impressively trained bird or two being flown to the lure around the fields locally. His younger brother Mark, the quieter of the two brothers, also loved his birds, though generally his were of the smaller variety. He spent most of what precious little there was of his spare time in a hide close to the copse where Hannah had recently come to grief, with a pair of binoculars, a flask of tea and a notebook.

On the day in question Ernie and his sons had been working in the thirty acre that sits adjacent to the Stanton Court Road and, now alone in the field, he was striving to finish ploughing ready for planting the following morning. It had been a very long day. He had finished just after 1am, had just drunk the last of his sugary tea, and after yawning for the fifth time in succession had decided to go home and allow himself the luxury of about four hours sleep before the morning milking at six. Trundling slowly to the edge of the field with his old transistor radio at full volume to keep him awake, he neither heard nor saw the speeding and lightless van approaching from the blind bend to his right.

Just about the point that Ernie's trailer pulled out into the road behind the tractor he let out a sixth exaggerated yawn, closing his eyes just for a split second.

Len, his eyes momentarily on his rear view mirror, did not see the half emerged machinery until it was too late to do anything other than pointlessly slam on his brakes.

Flynn's stolen van rammed into the moonlit blades on the side of the trailer doing at least fifty miles per hour; to the sickening sounds of metal against metal, and screaming engine. And the last thing Len Fidler ever saw with his terrified eyes, was the evil looking tip of a steel blade heading straight for his face.

*   *   *

The ambulance crew had quickly dealt with the terribly shocked but otherwise unhurt farmer before his son Matthew arrived to take him home. With the assistance of the fire brigade, the crew had then removed the gruesome remains of Len Fidler from more than one location inside the wrecked van, before the police took it away for in depth forensic examination.

One thing was soon discovered however. He obviously had not had very much luck at the car boot sale before he'd seen Jules Taylor in the playground at Yattley School, because most of the stolen items Tidbury had seen were still inside the bag they'd found in the back of it.

That same night the Coroner thankfully decided that it was not possible for either Danny or his mother to make a positive identification from what was left of Len, but luckily one had easily been established from his well documented police fingerprint files.

When it went to court, the Coroner recorded a verdict of Death by Misadventure.

Neither his widow nor his son had been present for the verdict.

Chapter seventeen

Flynn recovered consciousness while in the professional care of Jemmie Ryan in the Royal Berkshire hospital the following morning. Because of his injuries he was kept there for a few more days; with two broken ribs and one hell of a headache . . . though the pain from these eased significantly once Hector informed him that Len Fidler couldn't hurt Lizzie anymore.

He was taking strong pain killers and sleeping a lot, but even asleep he was desperate to see her. Her traumatised face haunted his dreams; wearing her white nightdress, wailing and crying and reaching out to him for help, with elongated arms and hundreds of distorted fingers. Each time this happened he awoke with his heart pounding, the bedding in a complete tangle and his hair clinging to his head in damp, sweaty tendrils.

*   *   *

The pub had been closed for a few days while Flynn was in hospital but once he returned home they had reopened with Donna and another of his regulars at the helm. Gareth, keen to help out in the only way he could, had been sending food down from the Royal Oak in huge metal containers for the Hart's less demanding customers and, keen to be kept informed, Flynn had heard that Gareth's lasagna was an instant hit, and that his sausage and onion gravy sandwiches had even managed to sway Jimmy away from his habitual cheese and pickle.

Knowing where Lizzie had been hiding out all the time now, Flynn had summoned up the courage and telephoned the Rectory in the hope of at least hearing her voice. Hector had answered though, and told him that she was in bed and asleep after having laid awake most of the night before, and that he didn't want to wake her. Not knowing that she had actually been lying awake feeling guilty at being worried about him, he forced himself to stay away; believing her to be grieving the loss of her husband, however difficult their relationship had been.

Danny had been up to see Flynn just as soon as he was fit enough to receive visitors; to thank him for saving his mother's life. It came as quite a surprise to Flynn how much Danny had changed in the weeks since everything had happened. He seemed so much more mature; more grown up. He was still quiet, but visibly less on the defensive, and more on the contemplative side now. Flynn told him about his own brother's violent death during the time known as 'The Troubles' in Ireland during the 1970's; after which the rest of the family had moved to the UK. Then it was as if Danny could really see how much they actually had in common. He'd really opened up, which had been a revelation in itself after his previous tendency to respond to anything Flynn said in words of one syllable or less, and they'd had a long talk.

'. . . And so I'm an only child too now Danny, just like you . . .' Flynn continued.

Danny was looking out into the car park where he'd been watching people come and go for some minutes. 'I'm not an only child though . . .' he said quietly, shifting from one foot to the other. 'I've got a sister . . . Anna . . . Did she never tell you?'

Flynn blinked in surprise but said nothing.

Danny turned away from the window to look at him, but not for long, obviously finding it easier to talk without eye contact.

'She's older than me . . . She ran away, years ago, because of . . . my . . . because of Len.'

'She never said a word to me about having a daughter . . .'

He shook his head slightly. 'Mum doesn't talk about her 'cos . . . well because he . . . wouldn't have her name mentioned after she ran away . . . and anyway Mum thinks she's safer where she is now . . .'

'Which is.?'

Danny turned to face him again, and shrugged his shoulders; hands thrust deep into the pockets of his jeans.

'Dunno . . .'

Flynn took a sip of his coffee and shook his head slightly as Danny turned back to the window.

Subject closed.

Chapter eighteen

Despite his frequent visits to Flynn, Danny was still spending the rest of his free, and now innocent, time at the hospital after what was now many weeks of lonely vigil by Hannah's bed: between Amy's visits with plastic boxes of contraband food for him and Hannah's father's daily visits of course. They'd moved her to a private room from the ICU because she was doing really well, the doctors had said. Her facial scars had healed over and she just looked like Hannah to him. The plasters and splints were off her limbs, and the physiotherapists were coming in every day to work on them to help strengthen her inactive muscles. Her hair had grown over the area that it had been shaved off for stitches to the point it was hard to see any scars at all now.

Just a matter of time they'd said. He was both impatient and terrified of what would happen when she finally woke up . . . and saw him there. But whatever happened he had to tell her. He knew that more than anything else.

After her father had gone home one day and Danny had returned from his usual hiding place to his vigil by her bedside, he'd found her teddy bear lying on her pillow; left there so that she would see when she woke up. Danny had taken to holding it himself ever since, finding both comfort in it, and from knowing how much it was loved by her: and loving that it smelled of her too.

After another long night and yawning widely from sheer exhaustion, he looked at the clock on the wall. It was just coming up to 10am. It would be hours before her father came back in: plenty of time for a quick snooze. He adjusted his position in the chair beside her bed, bent his arms and the teddy bear into a pillow and laid his head down beside the sleeping Hannah's right hand.

*   *   *

It was summer. She'd been lying in sweet scented grass in the sunny meadow for hours, and was now dozing blissfully up against a tree in the afternoon shade to the sound of the birds singing all around her; skylarks, chiffchaffs and wrens and, somewhere, high in the clear blue sky above her, red kites wheeled in the thermals and called to each other. A red squirrel ran up the bark of her tree and she heard its intermittently scratching and rapid ascent, occasionally pausing to listen and watch for danger, all the way to its dray the top. She could hear Beau cropping at the grass beside her; his bridle and harness clinking metallically as he contentedly munched the rich green meadow grass. Her mobile phone beeped incessantly, somewhere in the distance, but she couldn't be bothered just now; it was most probably Amy, or maybe Katie or Mel. She'd read her texts later.

She moved her right hand fractionally to pull at a strand of timothy grass to chew on its sweet and tender stem, but then her brows furrowed slightly; the timothy grass felt wrong. It should have felt long and spindly, with its seed feathers in a soft fan at the top . . . But this felt . . . warm and . . . wiry, and there was something . . . metallic . . . She felt a little further in her sleep and her fingers fought to grasp at the object that was so annoyingly just out of her reach . . . . But the sleep was too deep; and she couldn't bear to open her eyes to the bright sun, just yet.

What was it, this smooth metallic thing? She moved slightly to her side to reach it properly and felt for it again. Slipping her fingers through it she fondled it gently in the wiry, curly grass . . . Beau must have a cast a shoe . . . but no . . . it felt wrong . . . .

And then, in a momentary blink of her eyes, it was gone. The wiry grass and the ring were gone.

The ring . . . ? Yes, that was it! It was Danny's earring! But . . . why was it here, in the grass . . . it was wrapped secretly up in her hanky, in her coat pocket, surely . . . ? It must have fallen out when she . . . .

Her phone beeped again . . . it must be urgent. She really should wake up now . . . but it was so warm here, in the sun . . .

Danny shot up from where he'd been sleeping. He looked at her, lying there, still so pale and thin, still attached to one machine to the side of her bed, beeping incessantly, and fought back the desire to call out for the nurse. She'd moved; he was sure of it. He felt to his ear and touched the earring, and then his hand reached down once more, for hers, and took it.

'Hannah . . . it's me, it's Danny! I'm here . . . can you hear me?' he shook her hand slightly and lifted it to his lips, willing her fingers to tighten around his at long last, and kissed them tenderly.

After an age of seconds her eyelids fluttered; and finally, her hand moved in his. Then her long fingers wrapped themselves tightly around his, and stayed there.

'Hannah! It's me! Danny! Wake up . . . . Please . . . come on . . .'

The door opened behind him and Jemmie Ryan came rushing in at the noise, followed by Amy, and a nurse at her heels.

'Danny, what is it?' Jemmie said quickly . . . did she . . . ?

'She blinked! Honest! . . . and she . . . she's holding my hand . . . look! . . . a . . . and when I was asleep . . . with my head on the bed . . . she pulled my hair and . . . pulled at my earring . . . !'

Jemmie pushed past him and looked at the monitor behind her bed, then adjusted her position to allow for her pregnant belly and lifted one of Hannah's eyelids, shining a small torch held between her fingers. Hannah's pupil reacted to the sudden light and she made a very slight sound.

'It's Daddy!' he cried excitedly. 'She's tryin' to say Daddy!'

Jemmie replaced the torch to the top pocket of her lab coat and smiled as she turned back to him, putting a hand onto his shoulder to try and calm him down. 'Sounded more like Danny to me . . .' she said softly, before turning to speak to the nurse. 'Kimberley . . . would you please go and call Hannah's father to come immediately?'

'Yes Doctor . . . . of course . . . .' she replied with a grin.

'Thank you . . . .' Jemmie nodded as the nurse left the room and closed the door behind her.

'You'd better make this quick Danny . . .' she said with a conspiratorial grin. 'He'll be here before you know it . . .'

Her father arrived at the hospital within an hour of the nurse's call to him, and stalked into her room with his usual confidence, but with unusually bright eyes, only to find that blasted hooligan Danny Fidler sitting by her bed, holding her hand far too intimately as she sat back, pale but smiling against her pillows, while he whispered sweet nothings to her. Amy Palmer was standing by the window and went as pink as a peony with guilt when he looked at her too. Danny made as if to leap to his feet, but Hannah pulled him back and kept a tight grip on his hand.

'Daddy . . .' she said, with tears springing to her eyes despite herself.

Sir Christopher walked to the other side of the bed and reached down to kiss his daughter. 'Hannah, darling, I'm so . . . I'm so . . . .'

'I'm doing fine now Daddy . . . . please don't fuss . . . Danny has . . .'

His mood changed instantly and he stood as if struck at the sound of that name; thrusting his clenched fists onto his hips angrily. 'Hannah you do realise that this young . . . thug . . . is responsible for your being in this state? I can't believe you're actually . . .' he jabbed his head in the general direction of Danny, unable to actually look at him, and instead looked across the room; fixing his eyes on Amy. 'Did you know about this?' he demanded. Amy gulped visibly and looked to her friend for help.

'Amy is my friend Daddy, this has nothing to do with her . . . so don't look at her like that . . . this is between me and Danny . . .' She shifted her position slightly and looked at her father defiantly. 'Danny told me . . . what happened . . .' she said, swallowing for courage. 'I don't normally ride out alone . . . you know that . . . but Amy was away when it happened . . . And it wasn't even Danny's idea . . . . The car chase . . . . He tried to stop them . . . . And if he hadn't regretted his part in it and jumped out . . . of that still moving car . . . to come after me . . . to find me . . . and then rode Beau for help, I might have died . . . You should be grateful to him really . . .' Her pale face suddenly flushed but she still afforded herself a slight smile over to her friend who'd had the same thought at Danny trying to ride the enormous Beau.

'Yes . . . well . . .' Her father interrupted her a little less frostily, and stooped to shakily run a hand down the side of her face before kissing her tenderly to the side of one eye. 'That's as maybe . . . . Darling; can we put all that behind us now, and get you well . . . and home again . . . ?'

181

'I am sorry . . . sir . . . for my part in what happened . . . honest . . .' Danny looked him straight in the eyes as he spoke.

Sir Christopher snorted slightly. 'Creeping in here only since you heard she'd regained consciousness, you mean . . .'

'He's been here all the time Daddy . . . He just hides when you come in . . . So you couldn't have him thrown out . . .' she looked at Danny and smiled.

'How do you know that?' Danny looked at her incredulously.

'I heard you, sometimes, talking to me . . . and to Amy . . . and to my teddy bear once or twice . . .' she winked. 'And I heard a nurse telling you Daddy was on his way once . . .'

'Hiding from me were you? Couldn't face me, is that it?' He rounded on Danny, appalled at the way her eyes were now sparkling at that . . . thug.

'No, sir, I'm not afraid of you. I'm not afraid of anybody . . . but I did wrong and I wanted to put it right . . . . honest! I stayed because I wanted to speak to Hannah as soon as she came round about what really happened that's all . . . before you poisoned her against me . . .' He let go of her hand and stood up, equal in height to her father, but considerably thinner. 'I love your daughter sir . . . and she . . .' he looked into her eyes with his gypsy eyes shining with so much love that they severed all possible comparisons to his father for the first time in his life.

'I love him too Daddy . . . so you'd best get used to it . . .' Hannah's chin jutted up towards her father with a flash in her eyes that instantly took his breath clean away.

Beaten, Sir Christopher speechlessly looked across at the obviously thrilled and smiling Amy, nodded his head back at the pair of them in disbelief just once, and then abruptly left the room.

Ignoring Hannah's cries for him to come back and finding himself almost blinded by tears, he stumbled along the corridor with one hand against the wall to steady himself, as his heart pounded visibly through his shirt. At the very end of the corridor he turned into the open doorway of the day room, that was thankfully empty; but for the sound of the TV talking to itself in one corner. Then he sat down heavily and leaned forward, putting his head into his hands and breathing deeply before finally dissolving into racking sobs. Sobs that encompassed relief that Hannah had finally regained consciousness, rage at what he still considered to be her poor choice of boyfriend . . . rage at her friend for not keeping him informed and, above even all of that; grief. Grief that he'd just seen her mother in her so powerfully; she might have been lying there herself.

A sudden burst of game show laughter from the TV seemed to mock him without mercy, and he reached over for the remote control with a gasp of despair to turn it off. Then, tossing it back onto the table in front of him with a clunk, he sat back in the chair and put his hands over his face, shook his head slowly as he closed his eyes, and allowed the fortified barriers on that part of his life to come down inside his brain and remember . . .

Chapter nineteen

The plainly known Chris Derby had been almost twenty five years old when he'd fallen head over Saville Row heels in love for the first, and only, time in his life. She was Charlotte Wayne-Phillips, the nineteen year old only daughter of David and Rimini Wayne-Phillips, both well known local dignitaries and high flyers in the Rotary Club. He'd seen her many times before, of course. They'd crossed paths on many occasions, mostly due to the fact she was the best friend of his younger sister Arabella, and often because she was either on a horse at a hunt, or totally encased in an oversized green Barbour jacket, waxed hat and Wellington's, walking their three Golden Retrievers on the public right of way area on his father's estate. But he'd never seen her 'scrubbed up' in scarlet satin with a very impressive diamond tiara as she'd been at that hunt ball, almost twenty years ago now.

She'd outshone everyone else in the room that night, and try as he might, he hadn't been able to take his eyes off her. She'd been on the dance floor, laughing as she danced with that sandy haired oaf with no eyelashes friend of hers, the Honourable 'Wrong again' Rodney Copestake. Wrong again Rodney was so called because what ever he did or said, it was always wrong and therefore generally accompanied by a chorus of '*Wrong Again Rodney!*' from whoever he was with at the time, and he had such a nervous shake in his voice that it sounded as if he was constantly making a phone call from a helicopter or a car travelling on a bumpy road.

Sure enough, they hadn't been dancing for long before Charlotte suddenly stumbled under the weight of his clumsy foot on her open toes. Seeing his chance and marching away from his own companion for the evening mid sentence, he'd shuffled his way between the other couples on the dance floor with his arms loosely outstretched to avoid colliding too badly with anyone; reaching them midway though their dance. He'd tapped him once on the right shoulder, announcing quietly, whilst looking deeply into her surprised eyes, 'Wrong again Rodney . . .' before removing her neatly from his arms, and into his own. Mercifully, she hadn't brayed like a donkey when she'd laughed at his audacity either, like all the other girls he'd ever dated. In fact her shining eyes and her laugh had made strange things happen to his insides, along with her frankly hypnotic nipples, covered only by the merest layer of satin brushing seductively against his dress shirt; making him tingle in some very intimate places.

They'd become an item of speculation instantly, and he'd relieved her of what she'd assured him was her virginity at the first opportunity; which, he'd never forgotten, had been on a warm July night when he'd only been seeing her for a few weeks. Dressed that particular night for a formal dinner of his father's, but at the end of it with the ends of his bow tie draping elegantly from the collar of his dress shirt, she had been a vision in slinky green satin this time, with a plunging and obviously bra less neckline that had had him, (and all the other male guests at the table) transfixed on her nipples since she'd removed her coat on arrival. As soon as the dinner was over he'd sneaked a bottle of Bollinger and two glasses and they'd slipped away; running across the moonlit park giggling, her shoes in his hand, all the way up the hill, to the old Tithe barn.

Opening the old doors with great difficulty with both of his hands full she'd lunged at him with her tongue down his throat as soon as they'd made it inside, and grabbed enthusiastically at his bulging trousers, as his shaking hands fought to simultaneously untangle the straps of her shoes from one of them, and get the shoulders of her dress down with the other. Finally feasting his eyes on those delicious breasts and her astonishing nakedness when her dress fell in one movement to her ankles; (she'd worn no knickers either), he'd been so hopelessly over excited that once inside her he'd climaxed in about two minutes flat, on a bed of dusty straw, and as a family of barn owls hooted in disgust above them. Totally besotted, he had quickly recruited Arabella to help him mount a dedicated assault for the hand of the fair Charlotte, which in truth hadn't been in the least hard for the catch of the county and heir to the impressive Stanton Court Estate.

Within eight months of that first night and about a month before Charlotte's pregnancy would become noticeable, they'd had the society wedding of the year, with Litchfield soft focus photo studies of the stunning Charlotte bedecked in head to toe cream silk Chanel appearing in all the best magazines. They'd held the ceremony at St Nicolas church in Newbury but had a huge marquee for their reception in the grounds of Stanton Court, with a full orchestra, fireworks at midnight, and almost three hundred guests. And a perilously few months later their child, Thomas Christopher Desmond Derby, the grandson his father Desmond had been longing for, had arrived with only just enough time to claim a premature honeymoon baby.

Following the death of his father a few short months after Thomas' birth Chris adopted the more formal Christopher, and inherited the family seat. The beautiful Arabella meanwhile, had married one of his old Etonian friends after a whirlwind romance; one Lord Ralph (but pronounced 'Rafe') De Sales, and almost immediately became the mother of a beautiful baby girl they'd named Davina. This had all been much to Charlotte's dismay of course, because the newlyweds were now living very comfortably on Ralph's family Estate in Somerset: that could have been the moon, for all the fuss Charlotte made over her best friend's defection.

Christopher was in seventh heaven though. He had the wife of his dreams who simply adored sex, and he'd fulfilled his duty to provide a male heir in record time. 'Lottie' as she had now become, was undeniably beautiful; and despite being bereft at the loss of her best friend she took to her new roles of lady of the manor, and mother, with blue blooded British vigour. She was an excellent homemaker, a born mother, she had a good working relationship with the staff; indeed it was she who was responsible for employing the formidable Mrs Higgins to watch over them all.

Lottie was utterly brave and fearless when making decisions, with a devious way of making her own ideas sound like they'd come from her husband. She was clever too, and played the piano in the drawing room daily, and beautifully. She also loved to draw and paint, and thanks to her daughter, several of her

189

paintings were still on display in the house to this day; especially the pencil studies she'd done of the eight month old Thomas, which still had pride of place on top of her now silent piano.

Eight months old . . . that had been just before; before that terrible day when everything changed, for ever.

Back in the present Christopher blinked back the memories and stood to get a paper cone of water from the dispenser next to the TV.

He remembered thinking he should have known it was all going too well. By the time Lottie had gone into the nursery to see why he was so quiet, little Thomas had already slipped away; died in his sleep for no reason at all, and before Christopher could even make it home from work. Sudden Infant Death Syndrome they'd called it.

Utterly devastated, Christopher had fallen victim to his emotionally barren upbringing, stiffened his very English upper lip, buried his head in his work, and travelled abroad constantly. While the distraught Lottie, left to her own grief slipped into a prolonged and terrible depression, until she began seeking comfort from other sources, by which time her personality had changed almost completely.

Realising his mistake at leaving her alone for weeks on end, and try as he might to encourage her over the next two years; despite his best efforts, the damage was already done. Lottie had started to drink alarmingly and became more and more listless as time went on. She was given to long absences with no explanations and, without any appetite at all, she lost a frightening amount of weight. Her hair began to fall out, and even her periods stopped eventually. She was finally diagnosed with anorexia nervosa and chronic depression, and was sent to a private sanctuary near to her friend Arabella, to help her to overcome her problems.

When she returned home to her anxious husband almost two months later she seemed to have gained a resolve. She'd lost the dark shadows from under her eyes, put a little weight on, and she was better, for a while, so he'd taken her off on a Mediterranean cruise holiday in a last ditch effort to save their marriage. It was on that holiday that Hannah had been conceived, and on the discovery she was pregnant, at home almost two months later, Lottie had finally begun to try. She joined a pre natal gym class and took up swimming to get back some of her lost muscle tone. Together they'd decorated the newly located and commissioned nursery and bought a new pram and a new cot: all the things any new baby could ever wish for. When Hannah had been born, Christopher couldn't have cared less that she hadn't been a boy, and knew without doubt that they had turned the corner and put everything behind them, because Lottie had another child to love.

And for four years it had been just that way. Lottie seemed fully fit and well, with bright eyes, and she delighted in their beautiful daughter, constantly shopping for her and dressing her up in expensive clothes. She had a little play area built behind the house and could usually be found at least once a day with the delighted Hannah, pushing her on the swing or encouraging her to climb to the very top of the little climbing frame.

Now confident that Lottie was fully recovered, Christopher was able to concentrate more on his business career and began to spend longer periods away from home; travelling the world as managing director of his own highly successful international property development company. He excelled in everything he did in those days; soon becoming a millionaire, on paper at least: and all before his thirty fifth birthday.

Life at home on the face of it seemed to carry on as usual whether he was there or not and, once Hannah had started at the local school and she'd had some free time on her hands Lottie, to keep herself busy, became involved in as many local committees and causes that would have her.

When he was home, they continued to enjoy each other's company, or dined out with their many friends, and their sex life was, as always, healthy; but considering how long they'd been trying he'd been disappointed that there had been no further pregnancies because, though his daughter was the apple of his eye, he still secretly longed for another son.

In the day room he began to recall how his eyes had been opened as to what was really going on, and how he'd felt when he had overheard that conversation from the public bar in the Hart. The man, out of sight, and whose voice he had not recognised, was telling someone else how he'd seen Lottie's Range Rover parked in a secluded part of one of Ernie Jones' fields earlier that day, when she'd told him she had a WI meeting in the village hall. The teller of the tale had been walking his dogs apparently, and as he'd approached her car he'd noticed a previously hidden but distinctive orange motorbike that he recognised as belonging to one of the youths from the nearby Flowergarden Estate, was parked up alongside it. And they hadn't been reading a map in the back of that car together either, he'd announced raucously. In fact the windows were so steamed up he'd only known it was actually her in there with him by that huge rock of an engagement ring he saw on the back of the her hand sliding down the steamed up window: and by the empty vodka bottle she'd left on the grass by the car, of course!

Christopher had put down his glass with a shaking hand, and looked up into the eyes of Don Myers,

Flynn's predecessor at the pub, looking for some kind of a sign from him that the other man was spinning a tale. He was further shocked when Don's eyes had looked guiltily away, before he put down the pint he'd been pulling and then fled into the other bar. Something was whispered very hurriedly to whoever had been speaking; after which the conversation stopped abruptly, but Don hadn't returned. Christopher had downed the last of his whiskey, straightened his jacket and left without a backwards glance; just as Don's head peered tentatively around the side of the bar.

Intent on confronting her, and crazed once home to discover she'd taken advantage of Mrs Higgins and gone out again, he'd gone straight upstairs and ransacked her room and her bathroom, looking for evidence. In her bedside drawers he'd found a half bottle of whiskey: open, a packet of her favourite peppermints, a half empty packet of contraceptive pills, (that had at least explained her lack of fertility) and, he remembered with a swallow now, an open box of twelve condoms, with five of them missing. He'd had no option but to challenge her as soon as she returned home from wherever she was supposed to have been that night. Looking helplessly at her wedding rings finger in the vain hope she'd had her engagement ring stolen; she'd denied everything, of course. But her eyes were unusually bright, there were telltale traces of white powder around her nostrils, and her speech was very slurred. They'd had the most almighty row of course, during which she'd accused him, among other things, of loving his business more than he had ever loved her, and of being a 'woefully awful lover'. She'd fled the house once more, wild eyed and with her face flushed, stating that she would go to Somerset to spend a couple of days with Arabella, but on calling Arabella in search of his wife the following day, he found out that she had never arrived.

She'd returned home three days later, minus her car; reeking of alcohol, and looking terrible. On discovering that her husband was not home she'd apparently run upstairs two at a time, grabbed the largest case she could find and thrown her favourite clothes into it; tearfully announcing to Mrs Higgins that she was leaving him for a better life with another man; a man who truly loved her, and that she would send for Hannah once they were settled.

She'd left Hannah a letter to explain this fact, and entrusted Mrs Higgins to read it to her when the time was right.

Taking Christopher's beloved British racing green Aston Martin DB7 from the garage; less than an hour after she'd left the house she'd apparently lost control of it on a blind bend, on the wrong side of the road, after swerving to avoid a deer. The car had plunged down the embankment and into the fast flowing river Kennet by the weir at the bottom of the hill on the Yattley Road. Landing heavily, and upside down, she'd been dead when the witnesses got to her; her head wedged awkwardly against the roof of the car, and her neck visibly broken. There had been an open bottle of vodka in the car, and subsequent blood tests had soon found her to be almost three times over the drink drive limit.

It had all been hushed up of course and the old boy network had quickly joined forces to protect their own. As she'd died in Christopher's car reports were put around that Mrs Derby had earlier been the unfortunate victim of a bag theft in a local nail bar while she'd been having a manicure. The bag had contained her wedding rings and her car keys, and the female thief, presumably post manicure also and by now wearing her very expensive trophy rings, was then reported to have been the one discovered having sex on the back seat of Lottie's car by the man in the pub.

And nobody could prove otherwise because the motorcyclist Lottie had been seeing had been encouraged to leave the village and the area soon afterwards in return that his numerous speeding offences be conveniently 'forgotten'.

Confident that the cover up had been entirely successful Sir Christopher had instructed Mrs Higgins to deal with the letter that his wife had left, and he couldn't have cared less how now, any more than he had back then. As far as Hannah was concerned, her mother had been forced off the road by a drink driver on her way to a totally innocent 'bring and buy' sale in Yattley, and to complete the charade she'd been buried in the Derby's plot in the churchyard with a Portland headstone erected stating her prowess as a 'dedicated wife and mother'.

In almost twelve years nobody had ever told Hannah any of it, and Christopher would make sure that nobody ever would. In the years since therefore, she had learned to idolise her mother as a beautiful and accomplished woman cut down in her prime of life, insisting that her paintings and the drawings of her older brother should be always on display as a reminder of her.

And her Daddy had gone along to endure the ride.

Christopher's glazed expression slowly cleared as he blinked and came back to the present. Shaking his head abruptly to clear it before standing up, he drank the last of the water with a gulp and threw the paper cup into the waste basket. Then closing the door behind him, he left the hospital without a backward glance towards his daughter's room.

Chapter twenty

With Danny at her side Hannah continued to improve daily and was discharged from the hospital two weeks later. In conjunction with her continued physiotherapy and despite his reservations; her father, in the interests of her speediest recovery, grudgingly allowed him to visit her every day too, and even, once she could walk that far, let him and Amy take her down to the stables for an hour to see her beloved Beau.

Beau had been kept quiet in his indoor stall since the accident; while under the care of Ben Robinson, the local livestock vet for his cut leg. Despite his plush surroundings, he was beginning to get decidedly stir crazy indoors, and as Hannah tentatively approached on the arms of Danny and Amy, as if he knew she was coming, he was pacing his stall, whickering with impatience, and every few turns he would stop, ears pricked, and listen; every muscle in his body seeming to twitch with adrenaline. Hearing him, Hannah stopped just outside the door of the barn and called his name in her usual sing-song way.

'Pea-Beau . . . !'

Beau stopped pacing and whickered shrilly in reply, tossing his head and bouncing off his front feet in excitement. Fearing that he would try and jump the stall to get to her Hannah let go of her supporters and ran, slightly drunkenly, into the barn to throw her arms around her beloved friend who, instantly sensing she was still fragile, stopped jumping around and carefully bowed his head, contentedly puffing and nudging her in sheer joy at seeing her again, as she twisted her fingers in his head collar, and burst into tears at seeing him looking so well despite her fears.

Danny and Amy followed her into the barn, and while Amy went to pull a lead rope from a hook on the wall to take him back outside, Danny went across to say a dubious hello to the horse that had helped him save Hannah's life.

'He looks even bigger indoors than he did in the woods . . .' he laughed, nervously. 'He's enormous! Dunno how I even managed to get on . . .' He took another step forward; one arm outstretched nervously, to lay his hand on Beau's neck and pet him. Beau's eyes shifted from Hannah to look at him suspiciously; the muscles in his arched neck rippling slightly at the unfamiliar touch. Then as quick as a flash his ears shot back, his head tossed sideways in warning, and Danny was catapulted backwards, landing in a heap in the deep bed of wood shavings on the floor.

'Bloody hell he hates me!' he said, his voice shaking as he picked himself up and brushed his clothes off with shaking hands.

'No he doesn't silly . . . .' Hannah said, still giggling. 'Give me your hand . . . . He just needs to smell you first . . . make sure you're not a threat . . .'

'. . . or a vet!' Amy laughed.

Hannah took his hand in hers and offered it under Beau's nostrils to allow him to scent Danny properly and remember. Then his ears pricked up again and he whickered slightly.

'There you go Danny . . . Now he remembers you . . .' she said.

Amy reached into her jacket pocket for something and nudged Danny on the arm. Turning towards her, she was offering him a tube of peppermints with the top one pulled up ready to take. 'Give him one of these and he'll love you for ever . . .' she smiled.

Danny took the mint in the tips of his fingers and pointed it towards Beau's mouth; that instantly shot forward to snatch it away greedily.

'Bloody hell . . . !'

'In the flat palm of your hand for him Dan . . .' she laughed, 'or he'll still love you but he'll take your fingers off proving it!'

Standing at the French windows in his study and holding an elegant bone china cup and saucer of Earl Grey tea, Hanna's father was looking down towards the stable block, watching the three of them lead Beau out to the paddocks to join the other horses, and afforded a little smile at the way Captain; Beau's second in command in the stable pecking order, had torn across the paddock with a whinny of greeting to meet him. Albeit grudgingly, Sir Christopher could see the way that Danny was really trying to be worthy of his daughter; even from this distance he could see that gypsy smile and it was like all the troubles of the world had been lifted from his shoulders now that his father was dead. He held his chin higher, he looked much healthier and, he'd noticed yesterday, even his shabby appearance had improved a bit, and suspected that his friend Mrs Higgins had had a hand it that: though she denied everything of course. The boy smiled constantly when he was with Hannah too; which was a real revelation in the face previously so dark and brooding. The only thing still clouding his otherwise blue horizon, Hannah had confided, was his still not having seen his mother, and his desperate need to.

Hector had been in to see him only the day before to talk about a way to help the two of them. Following his talks with both of them it was apparent that neither of them felt that they could ever return to the house on the Flowergarden that held such terrible memories, and

201

so Hector had approached the council on their behalf, and though he'd said they were trying to be helpful, the problem was that social housing was in short supply and they could not guarantee re homing them in the area. With both of them obviously desperate to stay, Hector was wondering if he would consider letting them have number two; the vacant estate cottage in the village square.? It had two bedrooms and it was just sitting there since Mrs Cannings moved out . . . not earning him any rent . . . .

He'd agreed of course, despite his rather wicked first thought about getting neatly rid of Danny Fidler if he moved away. But mostly because years of working alongside Hector had taught him that it was nigh on impossible to say no to him when he was on a mission of mercy such as this.

Seeing Danny sweep his daughter into his arms through the windows now, he knew that at least she was happy about his decision, and had hugged him so hard this morning when he'd told her, that he'd almost lost his breakfast.

He averted his gaze with a sigh of resignation, took another sip of his tea and turned away.

Mrs Higgins was indeed responsible for Danny's physical improvement, having taken a bit of a shine to him since getting to know him better. On her day off she'd taken him on a trip to the second hand clothing warehouse in Newbury; a veritable Aladdin's cave near the Racecourse for very cheap bargains, to help him find some more respectable things to wear. Then she began to do all of his laundry for him to keep him in some semblance of clean and respectable in front of Hannah's father; the task being impossible for him living up at that camp.

She fed him secretly in the kitchen at night after he'd said goodbye and pretended to leave too, and huge platefuls of steaming casseroles and stews nightly found their way under his willing nose. She said that it was to keep out the night cold up at the camp, but really it was part of her one woman mission to get some meat on his skinny bones.

Chapter twenty one

The weeks passed by and the protest gathered pace. Paul Taylor had got his legal team hard on the case and they at least had got to the bottom of the agreement so far between Sir Christopher and Watsons: being that Watsons had so far paid only a minimal deposit in order to gain the option to purchase the land should the planning applications be passed. This was boxing clever and had obviously been despite Sir Christopher's attempts to make them enter into a proper contract: effectively leaving him desperate to overcome every possible obstacle in the way of the purchase, and them coming out without a hole in their pockets, either way.

As Hannah's health continued to improve Danny agreed to take her up to the protest camp one morning, in secret obviously, to show her around and to meet his friends.

Soon after they arrived Danny had to leave her for a few minutes to help repair one of the tunnels that had partially collapsed; but not before carefully settling her into a deckchair with a group seated chatting by the fire. DeeDee sat in a small group a little further away from the fire with her back to the others and was busy peeling vegetables, and only turned to say a quick hello before returning to her task. While they chatted to Hannah, Misty asked about her mother's absence from Stanton Court during her recovery.

'She died when I was very little . . .' Hannah said quietly. 'A car accident . . .'

'I'm so sorry . . . I didn't mean to pry . . . I just wondered where she was . . . .' Misty replied kindly, laying a hand on her shoulder.

Hannah smiled a sad little smile, paused for a moment, and settled one foot over the other comfortably. 'I don't remember much about her really . . . and what I do think I remember I might just have been told . . . She was very beautiful I do know that . . . because there's a family portrait . . . And she was talented . . . she played the piano . . . and she painted and drew . . . There are some of her sketches still in pride of place in the house . . . I love the ones of my brother, Thomas . . . He died before I was born . . . a cot death . . .'

'That's awful . . .' said Nigel, poking the fire with
a large stick. 'That's so sad . . . . And he's never met
anyone else . . . your father?'

'They were soul mates . . .' she said matter of factly.
'When she died it broke his heart. To this day he has
trouble talking about her without getting upset . . . So
we don't really . . . well . . . at least he doesn't . . . I like
to . . . it keeps her memory alive . . .'

She threw the stalk of coarse grass she'd been
playing with into the fire and brushed her hands
together briefly to remove the seeds. 'I suppose it's
because once you love someone like that . . . as much
as that . . . you can't ever look at anyone else . . .'

Listening quietly, DeeDee had long stopped
peeling potatoes; the peeler poised in mid air. As
Hannah finished talking, she placed it beside her on
the ground and looked into her lap as if staring at the
grubby flowers on her skirt. Then, looking at Hannah
over her shoulder briefly, she stood up and, obliviously
dropping her lapful of vegetable peelings into the fire,
that instantly began to hiss and spit, she ignored the
wails of protest as everyone sitting near it suddenly
became engulfed in thick grey smoke. A confusion of
arms waving the smoke away and a lot of coughing
and spluttering masked her swift exit from the scene.

Tindy turned and watched her disappear through
the trees in puzzlement; turning back to face Nigel who

was also watching her. As their eyes met he shook his head in bafflement and shrugged his shoulders.

If Tindy had chosen to follow DeeDee he might well have been very surprised indeed. She left the camp behind to make her way through the park, seemingly heading purposefully towards the house; intermittently stopping and glancing around to make sure she was still alone.

Reaching the back of the house eventually, she strode confidently across the terrace that surrounded it, and drew to a slightly breathless halt just in front of Sir Christopher's study windows, as if she knew just where he would be. Taking a reassuring breath in through her nostrils and breathing it out very slowly, she grimaced as she soundlessly tried the handle on the French windows. Finding them unlocked, she stepped through and, kicking off her muddy boots respectfully, her stockinged feet encountered their first experience of carpet for a many weeks. Her toes wriggled in the deep pile indulgently for a moment, and she afforded herself a little smile.

His deep mahogany and green leather topped desk was orderly. There was a computer whirring at one end of it, and a pile of letters sat in regimented order awaiting his attention alongside an expensive looking gold fountain pen. The only other articles to aid his daily work were a bottle of ink and a silver paper knife; that glinted in the sunlight as she turned to close the doors behind her.

On the coffee table over by the fireplace sat a wooden tray neatly set with a steaming pot of coffee, a little jug of cream, a bowl of brown sugar, and a single bone china cup and saucer decorated with a gold rim and a delicate ivy pattern. Gaining in courage at the sight of it she strode across the room, took the pot, and poured herself a drink. Adding a generous amount of cream, she sat herself down on the green leather chesterfield sofa that faced the door, and waited.

She didn't have to wait very long. A few moments later the door of the study opened and he entered the room with his concentration wholly absorbed by the stapled sheaf of documents that he held in his hands.

Stopping dead in his tracks when he looked up and saw the intruder however, his jaw dropped. Apart from the filthy skirt, the tattoos, and the ring through her nose, there was absolutely no mistaking her. She looked just like her mother.

'Davina?' he said incredulously.

'Hello Uncle Chris . . .' she said.

*   *   *

'Davina what . . . what the *hell* are you doing here? And . . . looking like *this*?' he spluttered. 'You're one of those damned protestors from the camp, aren't you?'

'Brilliant deduction Unc . . .' she said cheekily, crossing one leg over the other with a slight flair of one ankle.

'You've been sent down here to talk to me haven't you? I can tell you right now I have nothing to say to *any* of you lot!'

'That's not why I'm here . . . You shouldn't jump to conclusions . . .'

'Do . . . do your parents know about . . . all this?' Words tumbled from his mouth in dismay as one hand swept down the length of her to visibly illustrate his disgust.

Her chin jutted forward as her head came up indignantly.

'Give it a rest uncle, do . . . I don't go by the name Davina anymore . . . I'm known as DeeDee now . . . And please don't try to intimidate me because you don't. And no, this has nothing to do with the plans . . . I've come down from the camp to . . . to talk to you . . . privately . . .'

'I've just said I have nothing to say . . . to you or to . . .'

'. . . . About Hannah . . .' she said, ignoring his expression of surprise and continuing before he had a chance to stop her. 'I've just been listening to her up there talking about her poor dead mother and what a saint she was . . . and how much you still love her . . .' She paused as he continued to stare at her in disbelief; betraying her nerves by locking and unlocking her hands in her lap. 'Uncle Chris, you can't keep on deceiving her this way . . .'

He snapped out of his surprised trance and glared at her.

'What I choose to let my daughter believe about her mother is none of your damned business Davina . . .'

'She's my cousin uncle Chris and we're family so that makes it my business . . .' Her eyes glinted with indignation as they stared directly into his. He lowered his eyes first and did not answer, so she continued more assuredly. '. . . We might not see each other anymore . . . but that hasn't been our fault . . . the way you've shut yourselves off down here since aunt Lottie died . . . Like you're afraid or something . . .'

'I'm not afraid of my own sister . . . and I can't see how . . .'

'. . . Well she still thinks you've fallen out with her over it . . . How unfair is that? It wasn't *her* fault . . . She lost her best friend too remember . . . ?'

Doing his best to steer her off the subject, his voice faltered as a different thought struck him hard.

'Does Hannah know . . . that you're up there at that camp . . . ?'

Her voice softened slightly, but she still had a determined look on her face. '. . . No, she doesn't. I can't tell her who I really am, can I? Because she knows I'm old enough to remember . . . and then she'll

start asking me all sorts of questions won't she . . .
And I won't get involved in this tangled web of lies for
you . . . It's wrong . . . .'

'. . . Then I don't see why we have such a
problem . . .'

'Whether I tell her or not, it won't stop her asking
around . . . She already said she likes talking to people
about her . . . and you can be quite sure that *someone*
that remembers *will* put her straight eventually . . .
It's time you told her the truth, before someone else
does . . . however hard it is to say . . . and to hear . . .'

'She's perfectly satisfied with the story she's been
told, I can assure you of that . . .' he said shortly, turning
to the coffee tray and picking up the pot.

'There was . . . only one cup and saucer . . .
sorry . . .' she said, passing him her drink with just a
hint of embarrassment.

He took it and gulped down a mouthful of coffee,
pulled a face and turned to add some sugar.

'That's just what it is though, isn't it uncle? It's a
story . . .' she said quietly.

'You have absolutely no business . . .'

Losing patience with his stubbornness with a sharp
intake of breath she stood up suddenly, and gestured
one outstretched palm to make him stop.

'Oh come *on* . . . Now I know why Gone with
the Wind had an interval . . . ! Look, I don't *mean* to
be unkind and drag all this up . . . but you have to

understand she's old enough to start asking around . . .
and she *will* . . . she *is*. You must know that . . . It's only
natural . . .' She continued despite his 'subject closed'
expression. 'There are local people at the camp too
you know . . . older people . . . who will remember the
real story . . . just as well as I do . . .'

'You do?' he said incredulously. 'How can you?
You were just a child yourself . . .'

'Plenty old enough to listen to conversations
through the banisters . . .' she said more quietly, with
a sympathetic smile. 'But besides me there still *are*
plenty of other people around who know . . . there must
be . . . because scandal never dies . . . it just rests
uneasy. And anyway it wouldn't matter who tells her
would it? Because unless you do it first, it will be you
that she hates then . . . for lying to her . . . by painting
this sainted picture of her mother all these years . . . .
You've had your interval Uncle Chris . . . it's time for
act two now . . .'

He sat at his desk for at least an hour after she'd
gone, mulling over everything she had said. Finally,
picking up the house phone, he pressed the '0' for
housekeeper.

Chapter twenty two

Dizzy had taken the girls for a walk, away from the Rectory so that Lizzie could get a rest from their constant questions, and so that Hector could do some work on his Sunday sermon unmolested.

The move into number two Stanton Cottages in the square, though agreed, had been delayed by a few weeks on the advice of her doctor, because Lizzie was still on too much of a knife edge emotionally, and in her opinion certainly not ready to face going back to her old house yet in order to pack everything up and move out of it.

Lizzie's emotional knife edge was largely because she was worried about how Danny was coping with the news of his father's death without her. That and trying to keep her feelings for wanting to see Flynn under control for so recently widowed a woman . . .

On a promise to be away for a couple of hours, Dizzy and the girls were all now sprawled on a tartan car blanket and eating their picnic lunch on a hill about fifty yards or so away from the camp, totally fascinated by the rainbow of tarpaulin decorated tree houses, and by the exotic smells that filled their nostrils even from this distance. They sat transfixed as the tinkle of wind chimes drifted towards them, and watched a thin plume of smoke rise skywards in the airless July afternoon from the perpetual camp fire; the protestor's only source of heat for both washing and cooking.

The protestors were a familiar sight around the village now, and Batty knew most of them by name. She secretly imagined herself being able to live as they did drifting from camp to camp with their passion for the environment, singing and dancing and having lots of fun together, and not having to wear her scratchy and uncomfortable school uniform; but be dressed like the big girls in their colourful, shabby clothes and big, heavy boots. One of the big boys she'd been staring at one day had winked at her when he'd caught her neatly in the act; her eyes wide in amazement as he'd shuffled past her in his great army boots with no laces in them. He'd had a huge rucksack hanging on the back of his long green unbuttoned coat too, that had pots and pans hanging from it that jangled together when he walked; and his hair was so long it must have almost met his bottom at the back. He wore it in lots of strange, matted plaits twisted around his head and over his eyes, and he wore a black knitted hat that hung down at the back to hold it all like he'd hidden a picnic in there for later or something.

Batty took another bite of her jam sandwich and flicked away an inquisitive bug. 'Do you think they'll always live in the woods here Mummy?' she asked, rolling over onto one side and facing her mother.

'Well, not for ever darling,' she said. 'They'll have to leave eventually, one way or another.'

'What do you mean?' said Tesco, turning to face her too.

'You all know why they're protesting here don't you?'

Looby Loo took her eyes from the camp for a moment, removed her thumb from her mouth and looked at her mother seriously. 'It's because they want to save the trees from being chopped down to make way for the road and the supermarket isn't it?'

'It is darling . . . and if they succeed in saving the trees and stopping the plans . . . well then, they'll move on.'

'Where to?'

'They'll all go home again I suppose . . . or maybe they'll just move on to the next place that needs saving . . .' Dizzy finished rummaging in the picnic bag and passed Batty a bottle of made up orange squash.

'And if they don't save the trees, then the trees will be chopped down and so they won't have any trees to live *in* anymore . . . is that right too?' Batty was struggling to remove the lid so Dizzy reached over and, taking it back from her, twisted the neck of the bottle round in her cardigan for a better grip.

'That's right darling, they won't,' she replied, handing it back. 'Hold the cups for her Tesco, please. *Don't* try and pour out the drinks on the blanket Batty the cups will tip over . . . let Tesco help you . . .'

'I don't think anyone should be allowed to chop down trees . . .' Looby Loo said passionately, biting into a huge apple noisily. 'If all the trees get chopped down, like in the rainforests, then the wildlife won't have any habitat left to live in so they'll get succinct and there won't be enough oxygen for us to breathe because it's the trees that help to make it . . . And we'll all die because it won't rain as much and the earth will shrivel up because we should have left the world how God created it because he made it just right until man messed it up . . .'

Dizzy blinked at her daughter's rather neat synopsis of creation, climate change and environmental disaster, and gave her a hug. 'Extinct my darling not succinct . . . Well then it's a good thing there are people like this that remind us how much we need to take care of the world God created then isn't it?' she smiled encouragingly.

'I'd like to live in a tunnel to protest rather than a tree, Mummy,' Tesco said earnestly. I like trees but I'm not very good at climbing them. Batty's good at climbing trees, aren't you Batty?'

Batty gave her sister a hug and planted a rather exaggerated kiss on her cheek. 'I am good at climbing trees but I'm not as good at looking after the guinea pigs as you are, am I?' she said generously. 'They eat the vegetable scraps and weeds from the garden and that cuts down on waste in landfills . . . doesn't it Mummy? That's good too . . .'

Dizzy swallowed a giggle. 'Batty darling, you're priceless . . . and that was a lovely thing say to your sister,' she smiled, kissing the top of her head and giving her a tight squeeze. Batty squirmed and giggled and tried to break free until Dizzy released her, panting breathlessly, onto the rug.

They sat quietly for a few minutes until Tesco suddenly sat up and waved enthusiastically down towards the camp. 'Look there's Danny! Lizzie said he was living at the camp all the time now . . .'

Dizzy and the other girls waved, and Danny waved briefly back at them but quickly turned away and disappeared into a huge teepee style tent.

'Mummy, is Lizzie going to stay living with us like she wants to now that Danny's living at the camp and even though her nasty husband got all dead when

Ernie's machine chopped his head off?' Batty said suddenly.

Dizzy looked directly into Batty's eyes and she instantly blushed. 'When did you hear her say that Batty?'

'I heard her talking to you and Daddy in the kitchen . . . with the police lady . . .' she said sheepishly.

'You know you're not supposed to listen to people's private conversations Batty, I've told you that before . . .'

'I . . . couldn't help it,' she muttered quietly, 'I wanted a drink and I was waiting until the talking stopped before I came into the room . . . because Daddy said that's polite, isn't it? And I just . . . heard . . .'

'Don't you think that if Danny stays in the camp for ever that Lizzie would like to live with us for ever too?' Tesco asked, distracting her mother from further sisterly admonishments. 'I like her . . . she's lovely and she's good at telling us stories about when she was as young as us . . .'

'Listen to me, all of you . . .' Dizzy said sternly, sitting up again. 'Lizzie is still with us because she's not ready to live on her own yet. Her husband is dead, it's true . . . and it doesn't matter *how* he died Batty . . . it's bad to spread gossip like that, as you well know. The police asked us to look after her until she is strong enough to move into her new home, and because

Danny can't look after her on his own; he's very young and he has to go through all this too. He has his friends at the camp helping him, and he spends a lot of time with Hannah while she's getting better. Do you see?'

They all nodded.

'Danny loves Hannah now doesn't he Mummy?' Despite herself Batty looked excited at the prospect of some romance to dream about.

'That's just more gossip Batty, and we don't talk about other people like that, do we? It embarrasses them.'

'. . . Lizzie will get better soon though, now her husband can't hurt her anymore?' Looby Loo was lying on her stomach with her head resting comfortably on her bent up arms.

Dizzy turned to face her. 'She may take a while to get properly better darling . . . because what's happened has really hurt her . . . emotionally, as well as physically.' She gently moved a wisp of unruly hair from her daughter's eyes. 'But it's up to us to continue to make her stay with us as nice as we can, because being with us at the Rectory is still the best thing for her at the moment.'

'We have to do nice things for her and make sure she eats well and gets lots of sleep, because those are the things that help our bodies get well again.' Looby Loo said kindly.

'I drawed her a lovely picture yesterday . . .' Batty pulled her mother's arm around her shoulders and leaned in for a hug.

'Drew darling, not drawed . . .'

'Drew . . . I *drew* her a nice picture yesterday . . .' she repeated.

'And I make her cups of tea and try not to spill it in the saucer . . .' Tesco said earnestly.

'You're all doing brilliantly and I'm very proud of you,' Dizzy smiled. 'And we just have to keep being kind and reassuring her and then she'll get well again.'

Looby Loo had begun picking buttercups and daisies and held them up towards her mother in a small posy. 'We could pick a few more of these flowers and then she could have them in a little glass by her chair where she can see them . . .'

'That's a Lovely idea, Loo, let's do that on the way home,' she said, standing up and reaching down to tug at the edge of the blanket. 'Come on you lot. Off the blanket, it's time we went home . . . Daddy will be wondering where we've got to . . .'

As Dizzy began to gather up plates and cups Batty began to call excitedly as she saw Danny, the Amazonian Tindy, and the recently returned DeeDee making their way purposefully up the steep slope from the camp towards them.

'Hello, Danny!' Batty called, waving frantically at them. 'Mummy . . . ! Look!'

Dizzy stood with a smile and waited for them to approach. 'Hi Danny, how are you doing?' she said carefully.

He pulled a face. 'I'm ok . . .' he said. 'I feel . . . it's just weird that's all, with all that's gone on . . . and now I'm with Hannah and everything . . . But I don't really know how I should feel about my dad . . . And . . . I . . . came to ask you if . . . well if . . . is it all right . . . now she's not in danger anymore like . . . if I come and see my mum now, I mean, some time . . . I . . . I let her down when I should have been there . . . Please?' He looked so desperate she stepped forward and took his arm gently, as DeeDee took his free hand and squeezed it. 'None of it was your fault Danny . . . You couldn't watch over her 24 hours a day . . . and she knew that. She doesn't feel you let her down . . . I promise you. She's never said that . . . She's traumatized, certainly but . . . she misses you too . . . .'

Batty barged in to the conversation enthusiastically. 'Come for supper tonight, we're having shepherd's pie and there's *loads* of vegetables from the garden . . . Daddy says we could feed an army with them all through the winter!'

Dizzy sighed a little in apology but nodded. 'Yes . . . of course you can come . . . please come. She needs to see you now Danny . . . it would help her . . . really . . . and your two friends can come too if you'd like to?' she added, thinking he might be happier with

221

some moral support. Tindy and DeeDee both nodded gratefully at the mutually agreeable thought of a hot meal at a proper table with no couscous, lentils, or burnt bits in it.

'That's settled then . . .'

'We're picking her some pretty flowers for by her chair . . .' said Looby Loo shyly, holding up her wilting posy of buttercups and daisies.

Tindy bent his six foot six inch frame down to examine her flowers, pulling them gently vertical, but as soon as he let them go they flopped despondently back over her clenched fingers. 'They need to drink some water I think . . .' he chuckled, fascinating Looby with the way his hair beads danced when he laughed. 'Wild flowers like these get very thirsty once they are picked.'

'We'd better get home and get them in some water then Loo . . .' Dizzy said, nodding in agreement, 'See you all about six then?'

'Later Mummy . . . then we can stay up longer . . . it *is* Saturday . . .' Batty tried, hopefully.

'Six is late enough for you three . . . and Danny wants time to talk to his mum as well . . .' she replied firmly.

'Six it is then . . . and thank you for the invitation . . .' DeeDee said; taking Tindy's arm as his hair beads bounced in agreement.

'Thanks . . . Dizzy . . .' Danny said with a nervous smile. She nodded with a hopefully encouraging smile and a little rub on his arm as and they set off home, with occasional stops for the reinvigorated hunt for flowers for Lizzie's posy along their way.

*   *   *

Once back at the Rectory the children had put their little posy into an old honey jar by her chair very quietly, so that she could see them as soon as she opened her seemingly perma-closed eyes. Standing now with yawn and a stretch from yet another sleep that day, Lizzie stooped to smell the flowers, picked up the improvised vase and smiled, before she set off for the kitchen and a drink of water to ease her thirst.

Dizzy and the girls were in the kitchen preparing the supper as she stood and watched them unseen from the doorway. It was the sort of scene of typical family life that Lizzie wallowed in just now: Dizzy, feverishly preparing vegetables for her increased numbers this evening, Batty, cutting slices from a loaf of bread, with an admirable disregard for symmetry, onto an old wooden breadboard, Looby Loo mashing a deep pan of boiled potatoes with what looked like half a packet of butter and most of a pint of milk added, and Tesco laying the table, with the confident assumption that everyone sitting at it would be left handed.

Dizzy smiled in greeting when she looked up from her task to see her standing there. 'Shepherd's pie tonight . . .' she said, answering the unasked question from beside a mountain of sliced carrots and recently de podded broad beans from the Rectory veggie patch.

'Lovely . . .' Lizzie said, drawing their attention to the little vase by lifting it up in her hands. 'And thanks for the pretty flowers.' She placed it on a shelf on the dresser next to the table, then turning; she frowned slightly, as she noticed that Tesco had laid three too many places.

Dizzy stopped chopping carrots, wiped her hands on a tea cloth and laid a hand on Lizzie's shoulder. 'Lizzie darling, we met Danny this afternoon and he asked if he could come to see you . . . Do you mind awfully? He was with two of his friends from the camp . . . so we invited them as well . . . You've met Tindy and DeeDee? They seem really nice young people . . . students I think . . . They've been so good to him . . . and he seemed so pleased to have been allowed to come . . . He's desperate to see you . . .'

Lizzie surveyed the table, looked into the earnestly imploring eyes of the triplets who had all briefly stopped their tasks to look at her, and bit her bottom lip. 'Yes . . .' she nodded quietly. 'You're right. It's time.'

Chapter twenty three

Danny and his friends arrived just before six with two jars of chutney which caused much excitement, and a bottle of very murky looking homemade wine that Hector examined and accepted with well practiced sincerity. Danny, a bit pale, was shown straight into Hector's study where his mother was nervously waiting to see him, while the girls, as instructed before they all arrived, took Tindy and DeeDee into the garden to meet Bleep and Booster, the guinea pigs: speedily correcting Tindy who assumed they were being reared for food like his tribe kept their animals.

Hector opened the door to his study and motioned Danny in with an encouraging pat on the shoulder, closed it behind him, and returned to the kitchen to give his concerned wife a hug. 'They'll be fine . . . don't you worry,' he said. 'They both need this . . . They need to put this behind them if they're going to rebuild their lives together now and move into that cottage . . .'

Dizzy put down the tea cloth she was holding and put her arms around his neck lovingly. 'I hope so . . .' she said, before laying her head on his comforting shoulder and closing her eyes.

*   *   *

'Mum . . .' Danny blundered unseeing across the room and flew into her outstretched arms, all pretence of adulthood gone. 'I'm sorry . . . . I'm so sorry . . . I should've been there . . . I could have stopped him . . . .'

'Shh . . . it's all right, love . . . it's all right . . . it's not your fault . . . I never thought that! It was his fault . . . all of it . . . .' She pulled his head onto her shoulder and caressed his tousled hair, kissing him and rocking him like a baby as her own tears came. 'Stop blaming yourself . . . and anyway . . . it doesn't matter anymore does it? It's over now . . . it's all over now . . . He can't hurt me anymore . . . He can't make either of us feel that way anymore . . .'

They stayed that way for some minutes, holding on to each other and whispering the things they needed to say until Lizzie eventually led him to the sofa and they sat down.

His head moving slowly from side to side in disbelief, he gently traced the scar above her eye with his fingers, and ran his hand over her bristly scalp because, in an act of either bravery or defiance, she had decided not to wear the scarf any more.

'Your hair . . .' he said pitifully. 'Your lovely long hair . . .'

'It will grow again . . . it is growing again, look . . . That's the good thing about hair . . .' she ran her hands backwards and forwards through her bristles. 'And I always wanted to try it short anyway . . .' She practiced her brave smile and slipped an arm around his shoulders as he leaned into her, his arms wrapped tightly around her body as if he was afraid to ever let her go again.

'I wanted to kill him . . . every day . . . for years . . . since I was little . . . I wanted to kill him . . .' he said flatly.

'You don't mean that . . . it's just with all that's gone on . . .'

'I bloody do! I'm glad he's dead!' he sat up suddenly, his black eyes ablaze and sparkling. 'I'm glad he died that way . . . he deserved to die that way . . . I actually like to think about him dying that way and I hope he rots in hell for what he's done to you! For what he did to all of us . . . for making Anna run away and never come back . . .' his voice broke again and he sobbed.

227

She took his face in her hands and kissed him on the side of his mouth, gently wiping away the tears that were tracing down his cheeks with her thumbs. 'Don't let him do this to you anymore son . . . He's gone; so let him go . . . we both have to let him go . . . We have to . . .' She released him to snuggle once more into her shoulder. He breathed her smell in deeply and let it out slowly, looking into his lap and fretfully picking at the hole in the knee of his jeans.

'It's over . . .' she whispered. 'He can't hurt us anymore. We have to look after each other now Dan . . . we have to stay together . . . live together . . . We both need that . . .' she shifted position to look at him properly. 'And I need to let *this* family get back to normal again . . . They've been so kind to me . . . I could never begin to repay them for everything they've done for me . . . And you can't stay up at that camp for ever . . . can you . . . . Whether they get permission to build the road and the supermarket up there or not . . . all your friends will eventually move on won't they . . . .'

He spoke quietly as if he hadn't heard her. 'I tried to clean it all up . . . the kitchen . . . I did . . . but . . . it was like he was still there . . . watching me . . . I kept thinking he was going to come down the stairs . . . or in the front door . . . and all his stuff is still there . . . just as he left it . . . . I . . . I gave Flynn the RSPCA tin back . . . the money was still in it . . . I s'pose he couldn't get the top off . . . .' He lifted his face briefly to look at her: 'His bloody green jacket was still hanging over the end of the stairs . . . . right where he left it . . . . It was the first thing I saw when I walked in the door . . . I took it back outside and threw it in the skip on top of all that other rubbish!' He looked down, and then up again. 'I can't wait to move out Mum . . . I can't wait for us to be in our new house where he can't be . . . Then we can get rid of everything . . . every last little thing he ever touched that's to do with him, can't we? Then it would be a proper new start . . .' he smiled ruefully, giving her a little squeeze. 'Yeah I know . . . Another one . . . only it will be a real one this time . . .' He looked more hopeful for a moment but then he suddenly jumped up from the sofa as another thought struck him. 'I can't believe he hid up in the bell tower like a bleedin' coward and let me an' Baz take the blame for all those thefts . . . he'd have let us . . . me *and* Baz get sent down for that; wouldn't he!'

She pulled him back to her in a firm hug and rubbed his shoulders to stop him going any further. 'Well he never got away with it did he my love . . . I saw through 'is scheming . . . . and the police know it wasn't you now.' She leaned over and gave him a reassuring kiss on the top of his head, and smiled. 'Let's just see what the future holds for both of us shall we? We've got that pretty new cottage right in the square near the shops and things . . . so no more walking a country mile for a pint of milk or a stamp . . . And a cottage we can take joy in knowing he would have hated because he hated spiders almost as much as he hated thatched roofs . . .' she paused a moment to smile at the thought, with the merest of a glint in her eyes. 'So we can make that new start; you and me . . . please ourselves . . . just the two of us . . . yes?'

'And Anna maybe . . . 'Cos maybe now . . . we can try and find Anna . . .'

She shrugged a little. 'We don't know where she is, do we love? And she's a grown woman now . . . She's hopefully made a nice life for herself . . . Hector says she might even have a family of her own by now . . . and that I might be a granny and not even know it . . . !' she began to blink rapidly.

'I told Flynn about her . . . . Sorry . . .'

She smiled a slightly watery smile, and then gulped slightly as if unused to discussing her daughter out loud. 'Did you?'

A quiet knock at the door broke their train of conversation and Hector's head appeared around it tentatively. 'Sorry you two . . . but Dizzy says supper's ready . . .' Lizzie nodded and made efforts to stand up from the deep and saggy sofa. Danny pulled her up by one arm to a standing position and waited while she straightened her rumpled sweater.

'We're both so happy about the new cottage Hector . . .' she said with a smile, breaking the mood for good.

'Yeah . . . we can't wait to move in now; it's really great . . . Thanks mate . . .' Danny offered his right arm and Hector shook it with a little nod of his head in acknowledgement.

'No problem at all . . . People can be a little quick to misjudge him sometimes. He was happy to help you both actually . . . . after everything you've been through . . . and to make amends for accusing you of the theft at Stanton Court, Danny . . . And for helping Hannah of course . . . .' he winked slightly, but Lizzie caught it.

'Hmmm . . . and, um . . . talking of the Derby's, Dan . . . .' she said slyly. 'What's all this I hear about you riding a whopping great horse in a mission of mercy . . . and your bedside vigil for weeks with that young Hannah . . . . Nothing escapes me you know!' she tousled his hair playfully and Hector grinned; delighted in the change in her.

Danny blushed crimson as he straightened his hair. 'Mu-um!' he muttered; the teenager once more. 'Leave off . . .' But she noticed a definite twinkle in his eyes at the mention of her name.

She reached to kiss him on the cheek and whispered in his ear. 'She's a lovely girl love. You two will make a much better job of it. I feel it! You just have to remember . . . a girl likes to be told she's special every single day . . . As long as you really mean it . . . and you must always, always, treat her like a lady . . .'

Danny took her hand to lead the way for supper. 'You're special Mum . . . and I mean it . . .' he said, pulling her behind him with a little smile, into the kitchen to where everyone else sat expectantly, amongst the steaming dishes.

*   *   *

An hour later and it was as though they'd never been parted. The table was a battlefield of empty dishes and plates, and a ring of gravy with its blob solitaire marked where the jug had at some point stood on the tablecloth.

The meal over and the chairs in disarray around the table, Batty currently had everyone in hysterics with her impression of Sir Christopher's booming voice. DeeDee was in tears, clutching her hand to her chest as she coughed and spluttered. 'Oh dear . . .' she gasped, afraid she'd give her secret away, 'Oh Batty stop . . . please stop! It's quite uncanny!'

'He acts like he's king of the village or something . . . !' Batty said in disgust.

'Batty you're being very rude . . .' her father said, peering over the top of his spectacles as he wagged an index finger at her.

'Sorry . . . .' She muttered.

'If he *were* a king he might listen to the views of his people more . . .' Tindy said seriously.

'And you would know all about that my love . . .' DeeDee winked at him.

The table went quiet as all eyes fell on Tindy.

'I am not a king . . .' he said quietly, looking around at them all with a little smile. 'Not yet anyway . . .'

'You're a prince?' Hector's spectacles jumped up his nose in surprise.

Tindy flashed his whiter than white teeth in a very wide smile. 'My proper name is Matindy Mokele . . .' he said. 'My father is the head of our tribe at home; and that makes him our king . . . and I am his eldest son . . .'

'So that means you really are a real prince?' Tesco said; her eyes wide in awe.

'In our culture, I am, yes . . .'

'So that means you are really rich too then!' Batty said, jumping up from the table and sending her fork clattering to the quarry tiled floor.

'Batty, really!' her father said in exasperation, eyes cast to heaven at her lack of manners. Everyone laughed as Tindy reached under the table to retrieve the fork.

'Not anywhere near as rich as a royal family like you would expect certainly . . .' he smiled. 'But we get by . . .'

'And you've come to the UK for your education?' asked Dizzy, multitasking as she began to gather up the plates. DeeDee began to gather the ones from her side of the table and carried them to the sink.

'I have . . . so that I can take what I have learned home with me to help my people.'

'Do we have to curtsey when we see you? Like we did when Prince Charles came to Newbury and Daddy met him?' Batty asked, making everyone smile again.

'No you do not have to curtsey to me . . .' he chuckled, cuffing the tip of her nose with one finger before getting up to help Dizzy and DeeDee with the washing up. He had been seated with his back to the dresser, and turned slightly so that he could push his chair neatly back into place. Suddenly he froze and let out a loud squeak of surprise that was so much higher than his normal voice it stopped the conversation around the table in mid flow. He had picked up Lizzie's wildflower posy.

'We picked those for Lizzie this afternoon, remember?' said Batty. 'We showed them to you . . .'

'Not all of them you did not . . .' he said quietly. He was holding up the vase and pointing out two of the flowers. 'Where did these two flowers come from please?'

'We picked them on the way home . . .' said Tesco. 'Are they poisonous or something?' She looked a bit worried now.

'No, no,' he smiled. 'They are little orchids, little wild orchids . . .'

'Mummy said they might be . . .' she said.

'I just was wondering where you found them, that is all . . .' DeeDee noticed the slight quiver in his voice as he turned his head slightly to wink at her.

'Looby found them . . . on the Chalkies . . .'

'That's what everyone calls the chalk hills just up near the camp . . .' Dizzy said.

'Ah . . .' he replied with a slight nod. '. . . Near to the camp . . . ?'

'I did find them . . .' said Looby quietly. 'There's a place . . . it's a bit steep. On the hill where we have the Easter Sunday sunrise service . . . and we sit and watch the sun come up . . . and we sing *Jesus Christ is risen today* . . .'

'Then we all go to Saint Christopher's house and have bacon rolls and hot chocolate for breakfast!' Batty said enthusiastically.

'*Sir Christopher* Batty, not Saint Christopher!' Hector smiled.

DeeDee pulled her in for a soap sudded hug and kissed the top of her head.

'Mummy said I shouldn't have picked them if they're wild orchids . . . but they were so pretty and I liked the purple colour and the stripes that look like little insect's legs . . . When I saw them I knew Lizzie would like them because she likes purple best . . . it's her favourite colour, isn't it Lizzie?' She looked pleadingly across the table to see Lizzie smile at her in encouragement. 'And there were lots more of them and I did leave the rest . . . Will I get into trouble your Majesty . . . I mean, your Highness . . . ?' Looby stood up and slipped her hand into her mother's nervously.

'Just Tindy, Looby . . . same as always . . .' he smiled. 'But I might just eat you for *my* breakfast if you do not promise to show me where you found them on these *Chalkies*, tomorrow morning!' He grabbed her off her feet suddenly and sank his teeth into her sweater as she shrieked with laughter; tugging at the wool like a dog with a shell bead jangling growl. Letting her go finally and hugging her to him, he laughed his hugely sexy, deep and velvety laugh that always made DeeDee's toes curl. 'You, my beautiful girl . . . might just have found us the answer!'

'But . . . we can't go up there tomorrow morning . . . because it's Sunday . . .' Batty turned to her father hopefully, desperately not wanting to miss something as exciting as this. 'We'd have to miss church, wouldn't we . . .' she added imploringly, with her eyes as wide as saucers. Seemingly oblivious, Hector was peering at the little vase of flowers very closely.

'I think you can all be excused church tomorrow if it would help your cause . . .' he said, much to his daughter's relief, 'but I can't unfortunately . . . I've got an eight o'clock BCP communion . . . but Christopher *is* on duty for that as my Sidesman as I recall . . . so at least he'll be out of your way while you all go up there to see . . . .' Turning back towards the table he peered over the top of his glasses at Tindy with a squint. 'You're the botanist . . . so what are they then?' he asked, adjusting them on the tip of his nose for a closer look but looking completely baffled.

'Yes I am! And I did my dissertation on these as well! These, everyone . . . are called Late Spider Orchids, or *Ophrys Fuciflora* to give them their Latin name . . . and they are very, *very* rare! They are fully protected by your Wildlife and Countryside Act . . . And because of that the area they are found in, whether Sir Christopher likes it or whether he does not, is likely to be designated a Sight of Special and Scientific Interest. See this part here girls . . .' he said, stooping down to their level as they clamoured around the vase, 'this is the spider . . . and the markings on the petal just here . . . that is his legs . . . see? They were thought until a few years ago to be extinct in your country, until a few of them were found on grazed chalk hills in Kent . . . when the Euro tunnel was being constructed . . . The site in Kent has paths around it now for visitors that come from all over the *world* to see them! That is the key you see?' he swallowed hard, almost unable to believe his eyes. '*Grazed* chalk hills. Sir Christopher made this happen! He put his longhorns on the hills up there because the land was no good for anything else but grass to grow . . . and then the cropped grass lets the wild flowers flourish because the bees can pollinate them more easily . . . I am such a fool! I should have gone looking for rare plants up there before instead of hopelessly measuring tree trunks! It is so obvious! Steep in places, with calcareous rich chalk . . . nutrient poor soil that means he can't grow any crops up there . . .'

'In Thomas Hardy's day they were called 'ewe lease' acres because they couldn't grow anything on the land . . . so they just used to keep their sheep there . . .' Hector said knowledgeably.

'Sheep and cattle graze differently though Hector. Cows are selective and sheep will eat anything. The tubers for these orchids could have lain dormant under the soil for many years while the sheep grazed there . . . and only took their chance once the cows went onto the hills . . .'

'Do you honestly think these will be enough to stop them?' DeeDee was off her chair and looking at the orchids in disbelief.

'I think that they might be! They caused a lot of trouble for your Eurotunnel . . . they had to re route . . . but I will be out to check for myself first thing tomorrow . . . once Looby here has done her duty and shown me where she found them . . .'

Looby blushed crimson and hugged shyly into Tindy's trouser leg with her thumb in her mouth. 'I can

238

remember where they were . . . there was a sort of ledge in the side of the hill . . . just near the place where there are lots of rabbit holes dug into the chalk . . .' She yawned widely, remembering to put her hand over her mouth only when Hector raised his eyebrows at her. Tindy traced his fingers through her hair as he gave her a quick squeeze. 'Well now you must go off to bed and get plenty of sleep because I will be here to get you as soon as the sun comes up in the morning . . .' Then he performed a deep bow of respect, and opened the kitchen door for her.

'Come on you three,' said Dizzy decisively, 'time you were all in bed . . . it's almost nine o'clock.'

* * *

Once the service had started the following morning and Sir Christopher was safely out of the way; hopefully long before anyone else at Stanton Court would think they were up to something, Looby Loo and her sisters joined Danny and Tindy and an impressive, if shabby, procession of tree camp protestors, the three of them trotting to keep up and obediently holding hands with an adult to cross the roads, before making their way to the hills above the camp known locally as the Chalkies. Once in the right area Tindy took Looby's hand to lead him excitedly to the spot where she'd found the orchids; on the opposite side of a small hillock to the public footpath and nestled within a slight indentation in the chalk caused by years of prevailing wind and rain. There were twenty three of them in that location, and on closer inspection, another dozen of them elsewhere. Tindy was ecstatic as the numbers went higher as he counted, and called back to Jez, one of the other protestors, to bring his camera. Photographs duly taken by the keen photographer and transferred to his laptop computer, the protestors spread out to use their eclectic skills to see what else they could find.

Within half an hour a very excited DeeDee panted back up the hill towards the others, pulling another protestor, a girl called Sky, by the hand behind her.

'We've got . . . more good news . . . !' she panted, holding on to Tindy's arm with one hand for support and holding the other to her rapidly beating heart.

'There are Great Crested Newts in the flood meadow . . .' Sky panted . . . her eyes sparkling. She turned to point her arm down towards the road. 'Lots of them . . . . We saw five of them basking in the sun on a huge stone . . . right over the other side of the lane there . . . where it's really boggy . . . Over there . . .'

'You're sure Sky?' Tindy said, shielding his eyes from the bright sun to look in the direction she was pointing.

'No doubt about it . . .' she laughed. 'The most beautiful gold markings on the underside . . . just like blobs of gold paint . . .'

Tindy looked at her as his eyes pulled briefly together in a frown. 'The surveyors were in there weeks ago . . .' he said, 'I wonder why they never said anything . . . ?'

'Sir Christopher's surveyors you mean . . .' Sky pulled a face.

'Hmmm!' he said quietly, looking at DeeDee, who turned away from his eyes and stared pointedly at her feet.

Before Tindy could ask her what was wrong Jez held up his camera and shook it slightly to regain their attention 'Let's get down there too then!' he said cheerfully, setting off back down the hill towards the lane. 'I'm up for a good squelch in the meadow . . . !'

* * *

They all spent the next two hours searching the flood meadow for signs of Great Crested newts and other aquatic rarities. Photographic evidence then duly gathered, Danny, Jez and Tindy made their way with the three girls back to the Rectory, where Dizzy let them email their pictures to the DEFRA people, so that the first steps could be taken to stop the planning applications for the development in their tracks. As soon as he got wind of what was going on Sir Christopher called his team of legal advisors and accountants to an emergency meeting at Stanton Court to try and salvage the situation in any way he could before things got completely out of control, but once he'd received the first visitation from DEFRA even he seemed resigned now.

It was a devastating blow for the man in such financial difficulties within a global recession. Hannah felt torn to her heartstrings watching her beloved father age before her very eyes; staring in the face the responsibility for losing the family estate after more than three centuries of Derby stability.

The protestors held their breath for what felt like weeks while DEFRA sent this expert and that expert to the sites have a good look, and Tindy, despite his affection for Hannah, had no choice but to stick to his convictions and do everything he could to help them. This included, as Batty put it one afternoon on the way home from helping Danny and Lizzie move into their new cottage near the shop; '. . . Lots of men in suits and Wellington boots wandering around the flood meadows and the Chalkies looking excited . . .' And then they presumably all sat round tables arguing with the other two parties until, eventually, they gave their verdict. Despite everything he threw at it to try and salvage the applications, the land on Sir Christopher's estate was declared a Site of Special and Scientific Interest; with all the legal restrictions that come with it.

Watson's finally had no choice but to pull out of the deal and retreat, and celebrations rang around the village, quite literally, thanks to the bells of St Mary's; now that the diocese had allowed Hector's PCC to sort the dodgy stonework. Flynn and Donna also hosted a party at the Hart for the protestors and their supporters that went on way past closing time.

*   *   *

As the days passed by since the final decision was made Sir Christopher, never the most magnanimous of losers, had become more and more quiet and withdrawn, but Hannah would have been more than a little surprised to learn that she was completely wrong in assuming that she knew why. It was the recent run in with DeeDee, dragging skeletons from long closed dungeons that had been more responsible for dominating his current state of mind and, now unshaven and practically sleepless, he actually feared losing his daughter when he told her the truth a lot more than he feared losing their home. He was eating practically nothing despite Mrs Higgins' efforts to tempt him with his favourite steak and kidney pudding and banoffee pie. He was neglecting his duties at the church and in the parish and, after his meeting with his accountants yesterday, despite every effort being made on his part to try and save her inheritance from the banks, his worst fears had been realised and now the future of the family estate was certain . . . Stanton Court would have to be sold. Once he told her the whole sorry tale of his lies and deceptions, as now he knew he would have to, Hannah would most certainly leave him for letting her down, in every possible way; and no doubt run headlong into the arms of that blasted gypsy boy. Knowing in his heart that she would have every right to do it too, he knew he wouldn't be able to cope a single day without her: he was finished.

Hannah of course remained blissfully ignorant and tried everything in her power to try and reassure him to look on the bright side; that the sale could be viewed as a new start for them both without the responsibility, and running costs, of such a huge estate. Hector spent hours trying to coax him too, but he remained silent as to his real fears; his spirit broken. He was prone to long absences from his office now too, though Matthew Jones reported often seeing him as he flew his birds in the early mornings; wandering aimlessly on the estate. Utterly oblivious to any greetings along his way, and always with his head hanging low, his hands were always thrust deep into the pockets of his waxed coat, he said, and sometimes he'd even heard him weeping.

When she heard him tread on the loose floorboard as he crept past her bedroom door for the fourth sleepless early dawn in succession, Hannah decided to follow him to see where he was going and try to talk to him again.

Bare feet causing her to shiver on the cold flagstones, she silently watched him go into the boot room and put on his usual old Barbour waxed jacket, flat cap, and Wellington boots; then he collected a previously unnoticed coil of rope by the door and set off, heading across the park, and up the hill. Pulling her own coat and boots over her pyjamas quickly so that she could follow him, at first she thought he was heading for the camp; not that there was much of a camp now the battle was won of course. But at the top of the hill he suddenly veered in a different and more purposeful direction.

Keeping to the trees for cover as she ran up the hill, Hannah watched him as he made his steady way towards what was obviously his destination; the old Tithe barn. Not visible from the house at all, it had often puzzled her that her father had never seemed to care one iota about its upkeep; which was odd with it being such a beautiful old building, and so consequently it was almost derelict now and its approach was a tangle of brambles, weeds, and bits of it that had fallen victim to about a hundred years of weather. The barn used to play a major role on the estate and was the location that, in a bygone age, had been where all of the local tenants and farmers paid their dues to the Squire; and in wealthier times had held many a Harvest home and Christmas party for them too. Her brows knitted together in question as she watched him take a key from his pocket, insert it in the padlock, remove it, and go inside.

The hairs on the back of her neck stood bolt upright as she began to run.

Chapter twenty four

Inside the barn she immediately saw him sitting cross legged on a pile of long forgotten and dusty hay, in a spot that only he knew the significance of, with the coil of rope placed neatly on the floor beside him. Completely engrossed and not even aware of the slight squeak of the door hinges as she entered, he appeared to be reading a letter; its envelope lying open on the floor beside him. Assuming it to be a suicide note she swallowed and impatiently swept away her tears as they began to fall freely. He was visibly shaking with emotion now, with tears coursing down his stricken face; head swaying slowly from left to right as he read. Afraid, she spoke in barely a whisper.

'Daddy . . . .?'

He looked up slowly, not even jolting that she was there beside him.

'It's over darling . . . it's finished. I'm finished . . .' he said, his voice breaking and his breath nothing but a shallow wheezy rasp.

'It's not . . . Daddy you're not . . . I told you . . . it's a new start for us . . . . we can . . .'

'. . . And it's all her fault . . .'

Halted in mid calming flow she stared at him. 'Whose fault.?'

'Davina was right. She changed me . . . I never used to be a liar . . . She ruined our lives, both of us . . . . you and me . . . I was afraid . . .' he whispered, offering up the letter slightly to show her what he meant. 'I can't believe Mrs Higgins kept this all these years. I know I should have told you the truth . . . I was just afraid for you . . . of what it would do to you . . . and as the years passed by . . . I came to believe it all too . . . Sort of . . . I . . . so wanted what *you* believed to be true . . . as much as you believed it . . .'

'Daddy . . . I don't understand . . . what do mean you should have told me the truth . . . the truth about what? And what is that letter?'

He gave her a bitter half smile. 'I'm talking about your mother . . . . this letter is from her . . .'

Hannah took a small step backwards and leaned against a sturdy post for support.

Taking a very deep breath, he involuntarily looked up towards the broken roof as a sudden sound broke his concentration, blinking as daggers of sunlight exploded among the startled wood pigeons in the rafters; before returning his gaze to her widened eyes. 'The first time we ever made love was in here you know . . . your mother and I . . . .' He stopped with a half smile as he looked at her; his head cocked slightly to one side. 'I'm sorry . . . . I must be embarrassing you darling . . . but to be honest with you . . . .' Pausing again, he shrugged at the irony of the phrase, rubbing one thumb and forefinger across his eyes to wipe them. 'That's why I've left it . . . like this . . . the barn . . . derelict and falling apart . . . Just as our marriage was . . .'

'I don't understand . . . What ever do you mean? And what does that letter have to do with my cousin Davina, Daddy? I haven't even seen her since I was little . . .' she said, reaching out to take the letter from him, but he pulled it back towards him.

'No . . .' he said, swallowing. 'Not yet . . . I just need to explain . . .'

'It has my name on the envelope though . . .' she said, turning her head slightly to the side to read the faded handwriting.

After what felt like hours of silence broken only by the sound of the fluttering pigeons, he moved over on the hay and patted the ground beside him in a gesture to make her sit down with a shaking hand. 'Very well then . . . read it . . . if you must. And when you've finished . . . I'll talk to you about your mother . . . Set the record straight . . .' he said finally, and passed her the letter.

> *My darling,* she read.
>
> *I am going away from you, but just for a little while. And I promise it won't be for long my princess! I am going away to make a new life for us and I will send for you as soon as I can.*
>
> *You're too young to understand why I can't stay here anymore Hannah, but when you come you will have a new daddy who loves me, and he will love you too, so our lives will be happy forever.*
>
> *Until I send for you this has to be our own special secret, just like the ones we share when I put you to bed each night. So put this letter in your treasure box where no one will find it and be a good girl for mummy until I send for you*
>
> *Your loving mother*
> *Lottie*

Hannah began to shake, and tight within her grasp, the letter shook too.

'Was she saying she's leaving you for someone else?'

He nodded sadly as he closed his eyes; willing this to be over.

'This isn't real . . . . is it? It . . . can't be . . . because if it is . . . . then everything . . . you've told me about her all my life must have been . . . a lie . . .' She swallowed. 'I don't get this . . . I was too young to even read it . . . She must have known that . . . . Did she expect you to read it to me . . . or Mrs Higgins . . . ? She looked at him pleadingly and waited for an answer, but he said nothing. Her tone became harsher as the truth of it began to sink in. 'So you're telling me none of it was true now? And your little shrines to her . . . all over the house . . .'

'Your shrines Hannah . . . you made them all . . . I . . . I just didn't stop you . . .'

'And . . . if she was leaving you like she says . . . then why didn't she send for me like she says . . . ?'

'Because she died that same day . . .'

Hannah was re reading the letter as if for some hidden clue. 'So how did she really die then?' A sudden flash of horror crossed in front of her eyes. 'Daddy . . . you never . . . you didn't . . . because she was leaving you for . . . for someone else?'

He shook his head sadly and tried to put his arms around her, but she pulled away.

'She died in my car that day . . . just like I told you . . .' he said desperately. 'It's true, she was leaving me . . . for someone else, or so she says . . . but nobody ever came forward and I couldn't find any trace of anyone . . . serious. But Hannah . . . You have to know . . . It wasn't anything like you've believed all these years. She was a troubled woman when she wrote this . . . She drank . . . she was taking drugs . . . . Heroin and Cocaine . . . She had . . . . affaires . . .'

'No! No . . . you're lying . . . She drowned in the river when her car was hit by . . . by a drunk driver . . . you told me . . . you told me . . .'

He gasped as he struggled to compose himself. 'She *was* the drunk driver Hannah . . . she was driving under the influence when she came off the road that day . . . She never slowed down for the bend at all . . . There weren't any skid marks. She was dead when she hit the water . . . She didn't drown . . .'

'No! I don't believe you!' she screamed suddenly, throwing the letter in his face. 'Why are you saying all this? You're just . . . . She loved us both . . . everybody loved her . . . . She was an angel you said . . . you've always said . . . it broke your heart . . . losing her . . . .'

'It did . . . it did . . .' he gasped. 'I wanted to protect *you* from the truth . . . Protect the family name . . .'

'Family name?' she snorted. 'Protect yourself you mean . . . You're sitting there telling me she was nothing but a drunk and junkie! If all this is really true like you say . . . you were just ashamed of her . . . that's the real truth of it . . .'

'No . . . No . . . it wasn't like that at all! I loved her . . . I tried . . . I knew I should tell you all this as soon as you were old enough . . . but with each passing year it just got easier to run with the lies about how she died . . . because I couldn't bear that you would have your own heart broken as well. And by the time you *were* old enough you'd created this sainted picture of her in your head . . . She was your mother . . . and she loved you . . . so much . . . That was no lie Hannah . . . It was me she didn't love . . . it was me . . .'

Despite her confused feelings Hannah couldn't bear to see him so broken, and leaned in to pull him towards her as he finally collapsed in tears.

'And the . . . r . . . rope?' she said quietly. 'Did you think *that* would protect me from the truth too?'

'I thought it might be the answer to all *my* problems at least . . .'

'Well they say suicide is a selfish act . . .'

'Suicide . . .' he nodded, 'Indeed . . . and I might have proved it if you hadn't followed me up here . . . who knows?' He pushed the rope a little farther away from him with one foot. 'I doubt I could have done it once I allowed myself to think about you anyway . . . but I knew you'd find out about her some day, you see . . . and hate me for lying to you . . . and now Watson's, nor anybody else, can build on the estate, I've lost your inheritance too . . . In truth, by my badly thought out business deals over the years as much as the global recession . . . but it was all for you . . . really . . . it was all for you . . .'

'My inheritance?' she said vehemently, suddenly shaking him by his shoulders so his expensively bridged teeth rattled.

'Snap out of it Daddy! I don't care about bricks and mortar! When will you ever believe me! I want you . . . *you!* This hurts . . . it hurts so much . . . but at least I understand now . . . In fact this answers so many questions I've been puzzling about her all these years . . . like if you loved each other so much, why will *you* never talk to me about her? And why don't we ever see Aunt Arabella's family? She's your sister and you always said how close you were . . . and that she was Mummy's best friend . . .' She checked herself suddenly as something he'd said came back to her. 'And . . . while we're on that subject . . . What does all this have to do with Davina anyway . . . ? What does she have to do with any of this? You said she was right . . . Is it that she knows? Is that why you've become so afraid now . . . ? Is she threatening to come and tell me or something? I can't think why . . . suddenly after all these years . . . I wouldn't even know her if I saw her . . .'

He took a breath and looked into her eyes. 'You're right about that my darling . . . you didn't know her when you saw her . . .'

'I . . . saw her? When . . . ? Where . . . ?'

He sighed and gave her a sad little smile. 'She's been living at the camp all the time . . .'

'At the camp . . . ? But . . . I never met a Davina . . . I'm sure of it . . . .'

'She actually came to see me after she'd heard you talking about your mother up there . . . that day when Danny took you . . .'

She went pink in surprise despite herself and looked into her lap

'Yes young lady . . . I knew about that . . .' he paused, half smiling again. '. . . Davina was afraid for you . . . and that's why she broke her cover and came here . . . afraid that now you're talking openly about your mother some local resident would remember the rumours about the real story and end up telling you the truth of it . . . Not her . . . she wouldn't do that to you . . . but she *was* afraid that you would ask *her* if she told you who she is . . . she's old enough to remember her you see . . . and she said she couldn't lie to you . . .'

Hannah blinked in disbelief, and shook her head. 'But . . .'

'Davina is DeeDee, Hannah . . . DeeDee . . . her initials I suppose . . . Davina DeSales.'

Hannah couldn't hold it any more and put her head in her hands and cried, deep racking sobs of anger that shook her whole body.

'Get angry darling . . . but with me . . . not with her . . . she couldn't reveal herself for who she really is until she'd spoken to me . . . and she was right . . . I've been so wrong . . . deceiving you by letting you run with what you believe . . . It was up to me to tell you the truth . . . but you were so young . . . and then it was too late. But I was wrong . . . I see that. So now I have and . . . you know everything . . . I'm so sorry my darling . . . I'm so sorry . . .' He took her in his arms and rocked her, like the day her mother died and he'd had to tell her; the day their lives had turned into a web of lies . . . until now.

Chapter twenty five

Hannah had already arranged to meet Danny and their friends at the pub that same day, at lunchtime, and so it was swift that Hannah and her cousin stood recognisably face to face for the first time in over thirteen years. Oblivious to the chatter going on all around them, and to the exclamations of surprise from those that witnessed it, they embraced, breathlessly and with a lot of tears on both sides, and all became well between them without a word being said; such is the nature of the true family bond.

With everything now out in the open, at least to his daughter, and despite his looming financial crisis, Sir Christopher began to feel a little better with just their resultant homelessness to worry about. He had a bath and a change of clothes, and had a shave for the first time in over a month, and gradually he began to look more like the father that Hannah knew again. His accountant had assured him that after the sale there would still be enough money left to buy a house bigger than most people could ever dream of owning . . . so he tried to reassure himself that Hannah was right, as usual. He tried to reassure himself that this really was the ideal opportunity for a fresh start; away from Stanton Court, and away from all the bad memories it held. It was only bricks and mortar after all; well, Portland stone in actuality, but it still didn't matter a bit, in the scheme of things.

That's what he told himself.

They would go and live in France for a while, just the two of them, until the dust settled. He would have to sell his other properties, but he would retain their favourite one in Normandy, and then maybe come back to UK and live eventually . . . somewhere else. Anywhere else in fact . . . as long as it was far away, because if he knew anything at all, he knew he could never sit idly by and watch as someone else took over his Ancestral home and turned it into some five star hotel or health spa.

But the truth of it was that he knew it did matter. It mattered each time he walked the estate and heard the trees whisper their accusations in the wind; or when the rooks in their ancient rookery cackled and shrieked in laughter at his failure as he walked by.

And when, regardless of whether he ascended or descended the grand staircase, the portraits of his distinguished ancestors hanging there all seemed to follow him with the same, accusing eyes.

He was responsible for the failure of the estate. He was the one who had let them all down.

* * *

Over a sandwich and a glass of lemonade in the pub Hannah confided in her friends about the sale of Stanton Court now that the development had fallen through, and though by that time all but the most stalwart of the protestors had moved on to the next piece of England's green and pleasant land to be put under threat, the remaining few had spent the rest of the afternoon trying to think of ways to help their previous enemy and his lovely daughter to keep their family home.

Tindy looked more than usually thoughtful as everyone around him was chattering and throwing ideas around. Then he stood up and cleared his throat and, in the way that only he could, they all stopped talking and looked at him expectantly.

'I think you are all missing a very good point,' he said quietly. 'And that is that Sir Christopher and I have a lot in common.'

He ignored the guffaws.

'My family has been entrusted the care of our people for many generations, and so has his. In my culture he would be the head of his tribe in just the same way. Hannah said that he is very sad about what has happened and that everything he has done has only been done in trying to save their home . . . . He is not a cruel or a bad man . . . he just is just a worried man who fears that he will let down his family name; his ancestors . . . and I can identify with that. I think that he must simply be reminded of his role . . . and that we should help . . . by asking him to work with us, not against us.' He sat down again and leaned his face in closer towards them. 'I have an idea that we might discuss . . . that if I am right might be the answer to the problems of everyone in this village . . . and then maybe we could take it to him, and see what he has to say . . .'

*   *   *

After a long series of discussions and many sleepless nights worrying about whether they'd thought Tindy's idea through to the last possible problem Danny, Hannah, Tindy and DeeDee stood in Sir Christopher's study, nervously awaiting his arrival with their proposal in a black folder that Tindy held tightly under his right arm, which was about level with Hannah's head.

Whispering to each other in a bid to increase their combined confidence, the door finally opened and he entered the room, stalking past them all to sit behind his desk in his enormous leather wing chair that gave an indignant squeak as he sat abruptly down.

He made himself comfortable without saying a word, cleared his throat, rested his elbows on the arms of the chair, and brought his praying hands up to his lips, staring into eyes of the enemy.

'Well?' he said. 'What is it? I'm a busy man . . .'

'Daddy, please . . . We just wanted to . . . we have a really good idea . . . .'

'Hannah, let me . . .' Danny took her hand and squeezed it. 'Sir . . .' he paused, 'you're an intelligent man and we don't want to waste your time . . . .' He swallowed slightly with nerves, but raised his chin defiantly. 'We have an idea that will help you . . . help you to keep the estate . . . to keep your home . . .'

'Help me to keep my . . . .? What makes you so sure I want help . . . . particularly your help?'

'Daddy, please . . .'

'Uncle Chris . . . topher . . .' DeeDee corrected herself before making her way round the desk and lowering herself down to his eye level affectionately. 'Whatever you might think about the protest and everything that happened . . . we didn't do it for some kind of kick to cause trouble for you . . . we just wanted you, and everyone else to see that there's another way . . . a better way . . . without destroying the woods and flood meadows . . . and the chalk hills and everything that lives there . . . a way to work with nature . . . to let everyone enjoy, and learn to appreciate it.' DeeDee turned slightly to sit down on a chair by the window although he had not invited her to. The others followed her lead and sat down in various places too.

'I fail to see how that can be achieved Dav . . . ahem . . . DeeDee . . .' he said quietly. 'I've exhausted all possibilities . . . I've tried everything in my power . . . believe me.'

Tindy put the folder down on the desk in front of him and cleared his throat. 'There is another way, and if you will just spare us just a few minutes of your time we can show you . . . We have a proposal . . .'

'A proposal . . . ?'

'A proposal, sir . . .'

With more confidence than he was feeling Tindy opened the folder and drew out several documents, before looking directly at him. 'The people and the communities around Frincham are living in difficult times nowadays, and they really need your help, sir.'

His eyes glinted but he remained silent.

'By the Grace of God your family was given this estate and its people, and cared for them for many generations before you, just like my family has before me, and we think that you are the best and only man who can really give them the help they need now . . .'

Sir Christopher's brows went up in irony but he said nothing as Tindy continued.

'The orchids are just the beginning of what you could do here to boost the local economy . . . as well as your own . . . and with your permission we'd like to show you our ideas . . .'

'Go on . . .' he said, leaning forward slightly, despite himself.

Tindy pulled out a large and much folded piece of paper, opened it out to its full size and spread it on the desk in front of him. They all stood up to see the plans more clearly.

The title of the plans said in bold; 'Stanton Court Nature Discovery Park'.

'A picnic area?' he said dully. 'You want me to open up my estate to ramblers and weekend hikers you mean . . . ? Traipsing all over the place to see a few flowers, peering at us through the windows and leaving their litter everywhere . . . You'll be suggesting I bring in lions and giraffes and set up a wildlife park next . . .'

'Please forgive me but you are missing the point, sir. There will be lots of people coming here to see the orchids now that you have agreed them access . . . and it is a public footpath down where we are looking for the rest of the park already . . . all of this would be on the other side of the hills to your house . . . We are just saying that you could be taking advantage of a real opportunity when these visitors come. Your woods here are rich with wildlife . . . there could be nest boxes put up on the trees . . . and did you know there is an established badger set in there? It is huge . . . probably a hundred years old or more . . . and there is your fallow deer herd in the park . . . you could do tractor trailer rides to see them . . . and down here . . . where it is flat . . . you could set up a show ring . . .' Tindy chose to ignore the huffing coming at him from across the desk. 'You know that Matthew Jones from the farm keeps birds of prey?'

'I do . . . he flies them in the park sometimes . . .'

'Well . . . we have spoken to him and . . . he would be more than willing to do displays for visitors and maybe for a few school trips . . . His brother Mark will do the bird watching and wildlife walks . . . he would advise us about building a proper hide so people can watch and study the birds without disturbing them . . . and you could maybe ask the local Territorial soldier's Regiment to help you build an assault course down here . . .' he pointed, 'and maybe an adventure playground . . . and over here, near where it shows the café . . . there is already a little play area . . .' Hannah smiled over at her father as he briefly looked up at her. '. . . that could be brought up to current health and safety regulations and enlarged, for younger children . . . and Ernie from the farm suggested having a second farm shop down there near the entrance . . . that visitors would have to pass on the way in and out . . . and that local people could take advantage of and sell the things they make like . . .'

'Chutneys and jams from the WI . . . and cakes from the Mothers Union . . . and the Honeycomb Club's honey . . . !' Hannah butted in, knowing her father's fondness for all of them. 'Amy's dad can ask the other members . . . and Dizzy can see about the others . . . and we could sell Ernie's farm eggs . . . and maybe some fresh meat from Griffin's in the square . . . and we could have village barbeques too . . . and everyone could come . . . like in the old days . . . like you said Grandpa used to talk about . . .'

'And once you get established and people know about this place you could have a local farmers and growers market in the show ring . . . those are all the rage now everyone wants to buy locally . . .' Danny's eyes were sparkling.

Sir Christopher looked him in those eyes soberly. '. . . And one would suppose that all these visitors would come flocking through the village to this . . . discovery park . . . Tell me, how does your plan differ from mine with regard to the traffic problems you were protesting about . . . .?' he said tersely.

'This is different . . . see?' Danny said, pointing to the bottom of the map at a distance from the site of the abandoned supermarket. 'You could put your visitor's car park right down here . . . at the bottom of the hill . . .

they'd have to come the other way then 'cos it would be quicker . . . . right down there the nearest approach road would be off the motorway junction at Chieveley, instead of bringing everything through the village like before . . . On gravel would be fine . . . nothing else for that bit of land is there? It's too boggy, and Watsons weren't even interested right down there . . . probably because of the expense they'd have had pile driving the foundations . . .'

DeeDee smiled at him. 'And we wouldn't disturb the newts either because they are on the other side of the road . . . right over here.' She pointed.

Derby was standing up now, nodding his head slowly and following the trails of the pencil markings with one finger as Tindy continued.

'The local community hereabouts is very rich with country skills, sir . . . and those skills will die with the people that remember them, unless someone like you steps in. Villages in the 21st century are changing . . . With fewer full time residents and more houses being bought as second homes this close to London . . . we all know that the economy and livelihoods in villages is suffering, and it isn't just in Frincham, is it? Shops and businesses are closing and either going out of business altogether or moving to big towns like Newbury and Reading . . . and *you* could be helping businesses like Griffin's that remain . . . who want to keep Frincham's integrity alive in what we all know to be difficult times . . . and just think how you would be seen then? As someone who really cares about them . . . about their lives and their traditions . . . like your ancestors did . . . instead of someone who wants to drive the last nail into Frincham's coffin by bringing in a huge supermarket . . .'

'Hmm . . . yes well . . .' he looked up at Tindy briefly. 'I do care as it happens . . .'

They were all quiet for a few minutes to allow him to study the plans more closely. Eventually he followed them up to the top with one finger and pointed at an area so far undesignated. 'This is the old Tithe barn . . .' he had twisted the plans around for a better view, and as he pointed Hannah caught hold of his arm and squeezed it.

'Yes, sir . . . we hadn't thought of anything definite for that yet because we weren't sure about the state of it . . . and it's too far away from the rest of the site anyway . . .' Danny watched him studying the plans thoughtfully, and continued. 'It would be very peaceful up there though . . . if it was fully restored . . .' Danny was looking at Hannah now, who'd told him the building's much earlier history with her parents, and winked one sparkly black eye at her briefly.

Sir Christopher prodded the map with one finger. 'Well . . . it could be renovated and used for functions I suppose . . . . Like the sort of places Hector books for church camps . . . Then there could be camps for cubs and scouts . . . and we could host wedding receptions . . . that kind of thing . . . We could clear the shrubs that have taken over up there and use that area for the camp site . . . and put some lavatories in behind the barn . . . just here . . . .'

'That's a great idea Daddy! And then those visitors could come down and use the other facilities too . . . And we could have Gymkhanas and horse shows . . . Beau could . . .'

Just when they all thought they'd convinced him Sir Christopher suddenly straightened his back and shook his head decisively, taking a sharp intake of breath before interrupting her. 'Not so fast young lady . . . Let's not get carried away here . . . . This sort of thing would cost an absolute fortune to set up . . . . and may I remind you all that money is one thing this estate just doesn't have any longer . . . that *I* don't have any longer . . . . and it would need all sorts of costly planning permissions too . . .'

Before any of them had a chance to answer he carried on firmly. 'Besides . . . who on earth do you think would run it? It would take a huge team of people to cater for this many facilities . . .' He shook his head sadly as he looked around at them, arms now folded resolutely across his chest. 'I'm sorry everyone . . . but I'm no longer the wealthy person you seem to think I am . . . you seem to have forgotten that . . . I've lost everything . . . and I'm not even sure who I am anymore . . . I'm certainly not in a position to take chances like this . . .'

Tindy put a hand on his shoulder and assisted him back into his chair slowly.

'It was Gandhi who once said . . . *the best way to find yourself is to lose yourself in the service of others* . . . and in my culture we believe that, to give real service, you must add something to that which cannot be bought or measured with money: sincerity and integrity . . . and you are a man who has shown us plenty of that . . . We all know that you are a proud man . . . a man who is proud of his family name and his family history . . .'

Sir Christopher's eyes misted over and he looked away from Tindy's intense gaze, embarrassed. Tindy looked at the others briefly before continuing quietly.

'. . . and we also know that despite what happened between us, all you were trying to do was to hold on to as much of your heritage as you could for your daughter's future . . . But that is what we are asking you to do for these people too . . . help them to hold on to *their* heritage for their children's futures as well . . .'

'We could look into what kind of grants and government schemes might be available . . . and as for the team . . . that is where we would all come in . . .' DeeDee was speaking now. 'Despite what you might think, Uncle Chris, we are not just a bunch of . . . hippies . . .' she smiled shrewdly.

Tindy continued; 'We are just a group of people with a common goal . . . which is to preserve and save the environment that was entrusted to us by God . . . I am a Botanist, DeeDee here has a first class honours degree in Business Studies and is quite a financial genius . . . with very impressive organisational skills too, and Danny . . . and Hannah and Amy when they are not at school, would be in charge of the advertising and the bookings. Some of the other, former protestors are keen to get involved too, despite what you might think, and they are really keen to help you to achieve this. There is Jez . . . he is a photographer for your advertising posters, Billy and Finlay are both landscape gardeners with their own business . . .'

'We have a couple of builders and a bricklayer . . . a plumber . . . Two with degrees in animal husbandry . . .' said DeeDee with a grin.

'We've even got Tony Gillespie . . . he's a really good architect with some great ideas already . . . it was him that drew up these plans for us . . . And most of the others at least have retail experience from all of their summer jobs . . . . All you have to do is say the word and we will have a meeting to discuss it properly . . . all of us together sir . . . you included.' Tindy looked at the others and smiled, knowing that they had him.

Sir Christopher's head came up from the plans slowly and looked at them all. 'Well I have to say I'm not often speechless . . . but I think you might have the beginnings of a fine idea here . . . But the fact remains that even with financial help, it would still mean taking a massive chance . . . and my fingers are already burnt through to the bones with trying to save this estate . . . '

Tindy smiled and tilted his head slightly to one side. 'My people have a saying too sir . . . it is '*Zidele Amathambo* . . . ''

'Which means . . . ?'

'It means, literally, '*give yourself up, bones as well* . . . ' it means none of us can ever know how well something new might turn out . . . but if we really believe in something . . . then we should give our whole selves up to it . . . and take that chance . . . not just sit around wishing. We must *stop* wearing our wishbones where our backbones should be! You have the support of good friends . . . ' he added.

A collective sigh lightened the mood in the room as Sir Christopher smiled, finally.

It suited him.

'My backbone is right where it should be thank you, Tindy. I'll get my legal people to take a look, and see what they think of course . . . and then maybe . . . *maybe* we'll think about getting this meeting set up shall we?'

The tumble of lively conversation that broke out stopped abruptly when the door opened with a loud bang and a wobble of very valuable vase as Mrs

Higgins appeared with a large pot of tea on a trolley, along with a plate of fairy cakes and a rickety pile of cups and saucers, declaring that a lorry full of live chickens had lost its load eastbound on the M4 by the Heston services and that there were chickens flapping about and causing chaos on both carriageways.

Sir Christopher raised his eyes to heaven as he stifled another smile. 'Ah. Tea . . .' he said.

*   *   *

Because the seeds of such an exciting plan had actually come from the former protestors; courtesy of DeeDee the very shrewd business woman, the national press soon caught hold of the story and ran with it as something really positive to report on for a change, and once that happened, people were falling over themselves with offers to help.

It didn't seem possible that the once bitter enemies were now working together as a team to help save the house and the estate, but as each TV crew came to interview them all comfortably sharing the same sofas, and left again, and the weeks passed by with more and more good news coming in with each email, it really did look as though Sir Christopher had got many more people on his side now than he ever could have wished for. Even the banks had got on board and given him some more time, and offered huge new business loan to get the Discovery Park going, in return for taking on their accounts once it was up and running.

The local council had practically fallen over itself to obtain such a valuable local amenity and returned the successful planning application, with only some very minor recommendations, in record time. And because the majority of the park's 'discovery' features that were being advertised were already in place and had been for centuries, the construction of the site that was otherwise needed was soon enthusiastically well underway.

Sir Christopher, it seemed, had gone from zero to hero almost overnight, and the former protestors that had seen the story on the TV quickly responded to his invitation; returning in their droves to lend him a hand.

Now free to return to their former camp site in the woods, and making up the majority of the labour force, they worked hard, once more merely for the passion of it all . . . but this time with the addition of daily visits from their old adversary and his daughter with boxes of food. They even occasionally stayed at the camp for dinner . . . but one small leap of faith for the protestors was one giant leap for Sir Christopher, who usually arrived with a tube of Rennies hidden in his jacket pocket.

Chapter twenty six

Dr Jemmie Ryan gave up work at the hospital to concentrate on her impending motherhood once she couldn't reach over her patients with her stethoscope. Her own doctor told her she should now hang it up and she did this with a great deal of excitement once decided. Petite in stature, her pregnant stomach looked vast and out of proportion in her tiny frame, and Martin had even nicknamed her '*Weeble*' because he said she resembled one of those children's toys that wobbles but won't fall over. Once she had time on her hands for a change, the pregnancy nesting instinct very quickly kicked in, and she found herself waddling around the cottage sorting out drawers and cupboards and waging a war on dog hair. Jules arrived one morning to find her trying to get the vacuum cleaner up the narrow staircase, puffing and panting with exertion, and finally called a halt to her frenzied housework on the grounds of her personal safety.

After a surprisingly short discussion Lizzie was then employed to do her vacuuming and bending over the bath type cleaning until the baby arrived.

Martin played the role of doting husband very well, massaging Jemmie's back and bathing her swollen ankles and providing regular supplies of chocolate ice cream; her one weakness. As her due date approached she began to hate it when he went away on overnight jobs, as his profession of lighting engineer meant he quite often had to do. This included his absence the particular morning that she awoke just before eight with awful backache and a vicious muscle cramp in her left thigh. Cursing as she sat up in the bed sharply and in absolute agony, she missed his gentle hands and comforting words more than ever. Throwing back the duvet impatiently and apologising to her unborn child at such a rude awakening she eased herself out of bed to put her feet on the cool wooden floor, and once the cramp had gone she tottered yawning into the bathroom to relieve her swollen bladder. As she lifted her nightgown and sat down rather ungracefully on the toilet, the baby kicked her just behind her ribs, as it always did when she sat down and squashed it momentarily, and she spoke calming words to it again as she rubbed at her stomach tenderly.

Washing her hands at the washbasin while pulling a face at her bed hair in the mirror, she took the opportunity to slosh water onto her face and scooped some into her mouth to relieve her unquenchable thirst, before burying her face and hands in a towel and drying herself off.

Dipstick appeared at the bathroom door having heard her get up, and danced towards her with his tongue hanging out happily and his stumpy tail wagging in greeting. Realising he actually had an ulterior motive and needed to go in the garden, Jemmie reached up to the hook on the back of the bedroom door for her dressing gown and dragged it on with a yawn as the baby kicked again. She pulled a slight face, put one hand in the small of her back and stretched her aching spine.

'Oh baby Ryan . . . calm down . . . Tell you what . . .' she said, 'let's make some nice tea and have a biscuit while we let him out shall we?' She yawned sleepily again, never having been much of a morning person, unlike her mother who was always up with the lark and raring to go.

The belt redundant for the time being because the dressing gown no longer met in the middle by at least eight inches, she made her way slowly and sideways down the narrow staircase with her back wedged and sliding down the wall. Then, with her flip flop slippers flapping against her heels, she crossed the kitchen and turned they key in the lock, opening the back door with its usual, '*really must oil that later . . .*' squeak. The dog instantly pushed past her legs and tore off down the garden, barking his good mornings to the birds that up to that point were still roosting peacefully on the telephone wires; before gratefully cocking his leg up against his favourite dead shrub for a considerable time.

Back in the kitchen, Jemmie tipped the kettle over a mug and dipped her herbal tea bag a few times, glancing occasionally out of the window to see what the dog was doing and where, so she would remember to go out there later with a plastic bag. Satisfied that what needed to be done had been done and kicking the back door behind him, she turned to sit at the kitchen table and pulled yesterday's newspaper nearer, beginning to flick through it without much enthusiasm as she sipped at the tea. She looked up to the wall above the cooker and checked the clock; it was almost eight thirty now, and she wondered about calling Martin, who was staying the night with Marcus and Sam in London, to say good morning. As the thought struck her the baby kicked again, and this time she really winced as it suddenly tensed, and seemed to move right over to one side.

'Braxton Hicks contraction . . .' she thought, with a slight puff or two, and adjusted her aching back position until the baby relaxed again.

And now she needed to pee again . . . great.

Deciding not to call Martin while her back was hurting so much and the baby was being so active, Jemmie decided to try and calm things down a little. As she had to go back up to bathroom anyway, she thought she'd have a nice bath, with some of the bath salts she loved to indulge herself with. So she called the dog to follow her up and pulled up the door at the bottom of the stairs behind her as much as it would go with a broken latch to stop the draught.

A few minutes later she was back in the bathroom chatting companionably to Dipstick, whose tail was wagging as his chin rested on the side of the bath to watch the water swirling and frothing, and he was looking slightly puzzled as Jemmie happily sprinkled bath salts into the water. The door pulled to, the steam soon billowed, misting up the mirror and filling the room with a delicious smell of wild flowers as she slipped off her dressing gown and nightshirt and gingerly tested the temperature of the water with one big toe. Satisfied, she stepped carefully in and gradually lowered herself into the bath. The warm water instantly soothed her aching back, and she smiled as the baby fluttered when the sudden change in temperature reached it. As it calmed down and relaxed so did she, relishing her pregnancy weightlessness in the steaming water and closing her eyes luxuriously. Dipstick circled before he settled down on the bathmat beside her with a contented sigh.

She must have nodded off for a while, because the next thing she knew Dipstick woke her up with a sudden bark as he flicked open the bathroom door with his nose and tore off down the stairs.

Calling him, she winced as she realised that the pain in her back was ten times worse now, and as she came properly awake, to her horror she saw that the bath water, now barely tepid in temperature, had a distinctly pinky tinge. Shivering slightly, she pulled out the bath plug and struggled to stand herself up.

'It's only me!' Lizzie's voice echoed up the stairs as she spoke to the dog playfully for a few seconds.

'Lizzie . . . ! I'm in the bathroom . . . a . . . . and I think my waters have broken!' Jemmie shouted; her voice a lot more shrill than she had anticipated.

Lizzie was up the stairs in seconds, running breathlessly into the bathroom. '. . . All right if I come in, love? Is . . . is your bag all packed and everything?' She gulped at the sight of Jemmie standing there stark naked in the bath, puffing and panting, in very obvious labour.

Jemmie groaned involuntarily as she grabbed at Lizzie's shoulders; her whole body suddenly seized by a strong contraction so she couldn't answer her for a full minute.

'Not . . . sure there's . . . time . . .' she gasped.

Lizzie grabbed the folded towel draped over the corner of the washbasin and helped her out of the bath, leading her back in the bedroom and sending the dog back downstairs with a sharp command to get him out of the way.

'Should I phone someone . . . .? Shall I call Martin for you?' She asked, trying to keep the panic out of her voice. Jemmie was a doctor . . . everything would be fine.

But everything was not fine. Jemmie was in agony and totally unable to help her.

'This isn't right . . . this isn't right Lizzie . . . I need to be in the hospital . . . I need . . . I need an epidural . . . I need gas and . . . and air . . . oooh . . . oooh . . . Owwwwwch! I need . . . . I need . . . MAR . . . . TIN . . . !!!' Legs forcing themselves apart involuntarily Jemmie began to push on the way over to the bed.

Lizzie didn't have time to panic. Leaving her on the side of the bed for a second she ran to the airing cupboard on the landing and grabbed a rolled up picnic blanket and a pile of neatly folded towels.

'No! I need to be in the hos . . . pital . . .' Jemmie gasped, realising what Lizzie was preparing to do and totally losing her own capability of what to she was supposed to do next.

'Just lay down on this Jemmie . . . it's a picnic blanket but it's plastic underneath too . . . it'll protect your bed . . . .' Lizzie said wrenching the duvet to the floor by the window and throwing the picnic blanket on top of the bottom sheet.

'I . . . I . . .'

With slightly more confidence than she was feeling, Lizzie looked firmly into her eyes and said; 'Listen, I've had two children Jemmie, and in this instance I know what I'm doing more than you do . . . So just stop panicking and listen to me . . .'

Then she caught hold of Jemmie's shoulders and helped her to lie down, resigned and utterly compliant now. Once on her back, plumped up with pillows behind her shoulders and with a fluffy pink bath towel to cover her dignity, Jemmie was now free to deal with the matter in hand and began to push.

* * *

After many minutes of strange and unnerving sounds coming from his mistress upstairs, Dipstick, who was lying at the bottom of the stairs whining and panting, knew that something was very wrong and hated being banished out of the way. Hearing a sudden bark from outside in the lane he jumped up, tearing out of the back door that Lizzie had left half open, and out into the lane to find Jules and Barney on their way up the lane to the shops. Barney always barked hello to his best friend on the way past.

'Hello Dipstick . . . where's your mum?' Jules said with a grin as she reached down to ruffle his ears. But the dog didn't seem to be interested in greetings this morning; he just stood there with his stumpy tail wagging frantically, and whining. He ran back and forth from her to the driveway several times, running behind her and trying his best to get her to go inside the house.

Realising something might be wrong, Jules followed him.

Entering by the open back door and hearing nothing, she made her way to the bottom of the stairs and called up. 'Jemmie? Jems? Are you ok?'

'Mum!' Jemmie called. 'Mum . . . come on up . . . it's ok . . .'

Heading up the stairs with both dogs bring up the rear Lizzie took her completely by surprise by appearing at the top of the stairs, drying her hands on a towel.

'Come and see what your daughter just did . . .' she smiled.

Lying on the bed wrapped in a whole airing cupboard's worth of laundry lay Jemmie, and nestling in her arms, she could just see the tiny, sleeping face of her new baby daughter. The dogs shot forward for a sniff of the new arrival before Lizzie sent them both packing again and shut the door.

'This is Esther Elizabeth . . . .' Jemmie smiled tearfully. 'Essie . . . Lizzie just delivered her . . . thank goodness . . . because she was in too much of a hurry to get to the hospital . . . weren't you?' she kissed her baby's tiny head lovingly. 'So she gets an honorary mention on the birth certificate . . . I know Martin approves . . . . we just called him . . . he's on his way back . . . and Marcus and Sam and the twins are coming too . . .'

Jules was speechless.

'Essie . . . say hello to your Nanna . . .' Jemmie gently lifted her baby around to face her new grandmother and held her precious bundle out in her extended arms.

'Darling . . . she's perfect . . . . she's perfect . . .' Jules whispered, sitting down shakily on the edge of the bed and carefully taking the tiny baby from her daughter. Kissing Essie on the tip of her button nose, she turned to Lizzie, standing in the doorway, leaning against the frame with the towel still in her hands. 'Lizzie . . . I don't know how to thank you . . . .'

'My pleasure . . .' Lizzie said with a grin. 'Not sure it was in my job description, but hey . . . needs must as they say . . . It all happened a bit quicker than we expected really, didn't it Jemmie?'

'Jemmie smiled and gave her a conspiratorial wink. 'Just a bit . . .' she laughed.

Chapter twenty seven

One aspect of the project that had taken Sir Christopher more by surprise than any other was English Heritage's keenness to get involved in the restoration of the old Tithe barn, and it was the barn that seemed to be raising most interest in the press, both locally and nationally. It pleased him that it had taken on a rather pleasing female persona along the way too, and soon became referred to as 'She' or 'Her' by everyone. With her six impressive stone arches, half hammer beams and original flagstone floors still mostly sound; the truth of it was that if he'd been listening to her rather than wallowing in his own bad memories of her, she had long been screaming out at him to be restored. A few of the village's older residents remembered the harvest home and Christmas parties that they'd been to as children and longed to see her restored to her former glory too, and the 'Save the Tithe Barn' fund was growing by the day now.

Tony Gillespie, the former protestor that Tindy had mentioned as being an architect, had been so excited when he'd visited the barn that he'd offered his services to the newly set up Stanton Tithe Barn Trust for free in return for some publicity on their literature for his new boss' practice.

Once completed, his plans were displayed in the village hall for all to see, and everyone agreed that they were an ideal blend of the traditional, with a dose of innovation to bring her up to date a bit too. The vast roof, the exterior wattle and daub walls, the stone arches, and the floors were to be fully retained and restored, and the old grain bins were to be opened out into a huge rail fronted 'minstrel' gallery, so that the barn could be used for concerts as well because, he'd pointed out, that the acoustics in such a huge building were akin to a church. There was to be a stainless steel kitted out professional kitchen, a foyer with display area, cloakrooms, disabled facilities to comply with current building regulations, and a smaller meeting room was to be created, to square off the slightly odd shape at one end of the barn that was where the animal pens used to stand. To help with fundraising Paul Taylor had donated the recent and considerable proceeds of a sale of six of his paintings, and DeeDee had quickly discovered that many grants, from small local ones to potentially large ones were available to them for the barn from organisations such as the Heritage Lottery Fund and DEFRA.

The rest of the villagers were proud of this slice of their history and wanted to be involved in the restoration project too. Sarah Palmer had suggested setting up the Save the Tithe Barn fund in the first place and launched a local fundraising campaign; quickly taking the helm and using her wealth of fundraising ideas and resources. Having discovered that there were an awful lot of the original roof tiles lying where they had fallen in the soft landings that a sea of rampant nature had provided over the years in the immediate vicinity of the barn, she began with a roof tile sale on a sheaf of squared grid papers at ten pounds each: though she privately balked at the many thousands of squares that she'd have to get names in to cover the roof of such a large building. She organised cake sales, sponsored walks, sponsored swims, sponsored marathon entries . . . . Without much persuasion Flynn dedicated his still popular Tuesday curry and quiz night takings to the fund, and Amy and Hannah were recruited to go in regularly to help the children at the new afternoon club in the school design all of the posters for the advertising campaign.

After one of her persuasive visits Newbury buses helped the campaign hugely by reproducing some of the children's work on the back of all their buses to raise awareness to the fund, and soon the donations came flooding in as Thames Trains, the local supermarkets and the Newbury Round Table joined in and put the posters and banners all over the region.

Hannah and Danny spent many hours reading the heartwarming letters that accompanied the donations, with their tales of events held during barn's long history, and they decorated the walls of the site office with them until letter covered letter covered letter, by several layers, that all fluttered and chattered every time the door opened with another bag of letters from the postman.

The volunteers cleared all the debris, shrubs and the general invasion of nature, after which the restoration professionals came in to remove the roof and floors. Work then began to repair and make good the roof timbers by doing battle with wet rot, dry rot and woodworm, and a few things that appeared to be new to biological science.

Once the poster design campaign was over the children at the school began a long project to document the restoration in detail for posterity and made regular visits to the barn so that they could learn about its history, appreciate its historic value, and see how much work was needed to restore it to its original condition. As the work progressed Tony also led open days for the villagers and all comers who had sent donations or showed their support, so that they could be kept up to date. These proved hugely popular, and as the restoration work progressed the whole community seemed to grasp ownership of the barn and its history, and become excited about its future together.

The restoration seemed as if it might take for ever with months of numerous hold ups for weather and a myriad of other, unforeseen problems, but eventually the time came on a beautiful summer's morning when the keys were handed back by the builders, and the whole village turned out for an enormous barbeque party, courtesy of Griffins the butcher's, at the opening ceremony.

Patiently awaiting the celebration party the villagers watched as the requisite speeches were made by Sir Christopher, as chairman of the trust, Architect Tony Gillespie, Fund Trustee Sarah Palmer, local MP Peter Cooper, and representatives from the Berkshire Buildings Preservation Trust and the Heritage Lottery Fund. Until finally the moment that everyone had been waiting for arrived and Hannah Derby proudly cut the ribbon and put the key in the lock for the first time in almost seventy years. Her father didn't even try to hide his emotions as he effortlessly slid back the enormous doors, before bowing with an exaggerated sweep of his arms, warmly inviting the villagers and the team members into their new local amenity; with a glance over at Tindy just in time to see him mouth the words, *Zidele amathambo . . .*'

Chapter twenty eight

Jemmie and Martin's daughter Esther Elizabeth was registered as weighing in at seven pounds exactly, and Martin, on his rapid return from London, had ecstatically reported both mother and daughter as being 'utterly beyond beauty and compare' and Lizzie Fidler as, 'a complete star' on his Facebook page.

Dipstick quickly became besotted with his new charge, taking up guard duty next to the pram in the garden on nice days while she slept, resting his chin on the shopping tray underneath, and running in to raise the alarm once she woke up and cried for attention; and in the first few weeks of chaos he also became a dab paw at fetching missing items when Jemmie or Martin forgot them during the nappy changing routine.

Jemmie enjoyed being a mother but, unused to the limited social contact that came with the role she soon spent a lot of time wearing out the footpath between the cottage and her mother at Clearwater House, walking Dipstick and Barney around the lake and hearing stories about her own babyhood that she'd never heard in her life before.

It was during one of these walks that the subject of Lizzie Fidler came up again.

'Have you noticed the way Flynn looks at her in the pub, Mum?'

'What do you mean, looks at her?' Jules replied, coming up from the tray under the pram and passing her daughter a packet of baby wipes to deal with her daughter's sicky burp.

'You know . . . *Looks* at her . . .'

'You mean . . .'

'He *likes* her . . . Mum . . . . anyone can see it . . .'

'Really . . . ?' Jules said. 'Well it would certainly be great for her to have a decent man in her life for a change . . . but I'm not sure we should really interfere there . . . her husband only recently died and she's not really in the right frame of mind to start thinking about beginning a new relationship, is she . . . .'

'That's what I thought at first too . . . but then I saw her looking at *him*, and she didn't look much like the grieving widow to me . . . Anyway why should she? Losing that brute was the best thing that could have happened for her . . . Flynn's lovely, isn't he . . . ? Ideal for her . . . .'

'Jemmie! Speaking ill of the dead like that . . . *really* . . . . But . . . I do see your point . . .' she said with a smile. 'So you think she likes him too . . . ?'

'Yes I do . . . . but she's too shy or too insecure to do anything about it . . . so . . . I was wondering if maybe *we* can get her confidence up enough to . . . you know . . .'

Jules sat down on a favourite fallen tree adjacent to the path that was worn completely smooth, and Jemmie joined her, gently pushing the pram back and forth with a slight bounce to keep her daughter happy. An elderly couple with a dog stopped to admire the new baby and they got distracted talking to them for a few minutes.

'So what did you have in mind darling?' Jules said with a conspiratorial grin after they'd wandered on in search of their dog, that'd quickly lost interest.

'Well we were thinking it's time we organized the Christening for Essie . . . for one thing' she smiled, 'and maybe asking Lizzie to be a Godmother . . .'

'That's a lovely idea darling . . . She adores her and I know she would love that . . . but I don't see quite how that would . . .'

'Well . . . she'd need a new dress for that wouldn't she . . . ? Maybe . . . a new hairstyle . . . now her hair is long enough to take a bit of a style again . . . or maybe she could even . . . have a whole makeover . . . like . . .

you had . . . when you met that lovely Frenchman Michel . . . .?'

'And then have Flynn cater the reception . . . the pub wouldn't be big enough but . . . we could do it in the Tithe barn . . . so then he could see her . . . possibly . . . .?' Jules began to giggle.

'Possibly . . .' said Jemmie with a wink.

*　　*　　*

Later that evening and after they'd finished their supper; Paul and Jules were babysitting Essie so that her parents could go out for a romantic dinner at the Royal Oak. Having been waiting for the perfect opportunity to discuss the plan Jules put a tray down on the coffee table in the sitting room and turned to face her husband.

'Paul darling do you think you can stop bouncing that baby up and down for two seconds and look at me?' she said, offering him a bottle of baby milk with a smile. 'You'll make her sick again and she has to have this now . . . . I want to help Lizzie . . .'

Paul blinked at the sudden change of subject. 'Help Lizzie . . . ?' Putting his grandaughter into the crook of his arm comfortably, he took the bottle from his wife and helped Essie settle down to her feed. 'What do you mean?'

'Well Jemmie and Martin are thinking it's time to think about organizing Essie's baptism and obviously they would like to ask Lizzie to be her Godmother . . . and I'm sure that Lizzie doesn't have any money for a new outfit or anything . . . or to get her hair done . . . or do anything that I know she'd really like to for the day . . . and she'll feel embarrassed . . . .'

Paul nodded thoughtfully as he continued to feed his grandaughter.

'. . . So I want to help her to feel better about herself . . . sort of 'make her over' I mean . . . to help her regain her self confidence . . . Like . . . my friend Michel helped me . . .' she added quietly, 'in France . . . .'

Paul smiled a little at the memory of his first sight of the newly polished Jules almost four years ago, pursed his lips and nodded. 'Ye-es . . . I can definitely see why you would want to do that . . . .' A few seconds of contemplation later he nodded again. 'Do it,' he said decisively. Whatever it was that your French Yoda helped you to do . . . just do it!'

Jemmie and Martin went to see Hector the following week and arranged Essie's baptism for the second Sunday of the following month in the morning service. That gave an open invitation to everyone to join in the celebration, and also gave those concerned in the underlying subterfuge enough time to put it all together. Jules had already thought of the perfect plan, so Sam and the twins were recruited to come up to support and spend some time with Jemmie and Essie, in order to give her some free time to organise it. The Tithe barn also received her first big booking; for the baptism reception, which was to be catered by Donna, who had been briefed and was all for it, and the unsuspecting Flynn.

All that remained now was for Jules to persuade Lizzie to take a very giant leap of faith.

Jules got her opportunity just a few days later when Lizzie came over to clean the house as usual.

Jules was at home by design that day and happily on Nanna duty while Jemmie went to get her hair and nails done in a local hotel spa for a mummies' treat with Sam.

The twins, also under the care of their grandparents for the day, had gone down to the lake to feed the ducks with their grandad.

Essie was on Jules' lap in the kitchen contentedly sucking on a bottle when Lizzie arrived; pausing as she took off her coat to stoop down and admire the baby that she had brought into the world. Once she had set about her usual tasks it wasn't very long before Jules, heading for the stairs for a nappy change, found her studying Paul's portrait of her that was in pride of place on the dining room wall as she polished the table below it; her right hand clasping the large yellow duster that had been rather aimlessly swirling on the same spot for several minutes. Caught neatly in the act, Lizzie bit her bottom lip and smiled shyly. 'I can't help it . . . It's just that you and Paul are always so happy together . . . and he obviously loves you so much . . . I . . . just never believed married couples could be as happy as you two . . . especially after . . . you know . . . your troubles . . .' she was blushing with embarrassment.

Jules smiled at her and shrugged slightly. 'We're not in a film Lizzie . . . we do have the occasional squabble you know . . . it's not all fairytales and roses . . . believe me. It's just that I can stand my ground better now . . .' But seeing the ideal opportunity to talk to her about the idea, she patted the back of a chair. 'Lizzie, come and sit down for a minute.' She added an encouraging smile for good measure. 'I want to talk to you about something.'

Instantly nervous and thinking she was about to get the sack or something, Lizzie left the duster and wiped her hands down the front of her tabard. Stepping over a prostrate Barney who always seemed to want to be where she was she sat down slightly wide-eyed at the table with her forearms outstretched in front of her and her hands clasped together.

Jules laid one hand on top of hers to put her at ease.

'You remember when I told you it hasn't always been this way with me and my husband . . . ?' she said quietly. Lizzie nodded. 'There was a time for me when . . . well, I was in a . . . dark place . . . a lot like you . . . . Paul left me for . . . He left me for someone that he thought was the answer to all his prayers . . .' she smiled, ironically raising one eyebrow slightly. 'And when that happened, I . . . completely lost all my self-confidence for a long time . . . just like you . . .'

Lizzie was looking down into her lap now and playing with the hem on her tabard. Jules lifted her chin up with the tips of her fingers so that she could look into her eyes.

'I wanted to run away from everything too . . . so I took myself off for some . . . anonymous . . .' She pulled a rueful face about the press coverage at the time, and Lizzie nodded to show that she understood.

'. . . some anonymous peace and quiet. So . . . I went to the South of France and stayed in a villa that was owned by . . .' She paused again and took a deep breath. 'Let's just say . . .' smiling a little private smile, 'a . . . a very wise man . . . called Michel. And he . . . helped me to rebuild my confidence when he told me something . . . something that I've always lived by since; so I want to share it with you. He told me that he believed . . . he believes . . . that *all* women are special . . . and are born to shine brightly and confidently that they are special . . . like diamonds . . .

no matter how they grow up to be—tall, short, big or small . . . But sometimes . . .' she ran her fingers down the side of Lizzie's face gently; 'sometimes . . . the things that happen in our lives make us lose our shine . . . and then it's like we are ordinary pebbles instead. And dusty pebbles can't shine . . . can they?'

'I . . . I'm not sure I really understand . . .'

'Nor did I at first . . . don't worry,' she chuckled. 'Anyway, basically, what it means is that . . . now you're how shall we put it? . . . . free to be yourself again . . . it's time for a little assistance from your friends . . . We want to help you learn how to value yourself again . . . as an intelligent and beautiful woman . . . to see yourself as you once were . . . before Len . . . and before everything that he did to you . . . *everything* that has happened to you in your life to make you how you are now.' Jules took a deep breath, knowing that Lizzie was now transfixed.

'Somewhere deep inside here,' she put her hand across Lizzie's heart: 'there's a shiny you . . . desperate to get out.'

Reaching into her tabard front pocket Lizzie pulled out a tissue and wiped at her eyes, taking a minute or two before she spoke very quietly. 'I . . . know exactly who you mean when you talk about the shiny me . . .' she said, her hands trembling as she played with the tissue. 'She's called Beth . . . not Lizzie . . .'

Jules' eyebrows knitted together in puzzlement as her head tilted to one side to look at her. 'My mum always called me Beth . . . until I met Len and he preferred Lizzie . . . said it suited me better . . .' Deciding to explain properly, for the first time in her adult life, exactly what had happened to her before she met Len; she sat herself back in her chair and took a breath.

'My life changed for ever when my mum died . . . when I was sixteen. My dad . . . drank . . . and he killed her . . . He went to prison for it. And when that happened, me and my older brother Kevin . . . we were moved away . . . away from all our friends and . . . everyone that I . . . that we . . . loved . . . and I was put in care with foster parents . . . Kevin is older so he was on his own and we got separated when he went to live in Australia . . . We still exchange Christmas cards and that . . . But it's not the same . . . so I had nobody then. My dad is dead now . . . he died years ago . . . he got Hep . . . Hep . . . something . . .' her eyes cast downwards briefly as she tried to think of the word.

'Hepatitis?'

'That was it . . .' she said. 'He got it from the drinking . . . and he died; an old neighbour I stayed in touch with wrote and told me . . . and so I wrote to Kevin and told him. But by then he was settled in Australia so he wasn't planning on coming back, and I could never afford for us to go there. So because it was safe I moved back this way, with Anna, and got a place in a hostel in Reading until I could get a job and find somewhere permanent to live. If I could change anything in my life for the better now Jules, I'd like to do it as Beth again . . . but . . . I don't know how I can . . . not now . . .'

'If you want to be Beth then I'm going to help you find her . . . deep inside you, that's all. The way my friend Michel helped me . . .'

Lizzie still looked wary.

'It's basically just a bit of makeover, don't panic!' she laughed, as she pushed an opened envelope across the table towards her.

'What's this . . . ?' she asked, taking it gingerly.

'Open it and see . . .' Jules said with a smile.

Lizzie slowly pulled out a piece of thick glossy paper. Reading it, with her eyes gradually widening, she suddenly looked up and gasped, 'I can't accept this!'

Jules' mouth widened into a huge grin of pleasure: 'Yes you can . . . You do this and you'll come back shining like a fairy Godmother for Essie and waving the Hope diamond at the end of your wand, trust me! There'll be no stopping you!'

It was a booking confirmation for a very swish health spa called The Sanctuary. Nestling in almost thirty acres of parkland near Bournemouth, Jules had bought her five days of relaxing and luscious pampering treatments, leading right up to the day of the baptism, to help Lizzie rediscover her sparkle. Lizzie's face was a picture of disbelief, but she was already worrying one cuff of her shabby blouse nervously.

Instantly reading her mind Jules continued; '. . . and before you go home today, I'm taking you clothes shopping . . .'

Lizzie started visibly and her eyes widened in horror. 'I couldn't let you buy me any new clothes . . .' She shook her head but stood up involuntarily. '. . . and I can't let Flynn down at this short notice today either . . . not over lunchtime . . . what about the food?'

Jules laughed and gave her a conspiratorial hug. 'He knows . . . I spoke to him yesterday. DeeDee and Donna are going to cover your shift for you . . .

Come on Lizzie . . . I'm just asking you to trust me!'

A couple of hours later Jules marched the very apprehensive Lizzie out of Paddington Station and hailed a passing black cab to the Brompton Road. Heading for the shopping experience of a lifetime in Harrods, with seven floors and 330 departments to explore, Lizzie had hardly said a word all the way, and as Jules reached into her bag for her purse to pay the driver once he'd pulled up outside, she paused for a moment, laying a comforting hand on Lizzie's shoulder. 'I know just how you're feeling . . . .' Jules rubbed at her shoulder encouragingly. 'Don't worry I felt just the same to start with . . . but honestly, it's the best fun if you just relax . . . Come on, there's no time like the present is there?' She jumped out of the cab enthusiastically and took Lizzie's hand as she slid across the seat to join her.

Entering the vast shop to the sounds of fifty different languages from the hoards of people walking by them, Jules began the shopping extravaganza by dragging Lizzie by the hand into the lift to the first floor to the lingerie department, and repeated Michel's words of wisdom to her when he took her shopping in Cannes. She did it in an exaggerated French accent for effect. *The best way to feel good about yourself from the minute to wake up in the morning is to feel a little silk lingerie against your naked body . . .* Well he is a Frenchman!' She whispered cheekily.

The French stick insect shop assistant took a bewildered Lizzie to the fitting room, not batting an elegant eyelash at the state of her current underwear once she'd finally plucked up the courage to strip off, and fitted her with a selection of luxurious matching silk bras and panties, the likes of which she had never seen in her life before, even in a magazine at the doctor's surgery or the dentist.

Jules had been quite dizzy with excitement for days at the prospect of kitting Lizzie out just as she had been with everything she needed to become reborn. They left the Lingerie department an hour later with four carrier bagfuls of underwear and night wear, before setting off a bit further across the first floor for the ladies shoes department.

From there they headed to explore five floors of clothing collections and handbags, and by then Lizzie hadn't stopped talking.

Five hours later the exhausted pair were sitting with their shoes surreptitiously off amidst a veritable mountain of carrier bags in the Terrace Bar enjoying superbly fattening afternoon tea.

'I can't begin the thank you for all this . . . I could never repay you . . .' Lizzie was talking with her mouth full of the most mouthwatering cucumber sandwich, still in a daze of disbelief as her eyes scanned the bags on the floor beside them.

'It's my pleasure, honestly.' Jules grinned, taking a sip of her tea from the daintiest of bone china cups. 'If I can help you to feel as good about yourself as Michel made me feel . . . then I'd do it again . . . ten times over for you Lizzie . . . after what you've been through . . . and after what you did for our Jemmie of course . . .'

Lizzie sat and pondered how different she had looked in all the gilt edged mirrors, trying on all of these lovely things. Then she blinked; the ghost of a fugitive smile crossing her lips. 'Nobody will recognise me when I come home from that health spa will they?' she said shyly, looking up at Jules through her lashes. 'Not in all these lovely things . . . Flynn won't even . . .'

Jules put her teacup down in its saucer and took hold of Lizzie's hand, squeezing it in a conspiratorial way, mentally conceding that her daughter was right. 'He won't stand a chance . . .' she winked.

Lizzie smiled and stared into her own lap, burning with embarrassment; Lizzie thought, like some naive teenager.

Laying a hand on her shoulder to make her look up again, Jules said; 'You're fond of Flynn, I think?'

Lizzie looked at her for a second as if trying to think how she should respond, before saying quietly; 'I . . . I do . . .' And when Jules said nothing, encouraging her to go on by her silence, she seemed to gain a little in courage, having said it out loud for the first time. '. . . I know . . . you'll think he's too good for me . . . and I can't think why he'd give me a second glance . . .'

'I think no such thing Lizzie Fidler . . . and neither should you . . .'

Lizzie smiled at how cross Jules looked on her behalf. '. . . and anyway people will think it's too soon . . . won't they?'

'Poppycock!' she chuckled, picking up the china teapot.

'. . . well . . . I can't help the way I feel can I?'

'No, you can't . . .' Jules smiled, refilling Lizzie's teacup. 'And neither can he . . . he cares for you, Lizzie, anyone can see it . . . He saved your life that night too, didn't he? Thundering across the road to save you from being run down like that . . . without a thought for his own safety . . .'

Lizzie was silent for a few seconds, before adjusting her sitting position excitedly and looking straight into Jules' eyes.

'You know when people say that about . . . what's it called . . . that *De já vu* thing? Where you know you've done something before? Well . . . it's like that with him for me . . . .' She took a deep breath inwards, struggling to find the right words, before letting it out again slowly.

'It feels like I've known *Flynn* before . . .'

'What do you mean exactly?' Jules' lips paused on the edge of her teacup.

'I mean when he looks at me sometimes . . . it feels like I've always known him . . . He . . . makes me feel like . . . me . . . the real me . . . And when I get that feeling . . . it's just like my life with L . . . Len . . . never even happened . . .'

Chapter twenty nine

The Sanctuary was an imposing, ivy covered stone building at the end of a mile long, tree lined drive, and bordered either side by a carpet of green lawns and pristine and colourful flower beds in full bloom. Lizzie's eyes were wide as she saw, to one side of the road, an immaculately flat croquet lawn where four very tanned and intimidatingly glamorous looking people were busy playing a game. A little further along, and on the opposite side of the road, many more people were either swimming in or lying around an outdoor swimming pool.

'Looks great, doesn't it?' Jules smiled at her.

Lizzie pulled self-consciously at the skirt of her new Chanel dress with matching jacket and adjusted her toes in her squeaky new Jimmy Choo sandals.

'Lovely . . .' she said quietly, as she realised with a swallow that the young couple holding hands that they'd just driven past she'd seen before: last night on the TV—playing bitter enemies in Eastenders.

'Now listen to me . . .' Jules said, pulling into a parking place in a sweep and crunch of deep gravel.

Seeing the look on her face, Jules took the plunge.

'Everyone staying here, whoever they are, or they think they are, is here because, for one reason or another, they want to get off the world and relax for a few days . . . just like you. There is no difference between you and them; and you're all paid up to be here, just like they are . . . In fact . . .' she smiled, 'you're paid up more than they are because, with a little help from Paul, who's been here several times, I booked their Premier suite for you . . .'

'Their *what*?' she gasped.

'. . . their very best suite! You've got champagne, enough fruit to start a shop, choccies on your pillow, and towels that are probably four inches thicker than mine in the bathroom . . . and Paul says you have a veranda overlooking that lake over there . . . So get that chin up proudly, and keep it up Lizzie . . . because this is going to be a week you'll never forget!'

*   *   *

Lizzie swallowed very hard as she saw Jules drive away with a wave of her hand out of the car window and, gripping the handles of Jules' two Louis Vuitton trolley bags, tried to implement her advice about looking confident, even when you don't feel it.

Sunglasses on . . . check. Head up . . . check. Stretch your back up from your ribs and hold your shoulders back to walk tall . . . check.

And smile . . . . check . . . . sort of.

As soon as she took her first step towards the revolving doors a smartly dressed porter; a young Latino looking boy, appeared through them with a welcoming smile to take her bags.

Wearing black trousers, shoes she could see her reflection in, and a crisp white shirt; he also sported an emerald green waistcoat with 'The Sanctuary' embroidered in gold thread on a little pocket that was about level with what she'd immediately noticed was an impressively protruding set of Pecs.

Politely asking her to follow him through the doors, he led the way into a large, marble floored reception area with a domed glass roof in its centre that was trailing plants all down the walls. There were more huge plants in pots too, and a square of plush red sofas and armchairs in the centre where several people were seated reading newspapers and magazines, or drinking tea or coffee. One or two of them glanced up briefly as she was led towards the reception desk, but soon went back to reading.

She was just another smartly dressed and stressed out executive arriving, after all.

After she had been efficiently checked in and her luggage had been loaded onto one of several shiny brass trolleys lined up along one wall, the Premier suite Concierge appeared to greet her from an office behind the reception desk.

Introducing himself as Steven, he was dressed in similar black trousers and crisp white shirt to the porter, but he had an air of seniority about him, and his waistcoat was ruby red instead of the green.

Pulling the trolley along behind him easily with one arm, he escorted her through many a backwards glance from other guests; all obviously settled into the daily routine and wearing thick white toweling robes with matching slippers; down a long and kingfisher blue carpeted corridor past a shop and an impressive looking boutique, and pointing out her closest dining room on the way.

They soon turned a sharp right that swept along a glass walled walkway; the carpet eventually changing both colour and depth from the blue to a deep red, by which time they had walked to the very end of another corridor overlooking the lake.

There was only one door down this end of the corridor, she observed with a slight gulp and, opening it with a jangle of keys, Steven stepped inside and held it open for her to almost tiptoe nervously past him for her first view of her home for the next five days.

First door on the right, just inside the suite, was the bathroom. It was easily as big as her sitting room had been at Hyacinth Close, with large, sand coloured tiles throughout, and it had a pristine white bathroom suite with a freestanding roll top bath and shiny brass taps. A mountain of thick and luxurious towels, just as Jules had predicted, greeted Lizzie's bewildered but excited eyes too.

The enormous bedroom had twin, queen sized beds with snow white duvets standing out crisply against the mint green walls, and the triple aspect was adorned with full length curtains all cascading into elegant piles at floor level. On one of the beds sat a large plastic bag containing her brand new robe, embossed in rich gold lettering on one side, just above chest height, with *'The Sanctuary,'* and some matching slippers, . . . and the sharp eyed Lizzie immediately noticed that all the other, non Premier Suite, robes she'd just seen, had their lettering embroidered in dark green.

In the sitting room a white leather corner sofa with mint and black patterned cushions stood to one side of a set of doors that opened out onto a wide, semi circular sweep of veranda, overlooking the lake at the far end of the building. To the other side of the room sat a large entertainment centre with a plasma TV, and what looked like a Blueray player and some kind of expensive music playing set up.

'If you could see me now, Len Fidler . . .' she thought, with a gulp of disbelief, as one hand shakily removed an escaping hair from her eyes.

On the coffee table there was an envelope containing, Steven explained, her treatments timetable for her stay, and a list of organised trips and activities that she might like to be involved in too.

Once he'd finished showing her around the suite, Steven opened the champagne for her, pouring out an elegant glass flute, before taking it to her on a little silver tray, accompanied by a glass dish of fresh strawberries as she took advantage of the sunny early afternoon to sit outside.

And then he left her.

Once alone, Lizzie kicked off her shoes, took her champagne, and wandered down to the waters edge, raising her glass to her own reflection in the water.

'Here's to you Beth Edwards . . .' she whispered, and smiled a real smile for the first time in months.

Turning around to look back towards the suite she nodded contentedly.

I think I'm going to enjoy this . . . .' she said, to an inquisitive squirrel.

Chapter thirty

Flynn meanwhile, wondering how on earth he was going to tell her his secret and, needing something to take his mind off it, had set his mind on tracing her missing daughter.

He'd spent every available moment over the last three days secretly trawling the available information on the internet, and then hours on the telephone contacting the seventeen Anna Fidlers he found living locally, but none of them checked out based on what Jules Taylor had told him Lizzie had said.

He'd drawn a complete blank.

In the pub that evening Flynn gave Danny the disappointing news.

'Anna *Fidler*?' Danny said incredulously. 'She's not called Anna Fidler, Flynn, that's why!' he said with a grin. 'She never had Len's name . . . he never wanted her enough and she knew it. They never got on at all. She's Anna Edwards.'

'Edwards . . . ?' he said with a gulp.

'Yeah . . . Mum had her before she was married. I thought I'd said that . . . sorry . . .'

'No . . . you just said you had a sister so . . . I assumed . . .'

'No mate . . . she was four when my mum married Len, so she's just my half sister really . . . We don't look much alike either . . . I got my gypsy black hair from his side of the family . . . and she's got lovely red hair . . . a real head turner she is. My mum had her when she was younger than me . . . Some boyfriend she'd had but lost touch with. Sad really . . . she told me once she'd really loved him but never even got a chance to tell him she was pregnant . . .'

Danny picked up the two pints of beer that Flynn had just pulled and turned away to join Tindy at a table by the door.

Flynn turned away from his gaze to draw himself a shot of brandy from an optic on the wall behind him, taking a generous swallow.

His hands were shaking.

*   *   *

After a sleepless night and almost too nervous of what he was going to discover, Flynn tried the computer again.

Mercifully there were only two women called Anna Edwards listed as still living in the area, and one of them was far too old to fit the bill. He found the other one mentioned in more detail on a Google search as being a company director in a small computer software company in Newbury.

The only other director listed was called Philip Chamberlain; her last known boyfriend.

Bingo.

After over an hour of wearing out the bedroom carpet pontificating, Flynn called her office number and asked to speak to her and, twenty minutes later, he disconnected the call on his mobile phone with a smile. Standing up quickly, he clapped his hands together with a whistle as he grabbed his car keys from the hook by the back door; now desperate to find out, one way or another.

'Donna, love . . . I've got to nip out for an hour . . . . ok?' he yelled through the door to the bar, where she was in mid flow at a large table with four of the former protesters; now excitedly discussing their plans with her for the new discovery centre.

Just before closing time, the pub was otherwise empty.

Sally Breach

'Fine . . . .' She said, looking up briefly, and then in an afterthought she called after him. 'Oh . . . Flynn? If you're going to the cash and carry we're almost out of cheese and onion crisps . . .'

'I'm not . . .' he shouted back, with the side door already open. 'More on a bit of a mission actually . . . Tell you more later on!' and with a shout he was gone.

*   *   *

She had arranged to meet him in Victoria Park. She checked her watch again, adjusted her hair and her straight from work suit a little self consciously, and pushed the swing again. She felt overdressed and uncomfortable compared to everyone else there, all in their jeans and t shirts.

And she was here far too early, she knew it. But at least Daniel was enjoying himself, fresh from the child minders and delighted to see his mummy so much earlier than usual, and now kicking his little legs and arms on the baby swing, chucking with glee. She glanced around her; watching, not knowing who to look for or how to pick him out among everyone else, and wondering if she could even pick out somebody Irish just by his looks.

Where should she wait? Here? Not sure . . . she cursed herself for not being more specific with him on the phone.

The sound of the hatch going up at the little café drew her attention for a moment. Then the door at the side of the shop opened and the usual man appeared and began putting out a few tables and chairs. Slightly beyond the realms of middle age, he was a cheerful character, not very tall, a bit thin on top though well disguised with a bit of effort with his comb, and his rather impressive stomach was, as usual, encased in a long blue apron. Seeing her at the swings, he smiled and waved across to her, and she lifted an arm briefly in reply.

She was a real looker, that Anna he thought; tall, red headed . . . and feisty too; easily remembered. She'd given him as good as she'd got when he'd tried chatting her up that time . . . .

He hoped that she would come over and see him again, and pointedly lifted a basket of those little boxes of California raisins from under the counter that he knew she always bought for her little boy.

She checked her watch again. Still fifteen minutes, she realised with an impatient sigh, and continued to watch him as he now began setting out his shop, bringing up those little baskets of things from underneath the counter.

Once she could see he was properly open for business and deciding that a nice mug of tea would be just the thing to calm her down, she pulled the swing to a gentle stop and lifted Daniel out, pulling him up to her face for a kiss and a cuddle as his little arms went around her and his head rested against her neck happily.

Maybe the café was the more obvious place to wait anyway.

Flynn took his ticket from the machine and pulled into an available parking space in the Parkway underground car park. Checking his watch, he pulled at his rear view mirror and, for some reason, checked his hair. Leaving the car park on foot his eyes quickly scanned the park railings and located the gates, and on seeing the size of the park he swore under his breath at regretting to arrange where they should actually meet up. Just 'in Victoria Park' she'd said . . .

He could see from here there were lone women with children all over the place; playing with footballs and little tennis racquets, walking dogs, sitting on blankets and eating picnics . . . mothers sitting with other mothers . . . everywhere.

Then he remembered how her brother had described her; '*a real head turner with red hair . . .*' and silently prayed that she hadn't died it since he'd last seen her all those years ago.

He put his hands in his pockets to stop them shaking and walked purposefully through the gates, taking a deep breath and looking around the park for likely looking mother and child combinations, and trying not to look like a paedophile eyeing up the children. Seeing the playground come into view across the tennis courts, he headed in that direction and paused briefly by a young redhead with a little boy throwing bread inaccurately to the ducks in the concrete walled pond. Her eyes met his and he smiled slightly, but she looked quickly away and pulled her child closer to her body suspiciously.

Not her then.

Two more similar brief encounters had him retreating for the café, where he purchased a very welcome mug of steaming coffee and took a sip as he looked around for a free table.

Then he caught his breath sharply as he met his own eyes in a face that was otherwise an absolute blend of the both of them, looking straight at him.

Now he'd have to tell Lizzie his secret . . . so she could tell him hers.

* * *

Danny passed Hannah her glass of diet Coke and sat down at the table. 'What time did Flynn say be here?' he said, taking a long draught of his beer and carefully putting the glass down on its little cardboard coaster.

'Six thirty . . . don't worry it's only twenty past now . . .'

'Can't think what's so important . . .' he said quietly, pulling the curtain to one side and peering out into the car park, before swallowing a lump in his throat the size of a golf ball.

Hector and Dizzy were out in the beer garden with Paul and Jules and their family too, enjoying the rare treat of a quiet meal after the baptism rehearsal, as all the children played on the swings and Tesco pushed Essie's pushchair around the garden to keep her happy. Flynn's van pulled into the pub car park a couple of minutes later, closely followed by a second car that pulled in next to him, and Flynn stood by it for a moment waiting for the occupants to emerge. Dizzy and Jules were among the group of people that had their backs to them, and in the absence of much else to contemplate Paul was watching the children, so it was Hector who was watching Flynn curiously.

'Who's that he's got there with him then?' He said nosily, putting down his glass of shandy and wiping his mouth on the sleeve of his cardigan.

Dizzy and Jules turned around to see a well dressed young couple get out of their car, and as the man reached into the back of it to bring out a small child; presumably their little son.

'No idea . . .' Dizzy said turning to face her, but immediately struck by the young woman's striking red hair she turned back again. 'Jules . . . you don't think . . . .'

'It has to be . . . . He must have tracked her down . . . She looks just like her . . . apart from the hair . . .'

'Like who . . . ?' Paul said, turning around to see.

They'd all gone in the bar by now and, hearing a bit of a commotion coming from inside, curiosity got the better of all of them, so they went to investigate leaving Martin to watch over the children.

To find the young woman in floods of tears and wrapped very tightly in the arms of Danny Fidler.

* * *

'I think you must be Anna!' Jules said, putting out her right arm to shake hands once her brother had finally let her go.

Anna took it and shook her hand warmly.

'This is Mrs Taylor . . .' said Danny breathlessly. 'And this is Dizzy . . . and Hector. Mum delivered Mrs Taylor's daughter's baby on her own Anna . . . and . . . this is Jemmie . . . Dr Ryan I mean . . . and . . . um?' he faltered in his enthusiastic introductions, having never met the rest of Jules' family.

'This is my son Marcus . . . and his wife Sam . . .' said Jules, pulling them forward. 'And this . . . this is my husband, Paul . . .'

Anna gulped as she recognised him but quickly regained her control. 'It's lovely to meet you all . . .' she said with a smile.

She was well spoken, her air every bit the successful businesswoman, and Jules smiled to herself, knowing how proud her mother was going to be of her.

'We're here for little Esther's baptism tomorrow afternoon . . .' Sam said. 'And your mum is to be a Godmother Anna . . .'

'Flynn told me . . .' she said. 'He also told me you'd treated her to a few days on a health farm too . . . to get ready for it . . . that was nice of you . . . Mrs Taylor . . .'

Jules nodded. 'Jules, please . . . just a sort of thank you . . . for what she did . . . and to help her to get . . . .'

'Get over it . . . yes . . . I know . . . I read about the case in the paper . . . somebody left one on a bench on the railway platform on Reading Station . . . I read it . . . on the way back from a business trip to Holland.'

'But you didn't . . . feel you could come . . .'

'I wanted to . . . but after all this time . . . I didn't quite know how . . . I thought she wouldn't want me to come to her after . . . the way I ran away and abandoned her to her fate that night . . . the night Len tried to . . . .' She stopped and caught her breath slightly. 'I thought maybe it was just too late . . . all water under the bridge, you know? But then Flynn rang me out of the blue . . .

and told me how much she still misses me . . . and Danny here too . . . . so . . . Here I am . . .'

'Here you are . . .' said Danny incredulously.

'And who's this little one?' Anxious to change the subject before it got emotionally too much for her in the public bar, Hannah bent down and took the hand of Anna's son, shaking it slightly as he gripped her, and kissing the tips of his little fingers.

'This is Daniel . . .' said Philip with a proud smile. 'Our son Daniel . . .'

'You called him Daniel . . . ?' Danny said, turning to his sister with a blink.

She nodded and smiled a little bashfully. 'We couldn't call him anything else. I never told you this before Dan but . . . My earliest memory of you was peeping into the bedroom to see you on the night you were born. I was about six, it was twenty past two in the morning, and mum would have thought I was fast asleep . . . but I had crept out of bed to see what all the noise was.

I peeped round her bedroom door to see her there, sitting up in the bed, holding you. The midwife was there too, but her back was to you both as she put her things away . . . and Len was nowhere to be seen, I remember. Most probably drunk in a ditch somewhere . . .

Anyway, Mum was breast feeding you . . .' she smiled. 'I never saw anything like that in my life before.

I had no idea about babies or where they came from, I was too little . . . . and I was both wide eyed in shock, and totally transfixed by it. Then the midwife saw me hiding there and took me by the hand to tiptoe in and meet my new baby brother . . . Me in my little Ladybird dressing gown and matching slippers . . .' she laughed.

Danny grinned and put his arm around her shoulders, and all those gathered around her were silent as they listened to her story.

'. . . Mum didn't see me at first because she was so absorbed. Her face, Dan, it showed a look of such tender love . . . a mother's love . . . for you . . . that I never forgot it; not ever. Then, on the night after Daniel was born, and when Philip had gone home for some sleep . . . It was about that same time in the night when I was sitting up in bed feeding my new baby, and as I changed sides . . . I caught sight of my own reflection in the window next to my hospital bed . . . And I saw that very same look on my own face.' A single tear crept down her cheek as she caught her breath and swallowed.

'After that I explained to Philip that he had to be called Daniel . . . after you . . .'

Chapter thirty one

Getting a lot less self conscious in her anonymous white robe and slippers, and therefore able to really enjoy her daily pamper sessions that had so far included back neck and shoulder massage, a facial, some very smelly but rejuvenating body wraps, something called hot stone therapy, and an hysterical hydrotherapy session being at the wet end of a powerful spray jet hose; Lizzie was thoroughly enjoying her stay at the Sanctuary.

She had been asked if she would like to sit at a shared table when she arrived and had been having all her meals with the same three other women; all there by themselves and therefore willing to be open and friendly rather than eat alone. Though nervous at first sight of three women knew she would never get to spend time with on equal terms in her normal life, she was now happily getting to know them as soon

323

as she'd realised that they had no idea who she was either, or where she'd come from; a fact she was actually finding quite exhilarating.

They were Fiona, an IT consultant with her own company in London, who was wafer thin, tall, and ironed to within and inch of her life; but she had a giggle to set anyone off, and knew more swear words than even Lizzie had ever heard before.

Steph was a thirty something top rank hair stylist who Lizzie instantly hit it off with after introducing herself to her as Lizzie, Lizzie Fidler, which had stuck: Steph had worked with most of the glossy magazines, but had a shock of hair of a colour herself that God certainly hadn't thought of.

The last of the trio was Daphne, a glamorous great grandmother of at least eighty five who called everybody *dah-ling,* and who Lizzie could hear coming in her kitten heels at fifty paces before she even entered the dining room. Daphne was definitely the wealthiest of the three. Self described as a former Hollywood 'B list' starlet, she was positively dripping in bling and lipstick the colour of Satsuma's, and modestly described herself as '*never having reached higher than the echelons of second chorus girl to the right, but I married well.*'

She promptly proved this claim by pointing herself out as one of the chorus girls wafting tulle across the back of the stage in an old musical on the TV in the residents' lounge on their first evening together. Very obviously her; as Gene Kelly and actress she didn't recognise tapped and leapt at centre front of the huge screen, she had shrieked; 'O*h my dear GOD! Look Dahhhlings that's me!*'

. . . She also had blood red finger nails at least an inch long that made Lizzie think of Cruella Deville from 101 Dalmatians.

Surrounded by such rich characters, Lizzie had decided to reinvent her story rather than tell them her sorry tale. So she'd been treated to her stay at the Sanctuary by Paul Taylor's wife, a great friend of hers, (so far true, even if she was her cleaner . . .) after her marriage had ended recently. She had come for a few days rest and relaxation, to get pampered, recharge her batteries, and get ready to face the world again. Adding, with a surprising flash of wickedness, that she wanted to knock the man of her dreams off his feet at the same time, to get him to notice her existence . . . . This seemed to convince them easily enough, especially Steph, who instantly made it her mission in life to help by restyling her hair, to which Lizzie only agreed after being reassured that she wouldn't end up with anything like the colour of hers.

*　　*　　*

325

Lizzie's last morning at the spa was the day of Essie's baptism, and having persuaded the manager of the salon to let her have free run of the place, Steph set about sorting out Lizzie's hair with absolutely no idea of its sorry history.

Making a start by having shampooed and conditioned it she rubbed her hair vigorously with a fluffy yellow towel, dropping it into the chair beside her, and straightened her chair in front of the mirror. Then, taking a comb in one hand, she began to comb out the hair with a flourish and creating a neat parting down the centre.

Fiona, sitting on a tall stool and flicking through a glossy hairdressing magazine, stopped chewing a free toffee momentarily and turned the magazine round to show Lizzie a photograph of a young model with a huge scarlet pout and a mass of blonde frizz.

'Not on your life!' she laughed, wincing as Steph caught a tangle with her comb.

'Well honestly Lizzie . . .' Fiona said. 'You need something to cheer you up . . . you'll never catch his eye like this . . .' she said kindly. 'Don't get me wrong hun . . . but your hair takes layers to a whole new level . . . it looks like someone's been at it with the kitchen scissors or something . . .'

Lizzie swallowed and involuntarily looked away from her scrutiny. Her instant change of expression in the mirror did not escape Steph, who had not been a hairstylist for as long as she had without learning a thing or two about recognising victims, quickly continued: 'Some of these high street salons should be shut down for the way they cut hair you know . . .' and began to expertly pin Lizzie's wet hair up in sections with the aid of a handful of clips she'd attached to the hem of her t shirt.

Daphne stopped examining her faultless manicure for a moment and joined in. 'I see you more as a redhead . . . like Rita Hayworth . . .'

'No dye . . . I said no dye . . .' Lizzie said, suddenly looking up into the mirror again. 'I said you can style it, Steph . . . that's all!'

'I think it suits her this shade of blonde . . .' said Steph, her head to one side critically, 'but maybe a few strawberry lowlights would be good . . . give it a bit more depth . . . without it being too much . . . ?'

'What's a lowlight when it's a home?' Lizzie looked wary.

'Just a few thin strands done in a complimentary colour to your own . . .' she said reassuringly. 'We call them highlights if they lighten the colour and lowlights if they darken it . . .'

Fiona crossed her elegant legs again and turned her magazine round to face Lizzie once more, this time with a photograph that illustrated what Steph meant.

'I quite like that effect . . .' Lizzie said carefully. 'I quite like that style too . . . my hair is still quite short . . .

and its short enough to copy it . . . isn't it Steph?' it was a photograph of a woman similar in age to Lizzie, and her hair was an updated version of the classic bob cut, neatly layered to show off the shades of colour, and swept over to one side, slightly over one eye.

Steph took the magazine from Fiona and studied the photograph with her expert eyes, every now and again tilting Lizzie's head from side to side using her chin to steer it, as if imagining the style on her. Finally she nodded.

'I think we can do something like this . . . but maybe do you a bit of a fringe instead . . . get rid of these wispy bits that aren't quite long enough to do it like it is in the photograph . . . what do you think?'

'I think I like it . . .' Lizzie smiled at her in the mirror.

'Lowlights too?'

'Lowlights too . . . if you must . . .'

'No, Lizzie, *you* must . . .' she grinned.

'Trust her Lizzie . . .' Daphne said, rubbing Lizzie's arm to instill some confidence. 'A woman's hair is her crowning glory . . . She's going to make you look and feel fabulous once and for all . . . Dahling . . . .'

Chapter thirty two

Back in her room a couple of hours later, Lizzie zipped up her last bag, turned, and indulged in one final look in the mirror, and checked her watch before meeting her cab at reception in a few minutes. Excited more than she had ever been in her life; she knew she looked absolutely amazing.

Adding volume and density to a head of hair that looked a million miles away from the butchered scalp of the previous few months, the lowlights had done just as Steph had promised, taking years off her appearance simply with a clever haircut. The short style framed her pretty face perfectly, now totally devoid of worry lines thanks to a week of pampering, and the salon beautician's clever application of makeup.

With Daphne's help she had chosen one of the floaty Karen Mirren outfits that Jules had picked out for her, to wear to the baptism. It was a summer dress in a pastel shade of rusty red, with a matching jacket that brought out the lowlights in her hair brilliantly. It had a fawn coloured belt that complimented her heels and bag, and around her neck sat a necklace that Daphne had bought her from the Sanctuary gift shop. It looked like gold pebbles that caught the light and twinkled in the overhead light above the mirror, and its irony was not lost on Lizzie one bit.

'Twinkle twinkle shiny pebble . . .' she said, fingering the necklace one last time, and checked her watch once more.

Time to go.

A soft tap at the door hailed the arrival of Steven the concierge who had come to collect her luggage. Following him back the way she had come what seemed like months beforehand, and now knew so well, with sunglasses resting on the top of her glossy head instead of on her nose Lizzie now felt confident enough to stride forth without hiding behind them now. Her three friends were waiting on the plush red sofas under the sunroof in the reception area as she arrived there, all with their own bags and ready to go too. She twirled around to their whoops of joy as the hem of her skirt lifted above her knees to show off her newly waxed and San Tropez bronzed legs, and Fiona took her in her arms and gave her a tight hug.

One of the smartly dressed receptionists appeared at their sofa. 'Taxis for Miss Leighton and Mrs Goldwyn . . . .' she said cheerfully.

'That's me . . .' said Fiona from the depths of Lizzie's new hair. 'That's my cab for the station.'

'And me dahlings . . .' said Daphne, jangling her bling virtually from head to toe as she jumped up off the sofa with the ease of a woman half her age. 'That's my cab; all the way home . . .'

'You don't think she really married *That* Goldwyn . . . he as in MGM studios . . . ?' said Steph, pulling Lizzie back down with a conspiratorial whisper as the other two departed, chatting away about taxi drivers like they'd known each other for years.

'Well she did say she married well . . . .' said Lizzie with a grin, following Steph's gaze.

'Blimey . . . .' She laughed. 'A bit of a dark horse, that one . . . wasn't she?'

'She certainly was . . .' said Lizzie, stretching slightly to peer farther out of the door to see Daphne issuing orders to her taxi driver about her mountain of expensive suitcases.

'Bit like you, really Lizzie . . . ?'

Lizzie turned and looked into the eyes of her new best friend, and knew the game was up. She took a deep breath. 'OK . . . here it is . . .' she said with a sigh. 'He didn't leave me . . . my husband . . . he died . . . Crashed into some farm machinery on a dark lane trying to escape the police . . . after beating me up for the thousandth time and then hacking off my hair, with the kitchen scissors, as Fiona so rightly pointed out . . . and then he tried to kill me by running me down in a stolen van . . . .'

Steph blinked a few times and swallowed hard, simply putting one hand on Lizzie's shoulder as she squeezed it slightly.

'Don't cry for me Steph. He's not worth it. Worst of all . . . he cost me my relationship with my daughter . . . And all I really want to do . . . is go and find her now . . . and bring her home . . .' she said simply.

And as she spoke each word, the truth of it all hit her, and tears sprang to her own eyes before she knew it.

'Hey . . . hey . . . . don't cry Lizzie, Lizzie Fidler . . . you'll wreck your makeup . . . and I'll wreck mine . . . !'

'I'm not Lizzie, Lizzie Fidler either, really Steph . . .' she said, taking a calming breath and wiping her own tears away with a single swipe from two fingers. 'He preferred Lizzie so that's what he called me. I was Beth before . . . so now I want to be Beth again . . . Beth . . . Beth Edwards . . . that's who I really am . . . .'

'Ok Beth, Beth Edwards . . . then that's who you shall be . . . from today . . .' she smiled.

'Taxi for Miss Potter?' said the receptionist again, a few short minutes later.

'That would be me . . .' said Steph, standing up decisively. Taking Beth into her arms she held on tightly for a few moments, and then released her. 'While we're on the subject of confessions . . . I've just ended a going nowhere relationship with a married man and was here to sort out my head . . . So I'll be off men for a while. Or at least until I find one that can be mine, and just mine.

You have my mobile number and my email address, Beth, and I want you to promise me you'll keep in touch . . . because I want to meet up with you . . . and meet that daughter of yours . . . when you find her . . . understood . . . ?'

Beth nodded and hugged her back, before reaching down to grab the handle of her trolley bag.

'So who's coming for you then . . . the best friend . . . ?' Steph continued.

Beth smiled and looked down at her bag. 'No, I'm waiting for a taxi, like you. I'm on my way to her grandaughter's christening from here . . . the grandaughter that I delivered actually . . . But that's another story . . . . She's a friend certainly . . . the lady that paid for me to come here . . . but . . . well . . . that's another thing . . . I'm actually her cleaner . . .' she said, 'She sent me here to find my own sparkle . . .'

'Nothing wrong with cleaning, love . . .' Steph said affectionately. 'Besides, who am I to argue? I wash other people's hair for a living . . . I could tell you some pretty grimy stories too . . . But you've certainly found your sparkle . . .' she laughed.

*   *   *

A little over an hour later, the now to be known as Beth's taxi pulled up outside the church and she climbed out just in time to meet Dizzy coming out of the south door, checking her watch anxiously, to find her. Everyone else was inside and ready to begin the service.

'Lizzie!!' she exclaimed, stopping abruptly, with the breath totally knocked out of her, at the vision of shining confidence standing before her, straightening her dress and primping her hair.

Beth laughed and hugged her tightly with genuine warmth. 'I found my MoJo Dizzy . . . and my MoJo was me all the time . . . Beth . . . That's my real name . . . what I used to be called before Len . . . and I want to be known as again Beth now . . . Do you think that's ok?'

'It's more than ok with me . . .' she laughed, taking her arm and leading her into the church. 'Jemmie tells me you've never been baptised?'

'No, I haven't. My parents weren't churchgoers . . . they didn't really see the point.'

'Well if you're going to be a Godmother to Essie you'll have to be . . . So here's an idea . . . While we're baptising her . . . let's make it official for you too shall we . . . ?'

Chapter thirty three

Up at the Tithe barn Philip was helping Donna, along with Danny and Hannah, to put the finishing touches to the reception tables while Flynn and Anna were behind the bar getting to know each other better as they lined up a regiment of champagne bottles. They were getting along famously, Danny thought, looking over at them with a grin. She could certainly pass for being Irish . . . with that red hair of hers . . . and so like his too. They could even be mistaken for father and daughter if people didn't know better.

The plan to get Anna reunited with her mother was that all six of them were now smartly dressed as catering staff, and the barn itself looked magnificent, sparklingly new and still smelling of paint; holding its first function in many decades.

The plan to get Flynn and Beth together had been put on hold in light of recent events . . . but Jemmie and Jules' first sight of her in the church had left them very encouraged that that part might well look after itself at the same time . . . Unaware of what he was about to witness himself, Flynn checked his watch and gave Anna another hug. 'They should all be here any time now my love . . . you ready? You know the plan?' she nodded and turned to Danny, taking his hand and gripping it tightly.

'You ok?' he asked, kissing the top of her head. She nodded nervously, and worried at the nail on her left thumb in a gesture that jolted Flynn because once again, it struck him just how much she looked like her mother.

'Don't worry sis . . . she'll be blown away when she sees you . . .'

'And finds out she's a grandmother . . .' she said with a nervous giggle. 'Where's Daniel did you say?'

'Philip took him to the crèche in the back room . . . he's fine in there with the rest of the Taylor brood . . . and the Hardy-Mitchell's . . . Amy and her mum are running it . . . if Batty lets them . . .'

The sound of car doors banging outside in the car park and an absolute wave of chattering coming through the open doors heralded the arrival of the guests, and for several minutes the bar was a chaotic buzz of popping corks and laughter as the Bucks Fizz glasses chinked together in celebration. Now and again

337

Anna would glance across the room towards Danny, who was on sentry duty for their mother's arrival, but time and again he shook his head until finally, she looked up and saw him smiling, nodding discreetly at her while talking animatedly to a woman who couldn't possibly be their mum. Anna looked around for her again, but failing to see her anywhere, looked back at Danny, who was still grinning. Standing in front of him and with her back to the bar stood a tall, elegant woman in heels, wearing a stunning rust dress that fell just below the knee in elegant folds, and a jacket that must have cost a fortune. Looking harder, Anna knew she couldn't possibly be the downtrodden victim that Anna had last seen more than ten years ago, trying so hard to protect her from her step father by taking the abuse herself. The breath caught in her throat, and beside her, the breath caught in Flynn's, as he saw what she just had.

Taking her arm, he took the tray of glasses that she was shaking far too much to hold, and guided her towards her mother. Taking his cue, Danny took Beth's arm and led her out into the sunshine where it was more quiet, and over to the elegant fountain that had just been installed, and waited.

'Mum . . . you look amazing . . .' he said nervously. 'I can't believe it's you . . . honest . . . and fancy Hector re naming you Beth . . . that's so cool . . . makes it official like . . . . I like it . . . it suits you better now you look . . . so different . . . .'

'I'm still me my love . . .' she laughed, running her fingers down the side of his face. 'And I was thinking when I was away . . . now I'm feeling so much better . . . and we're all settled in at the cottage and everything . . . I was thinking . . . it's time . . . it's time we started looking for Anna . . . ?'

'A . . . glass of champagne for you madam?'

Beth turned and looked into the eyes of the waitress that had quietly crept up behind her, with Flynn at her elbow. She took the glass from the shaking hand momentarily, and then looked into the girl's eyes and gulped, looking first from one of them, and then back to other.

Taking her daughter in her arms as Anna dissolved into tears, Beth saw Flynn over her daughter's shoulder and for the first time, that unmistakable resemblance between the two pairs of eyes. The years finally fell away, allowing her to see him for who he really was.

Flynn turned away from her gaze to hide his own feelings and began to walk away, to leave the family to their reunion in peace.

'Not so fast Paddy Flynn . . . .' said Beth with a shaking voice, kissing Anna's face and taking her hand to hold onto for support.

Flynn's head turned back towards her as if on elastic. 'What did you say . . . ?' he said, with a gulp of his own.

Stepping forward though still holding Anna's hand, unable and unwilling to let her go again, she took hold of Flynn's hand with her free one. 'I said . . . not so fast . . . Paddy Flynn . . . I've got a bone to pick with you . . . .'

'You mean . . . it was him . . . all this time . . . ?' said Danny, realising the significance of what had just happened.

'What's going on, Mum . . . ?' said Anna.

'Well, well, well . . .' said Danny. 'This is so cool . . . . It's certainly a day for family reunions all right Anna . . .'

As Beth finally let go of her daughter so that she could allow Flynn to finally scoop her into his arms, Danny put his arm around his sister's shoulders and laughed at her expression. 'Brace your self sis . . .' he laughed. 'I think you just got reunited with *both* your parents . . .'

There was a long pause as a blackbird sang blithely from the willow near the lake. The sound of music and laugher drifted out from the barn, and the long grass shimmered in the breeze.

'Mum . . . is Flynn my Dad? Are you really saying . . . ?'

Danny took her by the hand and led her away. 'Let's give them a minute . . . we've got all the time in the world to play happy families now . . .'

The End

Epilogue

After Flynn told him the story of the double entry on the war memorial in the churchyard, Sir Christopher had taken the case to his heart and tracked down Jimmy Knapp's brother Wilf's grave for him, via the Commonwealth War graves Commission, to a tiny little war cemetery in Normandy, actually not far from their holiday house in Colouvray Boisbenatre. Then he had taken Jimmy over to visit him at last, and when Jimmie died peacefully in his sleep a few months later, his ashes were interred with his much loved half brother, in the corner of that foreign field where he'd been laid to rest in 1944.

Wilf's campaign medals were buried with him.

As well as losing such a memorable character in the village, the parish of Frincham with Yattley has changed an awful lot since the events of last year.

343

The park has opened and is proving to be a huge success. Beyond any of their wildest dreams, it is pulling the whole community together and brought in many thousands of visitors in its first year for the regular attractions. These include the Birds of Prey displays, donkey rides, tractor trailer rides to see the Fallow deer, a seasonal Butterfly safari, Early Bird dawn chorus and bird watching walks with Mark Jones, and migrant birds hide workshops with local members of the RSPB. River studies bring in schools and students from the local agricultural college to monitor habitat management, pollution protection, and the biological life of the river. There is pond dipping for younger visitors studying their national curriculum mini beasts, and volunteers from the village have discovered new keep fit regimes by holding team challenges such as invasive species clearance and path creation and management.

The Tithe barn is proving to be a hugely popular venue for all kinds of events and meetings for everything from wedding receptions and corporate events to church socials and Scout and Guide jamborees too.

After his boys decided to follow their own hearts Ernie Jones decided to retire and Stanton Farm has become part of the park project as well. Not that he has retired in reality of course, as the farm is now part of the attractions. Turning 100% organic with Ernie predominantly at the helm but the park footing his bills, heavy horses and other traditional farming methods are now used and are on show each day for the coach loads of visitors who come from miles away. In keeping with its original plans, these visitors arrive through the strictly advertised route from the motorway exit at Chieveley, and are then directed by big brown signs into the park without disturbing the peace of any of the local villages.

On the farm, National sheep dog trials, sheep shearing competitions, and feeding the lambs crop up seasonally, and a market garden has also been set up down there to provide fresh produce all year round for the park restaurant and Tithe barn; and for the ever popular farm shop that has also moved to the entrance/exit to the Park. Matthew and Mark Jones still work park time on the farm to lend their father a hand, but most of the labour force comes from the students at the agricultural colleges in Reading and Winchester, that are boosted by an annual influx of other students to help with the un-mechanized harvest; boosting the local economy further by frequenting the pub whilst camping at the park, or staying in local B & B's.

The majestic Tindy went home to Africa to take up his role as head of his tribe following the death of his father soon after the park opened. After a very tearful goodbye at Heathrow airport, DeeDee returned to the park but was disconsolate and quiet for weeks despite her cousin's attempts to cheer her up before leaving for university herself to study business management. After Hannah had gone, DeeDee became a bit of a workaholic at the park, regularly clocking up seventeen or eighteen hour days and burying herself in her work rather than think about her lost love. Her uncle, keeping a keen and watchful eye, was becoming worried that she was in danger of losing her feisty spirit for ever.

Unlike his niece however, he was secretly nurturing high hopes for DeeDee's love life. Often in her office he had soon noticed the frequency of Matthew Jones' visits for little if any reason, and the way he surreptitiously watched her at every opportunity. So to set things in motion in that department he suggested to the unsuspecting DeeDee that she get out from behind her computer screen and spend more time out in the fresh air in order to get some colour back in her cheeks. He encouraged her to help Matthew with the birds of prey displays in the show ring by taking over the commentary that he hated, and it showed. He of course had jumped at the idea, and so after a couple of afternoons in his company learning the ropes, DeeDee's educated voice was soon to be heard twice daily over the park sound system introducing each bird by name to the audience and providing a running commentary to their displays.

Before very long, (and specifically dated to one very hot day when he took his shirt off while setting up), DeeDee found herself dreaming less of Tindy at night, and more of Matthew's biceps and tanned farmer's shoulders, as well as his beautiful birds.

Matthew got his chance one morning in the aviary barn while they were returning the birds after their first display of the day. Frey the huge Eagle Owl fluttered his wings with excitement as usual when DeeDee let him go, but he had perched himself on a tree branch very near the floor so he sent up a cloud of dust and wood shavings into her face, setting her off coughing instantly, and before she could close them a speck of dust firmly imbedded itself in her left eye. Yelping in pain her hand shot up to protect herself as Matthew pulled her back out of the aviary and shut the door behind her. Taking her face in his huge hands, she looked up at him, blinking wildly and, though his hand was shaking, with as much tenderness as he could muster in the circumstances he gently removed the speck on the corner of a tissue from his pocket.

Wiping away a tear from her watery eye, she became acutely aware of how close they were standing to each other, and before he could say anything to break the spell she put one hand up to his face and looked deep into his eyes. He saw what he was looking for in her dusky blue eyes at that moment, and all around them the birds had fallen silent as if they were waiting until, as if magnetized, his lips finally found hers. His mouth tasted of peppermints and he kissed her with such strength of feeling that her knees buckled. She kissed him back with the confidence that she was thoroughly enjoying her last first kiss ever, and fell bait lure and gauntlet for his otherwise quiet charms.

After a bit of a whirlwind courtship that took everyone but her uncle by surprise, they had recently announced their engagement. In the middle of a display one sunny afternoon he sent Frey the Eagle Owl over to DeeDee as usual, but as the bird flew towards her outstretched and gauntleted arm, watching those powerful talons extended out in front of her body preparing to perch, the sun glinted on a ring on a little red ribbon draped around her neck. Once on DeeDee's arm the bird lowered her powerful neck so that she could remove the ribbon and gulp back tears of surprise. As Matthew came over to join her he dropped to one knee, in front of a hundred or so visitors, and asked her to marry him right into her visibly shaking microphone, to roars of applause and cheers when she said; 'Yes . . . !'.

Their engagement came as no surprise anybody who had seen them together, but a very big surprise to her parents, who had not.

With the success of the park Sir Christopher's financial worries are thankfully behind him, and with them, happily went his reserve. Now fully involved with the day to day running of the park, he is just as likely to be found up to his knees in water leading a team clearing the ever invasive Japanese knotweed down at the river as he is chairing the monthly park board meetings.

Since Hannah went off to university Danny is his right hand man these days and has become so loyal and useful to him that he was soon made Site Manager; on the condition that he has the occasional haircut, or at least combs his unruly head of gypsy black curls on a daily basis. Now earning good money, Danny can well afford to pay the rent at number 2 Stanton Cottages where he lives with his mum, but they still have it rent free, and live there fairly contentedly while Beth and Flynn's relationship continues to grow and Danny waits for Hannah to come home from university for her holidays to make his life complete again.

Anna and Flynn's relationship has blossomed as Father and Daughter and it is as if they had never been oblivious to their own existence. Anna has fully embraced the opportunity to call Flynn her 'Dad' and uses the term openly, and with frequency, and Beth knows how proud he is to have such a beautiful and accomplished daughter. Anna and her family have recently moved into a beautifully renovated old cottage near the pub in order to be closer to both her parents; and take advantage of their free and willing babysitting service, and their IT Company has taken on the software and management of the entire park's computers too, so they are frequent visitors there and, of course, at the pub.

Beth has become a pub landlady now, although she doesn't actually live there, and because she spends so much time with Flynn she quickly noticed that he refers to Danny as his son when talking about him these days. Though she'd seen Danny smile when he heard him say it, she secretly longs for the day that Danny accepts him as his new dad too.

*   *   *

Flynn and Beth's relationship is still a source of speculation around the village. She loves him, he is sure of that, although she hasn't actually said it, but despite his many hints in that area since the day she realised the truth about him almost a year ago, she always seemed to change the subject or make light of it; so much so that Flynn had begun to wonder if she would ever say yes if he asked her to marry him.

It wasn't hard for him to work out why. On the surface she was certainly a woman happily reborn; but he knew that what she had been through as a married woman had scarred her internally more than it ever had on her body. The years of abuse at the hands of her husband continued to haunt her dreams, and in the dark regions of her subconscious he and Danny both knew that she was still suffering from nightmares; waking up on those nights in a cold sweat and shaking. And although he was becoming a dab hand at reassuring her until she awoke properly on the rare occasions she actually stayed overnight at the pub, Flynn was out of his depth as to how to allay her deeply rooted fears. After Danny had reported one particularly restless night Flynn called Dizzy and arranged to see her in the pub while Beth was out collecting Daniel from *Watchtots*, Sarah Palmer's daily Crèche in the village hall.

It being a sunny afternoon and after she had collected them from school, Dizzy arrived with the triplets in tow and sent them out into the enclosed beer garden to play. Accepting the glass of lemonade that Flynn offered her, she sat down gratefully and took a long sip, before patiently resting the glass on a coaster. Well used to people bringing up difficult topics with the local vicar she said nothing and waited for him to speak first.

Taking a deep breath, Flynn finally took the plunge and told her what was troubling him as, unheard; Beth came back in through the side door.

Wiping her feet quietly on the door mat when she heard their voices coming from the bar, she quietly hung up her jacket and checked through the little window that Daniel was ok with the three girls outside. Her brows knitted as soon as she realised that Flynn and Dizzy were talking about her and her heart began to beat uncomfortably fast.

'. . . and although she says she knows I'd never hurt her . . . it's like deep, deep down inside, she feels she can't trust me . . . whatever I say . . . or do . . . not subconsciously anyway . . . If we disagree over something, no matter how trivial, and I raise my voice even a little bit . . . she . . . she gets this terrible . . . *hunted* look in her eyes . . . it's downright scary, Dizzy. I'm afraid for us . . . How *can* we have a relationship, a genuine one? With all the ups and downs that all couples have . . . if she can't cope with a cross word without thinking she's going to get another beating? It's like she's got no faith in me . . .' Flynn sounded desperately hurt and, in the hallway, Beth realised she had begun to cry.

Dizzy paused before she spoke again. 'Anyone can see that she cares very deeply about you Flynn . . . but, in abuse cases, it's really not that simple. The problems run much deeper than people often realise.'

'I do realise that . . . but . . .'

'. . . She didn't wake up one day an abuse victim you know . . . Len was all sweetness and light to start with . . . He treated her like a princess . . . she told me. The problems started once they married, and that's why she's . . . albeit subconsciously . . . so scared of being with another man. Len started when he became jealous of other men looking at her. She was a very pretty girl . . .'

'I know that too . . .' he said with a wry half-smile. 'She still is . . .'

Dizzy smiled at that before her face became serious once more. 'She told me he would just get angry at first . . . because you see Flynn; abuse is never about anger, it's about control. As the time passed he gradually increased that control over her, little by little, and she didn't see it coming. And she's scared she wouldn't see it coming again.'

'But she *knows* I'd never . . .'

'I'm sure she wants to . . .'

'But . . .'

'Flynn . . . women, and men, like Beth; when they are in the grip of something desperate like violent abuse, lose reality that their eyes are being taken from what the rest of us would see as the truth. Then they begin to believe that lie until that lie becomes their truth . . . and their whole life becomes wrapped around that lie. She doesn't see it like you and me, and you have to understand that.

Beth's lie ended the day that Len died, and she still has to realise it. Then she has to let that lie go before she can ever let the rest of her life go on. She needs to let go of all that pain to allow herself to live her life to the fullest, and she needs faith to achieve that. And despite what people think, faith is a bit of an irrational thing . . . It's not something you can assume she's got, just like that . . .'

'Faith, *irrational*? I'm a bit surprised to her *you* say that . . .'

'If faith, any kind of faith, were rational then, by definition, it wouldn't be *faith* would it? Faith means believing in something you can't see, or feel, or touch. Having faith in something is the ability to leap head first into the dark. Without fearing what's there . . . a leap of faith as they say . . . And remember, Flynn; with love you don't step into it, do you . . . you fall in. She needs the faith to know that she can now. All she's known of so called love most of her life has been bad things. But now she needs to believe she can have love . . . real love, marriage . . . everything. She can have anything she wants from her life now. It's her decision; her truth. She just needs faith to believe it now, and she needs your love; your patience, to help her. I'm sure she does love you Flynn . . . and that's a great start for someone like Beth . . . Gradually, she'll come to understand that she *can* love you, and *be loved* by you, without becoming a victim again . . .'

Dizzy paused to take a sip of her drink before continuing quietly.

'Hector always says God never promised us days without pain. Or laughter without sorrow or sun without rain . . . but He did us promise strength for each day . . . and comfort for our tears . . . and light for the way ahead. And I believe that if God brings you to something . . . then God will bring you through it too . . . And He will bring her through it too, Flynn . . .'

Out in the hallway Beth wiped her eyes with a crumpled tissue from up her sleeve.

'I believe He will too . . .' she whispered.

She'd never heard Flynn talk about his feelings like that before. And she'd never heard anyone describe exactly why she was feeling what she undoubtedly was, like Dizzy just had either.

After a few minutes, though still deep in thought, she went back outside and over to join Daniel and the girls in the play area. The girls were on the swings but Daniel was busy playing in the sand box; a large and bright blue plastic shell full of toys, and was tipping fine sand through the rose of a watering can over his little fingers as she sat down beside him. Absently, she raised her own fingers into the flow to allow the grains of sand to tumble though them. Daniel chuckled and refilled his watering can with the aid of a little red spade.

'. . . 'Gain Na-Na . . . 'gain' He held up the watering can as Beth dutifully raised her hand. Then shaking her head to clear it she looked at Daniel and smiled.

'Let's wet the sand and then we can draw some nice pictures in it . . .' she said, taking the watering can from him to fill it from the garden tap close by.

When Dizzy was drawn away by a phone call, and having promised faithfully to see the girls safely home, Flynn looked out of the back window to see Beth sitting with Daniel there, totally engrossed, and crept up behind her as she carefully raked over the wet patch before starting to draw him some flowers and shapes. Daniel pushed his fingers into the wet sand and seemed fascinated by the granules sticking to his fingers. Then before she knew it he had thrown his little arms around her neck to give her a very gritty kiss.

'Hey . . .' Flynn said cheerfully, stooping down to help her gently brush the sand off her face and settling himself down just behind her; one hand resting lightly on her left shoulder.

Daniel had lost interest in the sand now and toddled off to join the others, demanding to be put in the baby swing and pushed. They both grinned as Batty enthusiastically grabbed him under both armpits and hoisted him up awkwardly into the swing, before starting to push him.

'Not too hard Batty . . .' Flynn called.

Beth cleared her throat and picked up the sand rake to make a blank canvas again.

'Dizzy popped by . . . .' he said innocently.

'Yes . . . I saw she had . . . You looked deep in conversation together . . . so I left you to it . . . What did she want then . . . ?' she asked him, just as innocently.

'. . . Um . . . We had a long chat actually . . . Beth . . . ?' He faltered as she continued to trace her fingers through the sand. '. . . I wanted to ask you something . . . if that's ok.'

She nodded her head a couple of times but didn't look at him.

'Do you remember the reason why you loved me before . . . ?'

It wasn't what she was expecting. She stopped doodling and looked back at him before a smile slowly crept its way across her lips unbidden. 'Mmmm . . .' she said quietly.

He held his breath for several seconds before she spoke again. 'You were . . . very different, from any boy I'd known before. You were so . . . I don't know . . . mature I suppose . . . . compared to the boys in my year anyway. Irish too . . . I loved your accent . . . Still do as a matter of fact . . . .'

He kissed the top of her head, squeezing her shoulder gently.

'My friend Tracy Casey . . . Remember her?' she looked round briefly as he nodded.

'The dark haired girl Kevin fancied? Daft name she had . . .'

'It was . . . Don't know what her parents were thinking . . . .' She paused. 'Did he? Fancy her? Kevin, I mean? I never knew that . . . Anyway, that's the one . . . She was very envious of me . . . She was my only real friend, and the only one I dared tell we were together. There was no boasting or bravado in you like the other boys . . . I noticed that first about you. Well, apart from your accent . . . You were . . . still are . . . so considerate and . . . loving . . .' she blushed. 'You didn't think just of yourself . . . you always asked me . . . You still do ask me . . . what I think too. You've always treated me like a lady. And believe me . . . that's not something I was *ever* used to . . . until I met you . . .'

Flynn stretched out his legs on the grass so that he could slip his arm more comfortably around her waist. She adjusted her position so that her fingers could still play in the sand.

'And . . . in the time we were apart . . .' she continued; 'Did you ever think of me . . . ?'

'Every so often . . . every time I met another girl and she never matched up . . . I'm still single . . . did you notice?'

She smiled and pushed him backwards with her head, jokingly.

'So why didn't you let on that you'd recognised me when I came back then . . . ?'

'Because I could see your life was quite complicated enough . . . and I didn't want to make things any worse for you . . . if Len found out about me and you . . . So I just decided to help you . . . in the only way I could . . . By being your friend . . .'

'Well what about after . . . after he died . . . ?'

'I know I could have . . . but I didn't think it was the right time then either . . . and also . . . I wanted . . .'

He stopped briefly and turned her face toward his. 'I actually wrote to Kevin for some advice . . .'

'You did what? You mean you told him . . . about us?' she sat up suddenly. 'How did you even know where he was?'

'Danny found your address book when I asked him. Don't worry; Kevin said he knew anyway . . . He suggested I just give you some time . . . to find the missing piece within your heart that would bring you back to me . . . for good.'

'And it was you who found it . . . You found Anna . . . and opened my eyes . . . .' She looked away from him; across at Daniel giggling ecstatically as the baby swing sent him to and fro with his little legs kicking about happily.

'Flynn . . .' she said quietly, stopping the pretence. 'I know you're worried about me . . . and my feelings . . . and stuff . . . and I know you think I'm holding back so I don't let you close enough to hurt me . . .'

He leaned towards her and kissed her hair gently, but said nothing.

'I just want you to know that . . . I am *trying* . . . I really am. I feel so *close* to you now . . . more than ever . . . and knowing you're there for me . . . makes me stronger and braver every day . . .'

'*Close* to me . . . ?' he said, far quicker than he'd intended. He swung her round directly in front of him. 'Do you want to know what I reckon, Beth?'

'What do you reckon . . . ?' she said, slightly nervously.

'I reckon that *love* is what you're feeling. You *Love* me Beth Edwards . . . and I love you . . . I never stopped . . . and the trouble is that you're so *shite* scared of love that you can't say it. Because . . . Because you know it's everything it's cracked up to be. Just like I do. It's *never* going to be moonlight and roses all the time . . . . We both know it. And that's why you, why me, why *everybody* is so scared of it . . . But I know one thing more than you do . . .'

'What's that?''

'I know that love . . . *real* love . . . *is* worth fighting for Beth . . . Being brave for . . . risking everything for . . . Because the trouble is . . . my darling girl . . . if you don't risk it . . . you'll risk even more . . . *won't* ya?

Beth said nothing as she turned her eyes away from him. As her vision blurred she swallowed hard and sniffed. So Kevin had known about them all along. Funny he'd never said anything at the time: or since.

Flynn said no more; just sank his legs back down to one side with one arm still wrapped loosely around her waist so that he could lay his head on her shoulder;

while his eyes were more easily focused on looking over at the children.

Several minutes passed in silence.

'Flynn . . . ?' she almost whispered, eventually. He lifted his head to look back towards her face as she motioned with her eyes towards the sand.

His brows knitted together as he tried to make sense of the shapes she'd just drawn in the sand box.

But they weren't shapes. They were letters . . .

J . . . e . . . t . . . a . . . y . . . m . . . e . . .

OK . . . so the spelling wasn't right . . . But then again she couldn't speak any French, as far as he knew, schoolboy or otherwise. But it would still do very nicely, thank you.

*   *   *

The day dawned bright and sunny through a gap in the curtains as Beth opened her eyes, yawned, and pulled her brows quickly together. This wasn't her bedroom . . . .

Her eyes becoming used to light, she began to look around the room slowly. The curtains were wrong: they fell all the way to the floor. There was a door where there wasn't a door . . . and a dressing table . . . and a row of fitted wardrobes right along one wall.

A shaft of beckoning light fell on something hanging on the back of the door . . .

Then she remembered having come up a grand staircase last night that she'd thought even Daphne would have been proud to sweep down in one of her movies; and a smile crept its way slowly across her lips. She was in a bedroom room at Stanton Court.

Today she was marrying Flynn. Today came the last tick in the box towards making her whole.

Pulling her arms up above her head she indulged herself in a deliciously long stretch. Then, stretching out her limbs individually, one by one and catlike, a soft tap came from the other side of the door and a face appeared around it as it swished its way open over a thick cream carpet.

'Ah good . . . you're awake now, Mum . . .' said Anna. 'We were beginning to think you were going to stay there all day . . . .'

'I love this bed . . .' Beth laughed, 'I want to take it home with me . . .' Sitting up in the old four poster bed to greet her daughter with a creak a kiss and a hug, she gave her a squeeze of reassurance. 'But don't panic love, I'm not planning on lying in another minute . . . not today . . . . Even in my first ever four poster bed . . .'

'Come on then . . . up with you . . . your bath is run . . . and Steph is downstairs chewing the end of her comb gaging to get hold of you . . .' Anna said with a grin.

Three quarters of an hour later and post luxurious bubble bath, Beth tied the belt on her dressing gown and opened her bedroom door with a wide yawn. The sound of children's excited shrieks and giggles floated across what she'd noticed last night was a very wide landing, and Beth knew that Dizzy and Fiona must have already started trying to get them all ready. Peeping into the room that the children had all slept in she smiled as she saw the four mint green dresses and two perfect little grey suits hanging in a regimented row along the picture rail. Shoes sorted into six neat pairs lined the skirting right down one side as well.

Heading purposefully down the grand staircase, Mrs Higgins met her at the bottom carrying a silver breakfast tray with a snow white tray cloth on it and a little vase of freesias perched to one side.

'Oh . . . I was just bringing this up to you . . .' she smiled, 'but I see you are up and about now . . . and there's a letter on here for you as well . . . Young Danny brought it up. Such a lovely young man isn't he? It's an airmail letter I see . . .'

'Oh . . . really . . . ?'

'Tell you what; we'll go into the breakfast room . . . it's just along here . . . Follow me my dear. Everyone else has had theirs long ago so you can have the only little bit of peace you're likely to have today and then you can open it . . . see who it's from. The room faces east so the sun will be filling the room with bright new day for you . . .'

'That's a nice expression . . .' Beth said happily, falling into step next to her.

'One of my late mother's . . .' she said. 'She left me with enough of them to write a whole book.

Beth laughed as she followed the indomitable housekeeper through a nearby doorway.

'I still use some of my children's words that have crept into my vocabulary . . . I still say 'chipth' for chips . . . That was Anna, and I still say 'Utumnum' for cucumber . . . but I think that might've been me . . . .'

Mrs Higgins chuckled companionably as she set the tray down on the table to take everything off it, as Beth went over to the window to see the view.

The breakfast room at Stanton Court looked out over the park and to the chalk hills beyond. The view from this angle was neatly framed by a border of beautiful broad reach cedar trees; their branches sweeping right down to the immaculately cut grass like witches besom brooms just as if they'd been grown there to sweep up the annual autumn leaves.

Up on the hill in the distance she could just see the roof of the Tithe barn from here, and smiled at the thought that in just a few hours she would be seated inside there; or maybe dancing . . . but either way she'd still be married to Paddy Flynn . . .

Mrs Higgins picked up the sliver tray and closed the door quietly behind her as Beth settled down to her breakfast of warm croissants, butter and marmalade. She pushed down the plunger on the coffee pot as she made herself comfortable, and then, taking a shamelessly decadent bite of croissant, she brushed the crumbs off her fingers down the front of her dressing gown, told herself off and picked up her napkin; then carefully tore open the flaps on the blue airmail letter with a slight grin. She knew it could only be from one person.

Dear Beth He began.

I have to admit when Paddy told me you two were getting hitched I didn't stop laughing for almost ten minutes . . .

*   *   *

Her dress was on loan from Daphne Goldwyn's own wardrobe and was a piece of genuine history from her film career. A Christian Dior original with acres of cream chiffon folds, the gown was specially designed for one of her later movies and it was the exact one that she'd seen Daphne wearing in a soft focus 1940's publicity photograph on the wall of her Drawing Room in the beautifully rambling old house that she called home on a recent visit with her spa friends. They'd all been quite blown away when Daphne told them she still had it; 'In a trunk . . . up in the attic . . . somewhere . . .'

Then of course she'd brought the real thing down to Frincham 'for Beth to see'.

One look at the expression on her face and she'd known she was right to jump in that taxi and bring it, and she'd immediately insisted that Beth have it as her 'something borrowed' to get married in.

*   *   *

With Steph finished and her hair and makeup done, Beth was back upstairs getting dressed with Fiona's help and said a silent prayer of thanks for still being so rail thin that the dress actually fitted her. Like a glove in fact. Her fascinator 'hat' was made from fine feathers dyed to the exact colour of her dress with a little diamante for a bit of the sparkle she'd insisted on that Steph had woven into her hair so that it all looked absolutely perfect.

Fiona had found her a pair of elegant cream long satin gloves and lent her a single string of real pearls for her neck. Her shoes, made to order from the finest soft cream Italian leather, had been a present from Paul and Jules.

Batty had suggested she wear glass slippers of course, but it was decided that that would have been pushing the fairytale a little too far and that Italian leather would be much more comfortable for the bride to be wearing all day. Tesco had cheered her sister up by pointing out that glass slippers would have been too hard to dance in anyway because even Cinderella had lost one after all . . .

Hector and Dizzy had given Beth a white leather prayer book to carry into her new life as a happily married woman. The book had blue ribbon page markers so Beth had decided to carry it today in preference to a bouquet, for good luck. Inside the book Hector had written these wise words from Marie Louise Haskins: *And I said to the man who stood at the gate of the year: "Give me a light that I may tread safely into the unknown" And he replied: "Go out into the darkness and put your hand into the Hand of God. That shall be to you better than light and safer than a known way."*

*   *   *

When she was finally ready she found herself temporarily alone so she walked slowly over to the full length mirror in the corner of the room and studied her reflection closely for several seconds. Outside she heard the unmistakable sound and then saw a vehicle coming up the drive, and watched as it swung round to a halt in the deeply laid gravel. A few seconds later the front doorbell clanged impatiently on its chain and the sound of rapid footsteps coming up the grand staircase drew her attention to the door.

She turned around just as it opened.

'Your car's here . . . .' Mrs Higgins' face was quite pink with the exertion and she was puffing fit to burst the buttons down the front of her smartest jacket.

'Are you ok?' Beth asked with a concerned smile.

'I'm fine . . .' she puffed. 'Now come on . . . . Best foot forward . . . you don't want to be late . . . I don't hold any truck with that kind of tradition . . . it's rude to keep people waiting . . . You say noon on the invitations then you mean noon I say!' She fully extended one arm to encourage Beth to step forward and take her hand. Then for good measure she waggled her extended hand about a bit. Beth grinned and stepped forward to take it only too willingly.

'All you need today is to meet that Ernie Jones or one of his boys moving a herd of cows all down that lane and you'll get held up for hours . . . . That lovely man of yours will think you've changed your mind . . .'

'I won't be changing my mind on this one, don't you worry . . . The rest of my life depends on this, Mrs H!' Beth laughed.

*   *   *